MW01078299

Building Transformer Models with PyTorch 2.0

NLP, computer vision, and speech processing with PyTorch and Hugging Face

Prem Timsina

www.bpbonline.com

First Edition 2024

Copyright © BPB Publications, India

ISBN: 978-93-55517-494

LIMITS OF LIABILITY AND DISCLAIMER OF WARRANTY

To View Complete
BPB Publications Catalogue
Scan the QR Code:

Dedicated to

My beloved wife:

Sunita

and

My son **Percival**

About the Author

Prem Timsina is the Director of Engineering at Mount Sinai Health Systems, where he oversees the development and implementation of Machine Learning Data Products. He has overseen multiple Machine Learning products that have been used as clinical decision support tool at several hospitals within New York City. With over ten years of experience in the field, Dr. Timsina is a dedicated Machine Learning enthusiast who has worked on a variety of big data challenges using tools, such as PyTorch, Deep Learning, Generative AI, Apache Spark, and various NoSQL platforms. He has contributed to the field through more than 40 publications in Machine Learning, text mining, and big data analytics. He earned his Doctor of Science degree in Information Systems from Dakota State University.

About the Reviewer

Pratik Kotian is an accomplished professional with eight years of extensive expertise in Natural Language Processing, Machine Learning, Generative AI, and Python programming. With a versatile background spanning various sectors including technology, telecommunications, finance, retail, and more, Pratik has honed his skills across different domains. His experience encompasses leadership roles in research and development, technical consultancy, and team management. Currently, Pratik serves as a Manager at Deloitte, where he leads the Generative AI Team with a focus on pioneering innovative solutions for clients. In this capacity, he leverages his expertise to drive transformative initiatives, enabling businesses to unlock value through AI-driven strategies.

Acknowledgement

I extend my deepest appreciation to my wife, Sunita Ghimire, for her constant support throughout the process of writing this book. Special love to my son Percival for being a wonderful toddler and allowing daddy to work on the book.

I am immensely thankful for dedicated collaboration of reviewers, editors, and technical expert for revising and refining this book. Additionally, I am grateful to the entire BPB Publications team who have worked tirelessly on realizing this book.

My greatest thanks to all the readers who have supported this work. Your enthusiasm on this topic has been fundamental in bringing this book to fruition.

Preface

Lately, transformer architecture has appeared as a swiss knife for Machine Learning architecture. The transformer architecture is at the heart of most recent breakthroughs in Generative Artificial Intelligence. For instance, tools like ChatGPT and BARD, perceived by many as paving stones towards artificial general intelligence, are built on Transformer foundations. Thus, it is imperative for data scientists, ML Engineers, and Technologists to understand how this architecture can solve various ML tasks.

This book provides both theoretical and practical understanding of transformer architecture. Specifically, we will cover these ML tasks: **Natural Language Processing (NLP)**, Computer Vision, Speech Processing, Tabular Data Processing, Reinforcement Learning, and Multi-Modalities. Center to the book are four major ML tasks, each explored in depth across two chapters. The initial chapter lays the groundwork by discussing the conceptual understanding. Here, we discuss the inner working of transformer architecture to solve tasks and discuss the architecture of major foundational models. Following this, the subsequent chapters focus on the practical understanding of pre-training, fine-tuning and using open source models to solve the ML tasks. This book will demonstrate practical applications through several comprehensive, end-to-end projects.

To equip with comprehensive understanding, the book has dedicated chapters for Hugging Face Ecosystem, transfer learning and deploying and serving transformer models. We will also delve deeper into best practices and debugging transfomer model developed utilizing PyTorch and Hugging Face.

The pre-requisite for this book is basic understanding of PyTorch and deep learning. This book will benefit data scientists and ML engineers who are seeking to enhance their knowledge of transformer models and learn how to develop ML engines using the transformer architecture and Hugging Face's transformer library. It will also be valuable for developers and software architects looking to integrate transformer-based models into their existing software products. Additionally, AI enthusiasts interested in the latest developments in cutting-edge ML methods will find this book useful.

In summary, you will gain a conceptual understanding of transformer architecture and practical knowledge on how to solve various ML tasks using this architecture. Happy reading!

Chapter 1: Transformer Architecture – This chapter gives the readers an overview of the evolution of NLP models over time and how each previous development has influenced the transformer architecture. The majority of this chapter discusses the conceptual understanding of the transformer architecture, illustrating details on the encoder, decoder, positional encoding, and embedding. The chapter also explains to readers about different variations of the transformer architecture and their applications in solving NLP tasks.

Chapter 2: Hugging Face Ecosystem – This chapter provides a thorough understanding of the core functionalities and features of the Hugging Face ecosystem, specifically focusing on the transformers, datasets, and tokenizers libraries. The chapter explains how to use the Hugging Face ecosystem for using pre-trained models, fine-tuning existing models, and sharing your models. We will walk you through each step of this process, using practical examples, specifically fine-tuning the Dreambooth model (personalizing text to image generation).

Chapter 3: Transformer Model in PyTorch – This chapter will give the readers a detailed understanding of the PyTorch implementation of the transformer architecture, thoroughly examining its various components. This includes learning how to build models in different configurations, such as encoder only, decoder only, and the combined encoder-decoder setup in PyTorch. All of these concepts are explained through three projects implemented in Pytorch: 1. Classifier—IMDB sentiment 2. Text Generation—Shakespear poet 3. Machine Translation—English to German. This chapter is all about getting you comfortable and confident with how Transformer models work in PyTorch.

Chapter 4: Transfer Learning with PyTorch and Hugging Face – This chapter provides a complete picture of what transfer learning is, why it is useful, and where it can be used. We will showcase the transfer learning by building the real news vs. fake news project.

Chapter 5: Large Language Models: BERT, GPT-3, and BART – This chapter discusses the key concepts of **Large Language Models (LLMs)**. It will also discuss the key determinants of LLM performance. Additionally, we will look at the architecture of pioneering LLMs. We will conclude this chapter by showcasing how you can create your own LLM with your data.

Chapter 6: NLP Tasks with Transformers – This chapter will provide a detailed understanding of key NLP tasks and the corresponding transformer models used to solve these tasks. We will also discuss handling long sequences in transformers. We will explore these concepts through three projects: 1. Handling long sequences by chunking, 2. Handling long sequences with hierarchical attention, and 3. Generating Shakespeare-like text using GPT-2 and Tiny Shakespeare.

Chapter 7: CV Model Anatomy: ViT, DETR, and DeiT – This chapter will provide a foundational understanding of image pre-processing techniques and their significance in computer vision tasks. The chapter delve into the architecture and workings of the **Vision**

Transformer (ViT), **Distilled Vision Transformer (DeiT)** and **Detection Transformer (DETR)**. We will illustrate all these concepts by three projects.

Chapter 8: Computer Vision Tasks with Transformers – This chapter serves as a comprehensive understanding of various computer vision tasks and their applications. We will look at three main tasks here, namely, Image Segmentation, Classification, and Image Generation. We will explain these concepts through training and developing three machine learning models: 1. Food Image Segmentation, 2. Comparison of DEIT and RESNET, and 3. Dog Image Generation. → Mushroom, Bird.

Chapter 9: Speech Processing Model Anatomy: Whisper, SpeechT5, and Wav2Vec – This chapter provides a foundational understanding of speech pre-processing, and a detailed analysis of Whisper, SpeechT5, and Wav2Vec Architecture.

Chapter 10: Speech Tasks with Transformers – This chapter will provide a comprehensive understanding of various speech processing tasks and their applications in real-world scenarios. We will look at into three major tasks here: 1. Text-to-Speech 2. Automatic Speech Recognition, and 3. Audio-to-Audio. We will explain these concepts through real world projects

Chapter 11: Transformer Architecture for Tabular Data Processing – This chapter will look at the following architecture: 1. Google's TAPAS for quering the tabular data, 2. TabTransformer for Structured Data, and 3. FT Transformer for structured data. We will explain these architecture through real world examples.

Chapter 12: Transformers for Tabular Data Regression and Classification – This chapter explores the application of transformers in tabular data processing. We will also delve into the implementation of transformers such as TabTransformer, FT Transformer, and TabNet for solving classification and regression problems. The chapter illustrates these models by solving both classification and regression problems and comparing the results with XGBoost. In summary, the goal of this chapter is to provide a detailed explanation of how we can use Transformer Architecture for machine learning with structured data.

Chapter 13: Multimodal Transformers, Architectures and Applications – This chapter is an explanation of how transformers can handle multiple data types in a single model. We will discuss two major architectures: ImageBind Architecture (Meta's architecture that combines text, audio, IMU, thermal, depth, and image) and CLIP Architecture (text and image). This chapter also explains different multi-modal tasks.

Chapter 14: Explore Reinforcement Learning for Transformer – This chapter discusses the fundamentals of **Reinforcement Learning (RL)** and the most common tools in PyTorch, as well as the process of building an RL model. This chapter will walk you through developing a Trading Model using tools like Gym, Stable Baselines[3], and Yfinance. Additionally, this chapter illustrates two major RL architectures: Decision transformer and trajectory transformer, which are significant transformer architectures used in RL.

Chapter 15: Model Export, Serving, and Deployment – This chapter provides a comprehensive exploration of the machine learning lifecycle, focusing on model serialization, export, and deployment. Specifically, the chapter illustrates exporting PyTorch models to interoperable formats like ONNX, as well as the usage of PyTorch Script and Pickle. The chapter also provides a practical illustration of serving a PyTorch model using FastAPI and sharing model through Hugging Face. The goal is to equip readers with the knowledge and tools needed to efficiently export, serve, and deploy machine learning models.

Chapter 16: Transformer Model Interpretability, and Experimental Visualization – This chapter discusses the concepts of model interpretability and explainability. The chapter explores various tools that can be used for model interpretability and explainability. It provides a practical example of using CAPTUM for interpreting transformer models. Additionally, the chapter showcases how to use TensorBoard for model visualization, logging, and interpretation

Chapter 17: PyTorch Models: Best Practices and Debugging– The chapter discusses practical guidelines and best practices for building transformer models using both the general PyTorch Library and the Hugging Face Library. It then discusses a structured approach to debugging PyTorch models. The chapter illustrates all these concepts through real-world examples.

Code Bundle and Coloured Images

Please follow the link to download the
Code Bundle and the *Coloured Images* of the book:

https://rebrand.ly/hydtz8g

The code bundle for the book is also hosted on GitHub at
https://github.com/bpbpublications/Building-Transformer-Models-with-PyTorch-2.0.
In case there's an update to the code, it will be updated on the existing GitHub repository.

We have code bundles from our rich catalogue of books and videos available at **https://github.com/bpbpublications**. Check them out!

Errata

We take immense pride in our work at BPB Publications and follow best practices to ensure the accuracy of our content to provide with an indulging reading experience to our subscribers. Our readers are our mirrors, and we use their inputs to reflect and improve upon human errors, if any, that may have occurred during the publishing processes involved. To let us maintain the quality and help us reach out to any readers who might be having difficulties due to any unforeseen errors, please write to us at :

errata@bpbonline.com

Your support, suggestions and feedbacks are highly appreciated by the BPB Publications' Family.

Did you know that BPB offers eBook versions of every book published, with PDF and ePub files available? You can upgrade to the eBook version at www.bpbonline.com and as a print book customer, you are entitled to a discount on the eBook copy. Get in touch with us at :

business@bpbonline.com for more details.

At **www.bpbonline.com**, you can also read a collection of free technical articles, sign up for a range of free newsletters, and receive exclusive discounts and offers on BPB books and eBooks.

Piracy

If you come across any illegal copies of our works in any form on the internet, we would be grateful if you would provide us with the location address or website name. Please contact us at **business@bpbonline.com** with a link to the material.

If you are interested in becoming an author

If there is a topic that you have expertise in, and you are interested in either writing or contributing to a book, please visit **www.bpbonline.com**. We have worked with thousands of developers and tech professionals, just like you, to help them share their insights with the global tech community. You can make a general application, apply for a specific hot topic that we are recruiting an author for, or submit your own idea.

Reviews

Please leave a review. Once you have read and used this book, why not leave a review on the site that you purchased it from? Potential readers can then see and use your unbiased opinion to make purchase decisions. We at BPB can understand what you think about our products, and our authors can see your feedback on their book. Thank you!

For more information about BPB, please visit **www.bpbonline.com**.

Join our book's Discord space

Join the book's Discord Workspace for Latest updates, Offers, Tech happenings around the world, New Release and Sessions with the Authors:

https://discord.bpbonline.com

Table of Contents

CHAPTER 1
Transformer Architecture

Introduction

Imagine you are a software engineer working on an exciting project and searching for a programming language to help create software quickly and efficiently. You hear about a revolutionary new type of language that is the Swiss knife of programming language: this language is most efficient in creating **Machine Learning (ML)** models—plus, this programming language creates stunning websites faster than other web development frameworks and supports hardware programming. Furthermore, its performance in network programming and other related tasks is also outstanding. Would it not be interesting to learn about this powerful programming language?

Similar developments can be observed in the world of ML frameworks. The transformer architecture is an incredibly versatile ML architecture. Transformers were initially developed for **Natural Language Processing** (**NLP**). Due to their superior results, this architecture has rendered other NLP architectures like RNN and **long short-term memory networks (LSTM)** obsolete. More recently, transformers have begun impacting other ML fields as well. According to SUPERB (**https://superbbenchmark.org/leaderboard**) the best foundational model for speech processing is also based on the transformer. Furthermore, transformers have shown excellent results in computer vision and other machine learning fields as well. Therefore, transformers have the potential to converge all AI frameworks into a solitary, highly adaptable architecture.

In this chapter, we will look into the **base architecture** of this versatile machine learning in depth. The chapter specifically focuses on understanding the original transformer architecture proposed by *Vaswani et al. (2017)*. Since the transformer was originally proposed for NLP—we will understand important NLP models and how the transformer was influenced by those models.

Structure

This chapter covers the following topics:

- Chronology of NLP model development.
- Transformer architecture
- Training process of transformer
- Inference process of transformer
- Types of transformers and their applications

Objectives

This book chapter intends to provide readers with a broad understanding of the evolution and significant milestones in the development of NLP models, with a special emphasis on the transformer architecture. It seeks to offer an in-depth examination of various NLP models, drawing comparisons and highlighting the distinctive ways in which the transformer model addresses the limitations of its predecessors. A key focus will be placed on investigating the essential components that make up the transformer architecture. Additionally, the chapter aims to educate readers about the different variations of the transformer model, showcasing their broad spectrum of applications in the field of NLP. The overarching theme of this chapter is to trace the journey of NLP models' development, culminating in the rise of the transformer as a ground-breaking innovation in the landscape of language processing technologies.

Chronology of NLP model development

The transformer was originally proposed for NLP, specifically machine translation, by *Vaswani et al.* in 2017[1]. It is currently the most popular and effective model in NLP, as well as other wide-ranging tasks (speech processing, computer vision, and others). However, the development of the transformer was not a sudden occurrence. In fact, it was the culmination of years of research and development in NLP models, with each model building upon the previous ones. Let us examine the chronological history of different NLP models. This is important because as we understand the transformer architecture,

---

[1] Vaswani, A., Shazeer, N., Parmar, N., Uszkoreit, J., Jones, L., Gomez, A. N., ... & Polosukhin, I. (2017). *Attention is all you need. Advances in neural information processing systems, 30.*

we will be able to contextualize it within the historical development of NLP models, their shortcomings, and how transformer is unique and versatile.

In the upcoming section, we will explore the timeline of NLP model evolution and contrast various NLP models. *Figure 1.1* shows the chronology of NLP research:

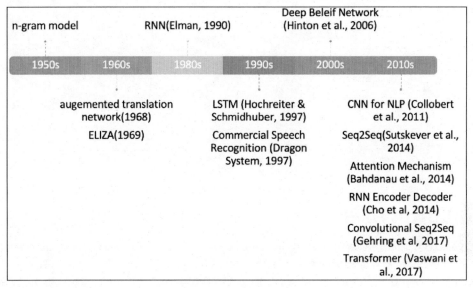

Figure 1.1: *Chronology of NLP models development*

The transformer model was the culmination of all the previous research developments. *Vaswani et al.*, cited a few of that original research. Specifically, *Vaswani et al.* cited the following research, and the transformer model seems to have been highly influenced by them.

In the following sections, we will discuss a few of the most important NLP models, their benefits, and their shortcomings.

Recurrent neural network

First, let us discuss the concept of next-word prediction. For instance, let us say we have a sentence, *The color of the sky is …*. Based on the information already processed by our brain, we can predict that the next word in this sentence would be *blue*. However, this prediction is not solely based on previous words, but rather on multiple preceding words.

Traditional machine learning algorithms, such as linear regression and multilayer perceptron, are not equipped to store previous information and utilize it for predictions. These algorithms do not have the capability to retain information from prior inputs. Here, recurrent neural networks come into play, which is capable of retaining prior information and utilizing it for making accurate predictions.

Figure 1.2 shows the structure of RNN. Here, each cell takes the output of its previous cell as its input. This allows the network to retain information from previous time steps and incorporate it into the computation at each subsequent iteration:

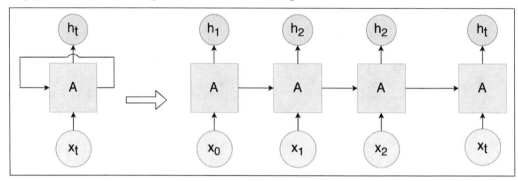

Figure 1.2: *RNN structure*

Limitation of RNN

Let us consider the following example: *England is my hometown. I spent my whole life there. I just moved to Spain two days ago. I can speak only one language, which is ....* In this example, the next word is *English*. The most important contextual word, in this case, is *England*, which appears at the beginning of the sentence. However, in some cases, the relevant information may be located far away from where it is needed in an RNN. For example, in this case, the gap between the relevant information and the predicted word is about 26-time steps, that is, *England* is at time step 1, and the predicted word is at time step 27. This large gap can pose a problem for RNNs, as they may not be able to retain contextual information over such long sequences, or the weights associated with that information may become very small. This is due to the structure of RNNs, where the gradients can become very small or even zero as they are repeatedly multiplied by the weight matrices in the network. This can make it difficult for the network to learn and can cause training to be slow or even fail altogether.

LSTM

A
RNN +
Memory & Forget
Gates

To overcome the issue of the vanishing gradient problem, LSTM was introduced.

In contrast to RNNs, LSTMs have a memory gate that allows them to store information about long-term dependencies in data. Furthermore, they possess a forget gate which helps filter out unnecessary information from previous states.

Another advantage of LSTMs is their low likelihood of encountering the problem of vanishing gradients. This occurs when gradients become very small or even zero during backpropagation, making it difficult for the network to learn. LSTMs address this issue by employing gates that regulate information flow through the network, allowing it to retain relevant details and discard irrelevant ones. *Figure 1.3* shows the comparison of RNN and LSTM structures. As compared to RNN, LSTM structure is complex:

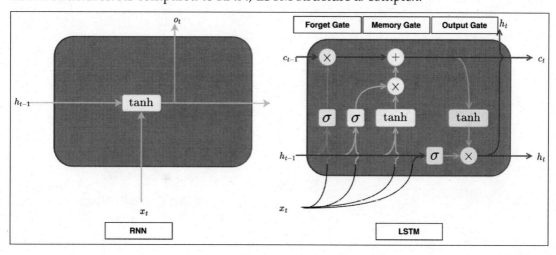

Figure 1.3: *Comparison of RNN and LSTM*

Limitation of LSTM

Limited ability to handle long sequences: Even though LSTM has a memory gate, they still struggle to handle long sequences. This is because they use a fixed length hidden state, which may be a problem if the input sequence is very long.

LSTMs process sequences sequentially, this can be slow and limit the ability to parallelize computations across multiple processors.

Cho's (2014) RNN encoder decoder[2]

The RNN encoder-decoder model is a sequence-to-sequence algorithm. It has three major components. Let us explore the components of an RNN encoder-decoder model with an example of English-to-French translation:

- **Encoder**: This is an RNN that encodes a variable-length input sequence (in this case, an English sentence) into a fixed-length vector.

- **Encoded vector**: The fixed-length vector output by the encoder.

- **Decoder**: This is also an RNN that takes the encoded vector as input and produces a variable-length output sequence (in this case, the French translation of the English input sequence).

---

[2] Cho, K., Van Merriënboer, B., Gulcehre, C., Bahdanau, D., Bougares, F., Schwenk, H., & Bengio, Y. (2014). Learning phrase representations using RNN encoder-decoder for statistical machine translation. *arXiv preprint arXiv:1406.1078*.

Q: For which Task is enc-dec beneficial?
Q2: Limitation of Bradais 2014 Attention?

6 ■ *Building Transformer Models with PyTorch 2.0*

The encoder-decoder model is especially beneficial for tasks such as machine translation and speech recognition, where the input sequence and output sequence may be of differing lengths. *Figure 1.4* illustrates a simplified representation of the RNN encoder-decoder model:

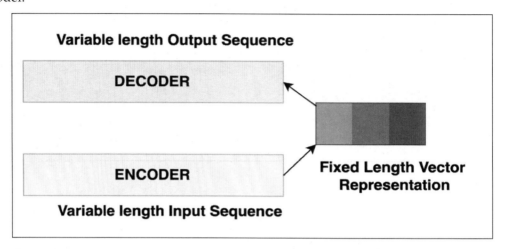

Figure 1.4: *Simplified representation of Cho's encoder-decoder model*

Limitation: The major limitation is vanishing gradient problem. The model generates a fixed-length vector representation of the input sequence using the final hidden state of the encoder RNN, which can result in the loss of important information from earlier time steps.

Bahdanau's (2014) attention mechanism[3]

Bahdanau's 2014 paper on attention mechanism introduced an extension to the RNN encoder-decoder model. It is also the encoder-decoder model with the addition of attention. Let us discuss what the attention mechanism is:

- It allows the model to selectively attend to certain parts of the input sequence that are more relevant to the output while ignoring others that are not as relevant.

- For example, in machine translation—the attention mechanism allows the model to focus on the most important words or phrases in predicting correct translation.

- In essence, the attention mechanism mimics human cognitive behavior by focusing on the most important words while filtering out noise.

Limitation: The major limitation is *Bahdanau's* mechanism is a local attention mechanism that only looks at a subset of the input sequence at a time. This works fine for the shorter sentence. However, performance reduces significantly if the input sentence is long.

---

[3] Bahdanau, D., Cho, K., & Bengio, Y. (2014). Neural machine translation by jointly learning to align and translate. *arXiv preprint arXiv:1409.0473.*

Let us summarize the important concept based on the above four architecture:

- The encoder-decoder approach is effective because it can handle different lengths of input and output sequences, which is often the case in machine translation and other NLP tasks where the number of words in input and output sequences may differ.

- Attention-mechanism is a crucial component in this approach because it enables a neural network to concentrate on specific parts of the input data that are essential for the task being performed. This helps the network to capture the relevant information more effectively, leading to better performance on various NLP tasks.

In the next section, we will discuss the transformer architecture and understand how encoder-decoder architecture and attention-mechanism are the major components of transformer architecture. *+ positional encoding*

Transformer architecture

There are many variants of the transformer; however, in this section, we will discuss the original transformer architecture proposed by *Vaswani et al.* (2017). They proposed the architecture for machine translation, (for example, English to the French Language). Let us highlight the most important aspects of transformer architecture before going into detail:

- Transformer uses an encoder-decoder architecture for machine translation.

- The encoder converts the input sequence into a sequence vector, with the length of the vector being equal to the length of the input sequence. It consists of multiple encoder blocks.

- The decoder also consists of multiple decoder blocks, and the sequence vector (output of encoder) is fed to all decoder blocks.

- Multi-head attention is a primary component of both the encoder and decoder.

- Positional encoding is a new concept introduced in the transformer architecture that encodes the positional information of each input token, representing its position in the input sequence.

Figure 1.5 shows the transformer architecture:

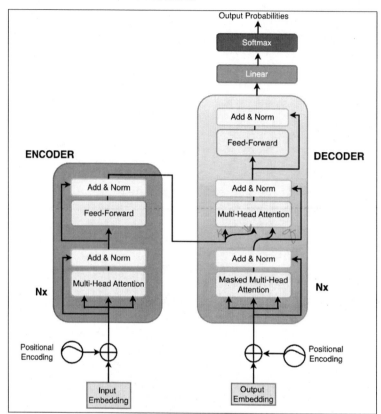

Figure 1.5: *Transformer architecture*

Embedding

As shown in *Figure 1.5*, the input sequence in the transformer is represented by an embedding vector. Embedding is the process of representing a word or token as vectors of fixed length.

Before we go in-depth about embeddings, let us understand how the text was traditionally represented in NLP. This will help us appreciate why we use embeddings. Traditionally, textual data in machine learning has been represented as n-gram words. Let us consider the example of 1-gram: if the total sample has 50,000 unique words, each input sequence would be represented with a 50,000-dimensional vector. We would fill these dimensions with the number of times each word appears in the specific input sequence. However, this approach has several problems:

- Even for small input sequences (for example, those with only two tokens), we require a high-dimensional vector (50,000), resulting in a highly sparse vector.

Q: Why are positional encodings more important in transformers as
gopere l to, say, RNNs !

Transformer Architecture ■ 9

- There is no meaningful way to perform mathematical operations on these high-dimensional vector representations.

Embedding overcomes those challenges. Embedding is a technique used to represent the word or sequence by a vector of real numbers that captures the meaning and context of the word or phrase.

A very simple example of embedding is taking a set of words, such as [cabbage, rabbit, eggplant, elephant, dog, cauliflower]; and representing each word as a vector in 2-dimensional space capturing for animal and color features. The embedding is shown in *Figure 1.6*. The final embedding vector may look like as follows:

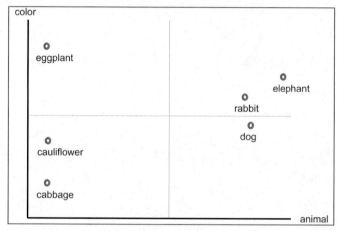

Figure 1.6: Embedding plotting

```
[cabbage, cauliflower, eggplant, dog, rabbit, elephant]=[[0.2,0.1],
[0.2,0.3], [0.2,0.8],[0.8,0.4],[0.75,0.6], [0.9,0.7]
```

We can see that the first dimension of cabbage and cauliflower is almost the same, as both represent vegetables. They are located nearby in the first dimension. Also, we can perform addition and subtraction on these embeddings because each dimension represents a specific concept, and tokens are near if they represent similar concepts.

Interestingly, in the real world, we mostly use a pre-trained model like BERT or word2vec, which has been trained with billions of examples and extract large dimension of feature (BERT use 768 dimensions). The embedding is highly accurate as compared to n-gram and offers greater flexibility during NLP.

Positional encoding

Positional encoding in a transformer is used to provide the model with information about the position of each word in the input sequence. Unlike previous architecture (like LSTM) where each token is processed in sequence (one by one); the transformer processes the input tokens in parallel. This means each token should also have positional information.

Let us understand how positional encoding is done. In the *Attention is All You Need* paper, the authors use a specific formula for positional encoding. The formula is as follows:

$$PE(pos, 2i) = \sin\left(\frac{pos}{10000^{2i/d}}\right)$$

$$PE(pos, 2i+1) = \cos\left(\frac{pos}{10000^{2i/d}}\right)$$

$PE(pos, 2i)$ and $PE(pos, 2i+1)$ are the $i-th$ and $(i+1)-th$ dimensions of the positional encoding vector for position pos in the input sequence.

pos is the position of the word in the input sequence, starting from 0.

i is the index of the dimension in the positional encoding vector, starting from 0.

d is the dimensionality of the embedding (512 in the original architecture)

This formula generates a set of positional encodings that are unique for each position in the input sequence and that change smoothly as the position changes.

It is important to understand that there are 256 pairs (512/2) of sine and cosine values. Thus, i goes from 0 to 255.

Let us unpack the formula:

$$PE(pos, 0) = \sin\left(\frac{pos}{10000^{0/512}}\right)$$

$$PE(pos, 1) = \cos\left(\frac{pos}{10000^{0/512}}\right)$$

$$PE(pos, 2) = \sin\left(\frac{pos}{10000^{2/512}}\right)$$

$$PE(pos, 3) = \cos\left(\frac{pos}{10000^{2/512}}\right)$$

$$|\ \square\ |$$

$$PE(pos, 511) = \cos\left(\frac{pos}{10000^{511/512}}\right)$$

The encoding of first word (position=0) will be:

$$PE(0, 0) = \sin\left(\frac{0}{10000^{0/512}}\right) = 0$$

$$PE(0, 1) = \cos\left(\frac{0}{10000^{0/512}}\right) = 1$$

$$PE(0, 2) = \sin\left(\frac{0}{10000^{2/512}}\right) = 0$$

$$PE(0, 3) = \cos\left(\frac{0}{10000^{2/512}}\right) = 1$$

$$| \square |$$

$$PE(0, 511) = \cos\left(\frac{0}{10000^{511/512}}\right) = 1$$

Thus, positional encoding of the first word will look like [0,1,0,1,...1]. The positional encoding for the second word will look like [0.8414,0.5403,0.8218,..]. If the embedding is of 512 dimensions. The position encoding vector looks like:

$$Positional\ Encoding\ Vector = E\Big[[size = 512],[size = 512],[size = 512],\ldots\Big]$$

Model input

As depicted in *Figure 1.7*, model input is the pointwise addition of positional encoding and embedding vector. Let us understand how we achieve this.

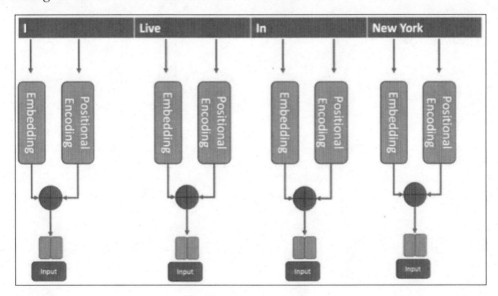

Figure 1.7: Model input

To represent "I Live In New York" with a tokenized length of 5, we add 1 tokens.

[' I,' Live', In, 'NewYork', <pad>]

At first, each token is represented by Integer. Here, word *I* is represented by 8667, *Live* is represented by 1362 , *In* is represented by 1300, *New York* is represented by 1301 and *<pad>* represented by 0. The resulting will be

IntegerRepresentation = [8667, 1362, 1300, 1301, 0]

We then pass these tokenized sequences to the embedding layer. The embedding of each token is represented by a vector of 512 dimensions. In the below example, the dimension of the vector *[embeddingtoke8667]* is 512.

Embedding
=[[embeddingtoken_8667], [embeddingtoken1362], [embeddingtoken1300], [embeddingtoken1301], [embeddingtoken0])

Finally, we perform the pointwise addition of Embedding and positional Encoding before feeding into the model.

PositionalEncodingVector
= [[size=512], [size = 512], [size = 512], [size = 512], [size = 512]] +

Embedding
= [[embeddingtoken_8667], [embeddingtoken1362], [embeddingtoken1300], [embeddingtoken1301]*

[embeddingtoken0] =

ModelInput = [[*size* = 512], [*size* = 512], [*size* = 512], [*size* = 512], [*size* = 512]]

Encoding layer

The encoder layer is a crucial component in the transformer architecture, responsible for processing and encoding input sequences into vector representations. Refer to the following figure:

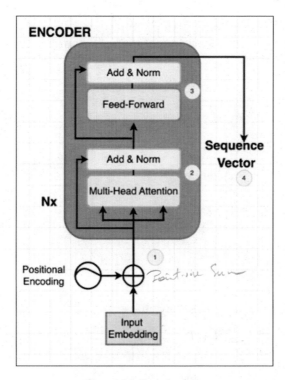

Figure 1.8: *Encoder layer*

Let us understand each subcomponent of the encoder layer in detail:

- **Input to the encoder**: The input to the first layer of the encoder is the pointwise summation of embeddings and positional encoding.

- **Multi-head attention**: A key component of the encoder block in a transformer is the multi-head self-attention mechanism. This mechanism allows the model to weigh the importance of different parts of the input when making a prediction. In a later section, we will discuss the details of multi-head attention.

- **Add and norm layer**: The add layer, also known as the residual connection, is used to add the input to the output of the previous layer before passing it through the next layer. This allows the model to learn the residual function, which is the difference between the input and the output, rather than the actual function. This can help to improve the performance of the model, especially when the number of layers is large. The norm layer normalizes the activations of a layer across all of its hidden units. This can help to stabilize the training of the model by preventing the input from getting too large or too small, which can cause issues such as vanishing gradients or exploding gradients.

- **Feed-forward**: The output of the multi-head self-attention mechanism is fed to the input of the feed-forward layer. Additionally, a non-linear activation function is applied. The feed-forward layer is important to extract the higher-level feature from the data. We also have add and norm layer after the feed-forward layer. The output of this is fed to next encoding block

- **Encoder output**: The last block of the encoder produces a sequence vector, which is then sent to the decoder blocks as features.

Attention mechanism

The attention mechanism has emerged as a versatile and powerful neural network component that allows models to weigh and prioritize relevant information in a given context. Its core concepts, self-attention, and multi-headed attention are instrumental in enabling the transformer architecture to achieve remarkable results. Let us delve into these concepts in more detail.

Self-attention

Self-attention mechanism is the key to the performance of the transformer. Let us understand how it works. Consider the following two examples:

> *Rabbit ate the carrot because it was hungry.*
>
> *Rabbit ate the carrot because it was tasty.*

What does *it* refers in each sentence. We cannot answer just by understanding the location and structure of the sentence. According to *Vaswani et al.* (2017): Meaning is a result of relationships between things, and self-attention is a general way of learning relationships.

Self-attention calculates the relationship weight between each token in the input sentence. Through this mechanism, the model understands the meaning of the input sentence.

Let us look at the attention calculation for "*it*" in both sentences. *Figure 1.9* demonstrates the calculation of relationship weights in the self-attention mechanism. In the first sentence, when we are processing the word "*it*" the model provides more weight to the rabbit than other words, whereas, in the second sentence model provides more weight to tasty.

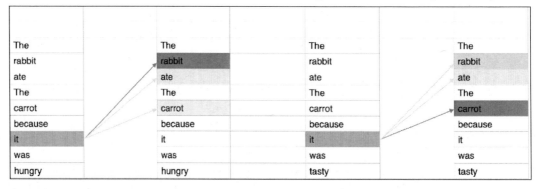

Figure 1.9: Self-attention mechanism

Multiheaded attention

Instead of using just one attention head, self-attention block use multiple heads. Each head uses different parameters with a different focus to extract different features from the input.

Figure 1.10 depicts the same example again with two attention heads. **Head1** is represented in the diagram in red, whereas **Head2** is represented in yellow. We can see that different heads are capturing different contextual relationships:

		Head1	Head2				Head1	Head2
The		The	The		The		The	The
rabbit		rabbit	rabbit		rabbit		rabbit	rabbit
ate		ate	ate		ate		ate	ate
The		The	The		The		The	The
carrot		carrot	carrot		carrot		carrot	carrot
because		because	because		because		because	because
it		it	it		it		it	it
was		was	was		was		was	was
hungry		hungry	hungry		tasty		tasty	tasty

Figure 1.10: Multi-head attention

Decoder layer

The decoder has a similar structure to the encoder but with an additional component called the masked self-attention mechanism. Let us look at the decoder architecture in detail:

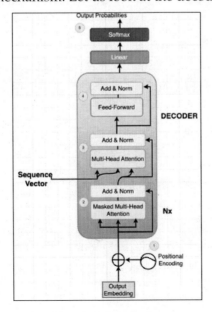

Figure 1.11: Decoder layer

- **Decoder input**: During training, the input to the first layer of the decoder are pointwise summation:

  o Embeddings of the target

  o Positional encoding of the target sequence.

- **Masked multi-head attention**: The key difference between masked multi-head attention and regular multi-head attention is that in masked multi-head attention, certain parts of the input sequence are masked or *blocked* so that the decoder cannot see them when generating the output sequence. The positions of the input sequence that correspond to the future target tokens (the tokens that have not been generated yet) are masked. This is required because:

  o Decoder works on generating one word at a time.

  o We only show the word until the current position; thus, the decoder will not be able to see the future targets that need to be generated.

  o As shown in the diagram, the input to the masked multi-head attention is vector generated by step 1--pointwise summation of

    ▪ Embeddings of the target

    ▪ Positional encoding of the target sequence.

- **Multi-head attention**: As you see in the diagram, the input to the multi-head attention mechanism in the decoder is typically the output of the encoder and the previously generated tokens in the output sequence. Instead of just the first decoder block, all decoder blocks receive the output of the encoder because:

  o The model can ensure that information from the input sequence is propagated through the entire decoding process.

  o The model is effectively regularized since each decoder block has access to the same information. This can help to prevent overfitting and improve the generalization performance of the model.

- **Feed-forward**: The output of the multi-head self-attention mechanism is fed to the input of the feed-forward layer. Additionally, a non-linear activation function is applied. The feed-forward layer is important for extracting the higher-level feature from the data.

- **Linear layer**: In transformer architecture, the linear layer in the decoder is a component that is used to produce the final output of the decoder. The input to the linear layer in the decoder is the output of the final layer of the decoder. Additionally, the SoftMax activation function is applied to generate the probabilities of the next word in the sequence.

Training process of transformer

The training process of a transformer for machine translation typically includes the following steps:

1. Data pre-processing and Generating Positional Encoding of Input and target.

2. Passing through the encoder and decoder layer.

3. Loss calculation: The generated output sequence is compared to the target output sequence, and a loss value is calculated using a loss function such as cross-entropy.

4. Backpropagation: The gradients of the loss with respect to the model's parameters are calculated using backpropagation.

5. Optimization: The model's parameters are updated using an optimization algorithm, such as Adam, to minimize the loss value. Repeat steps 3-7 for multiple epochs until the model's performance on a validation set stabilizes or reaches a satisfactory level.

It is also worth noting that during the training process, the model is exposed to large amounts of parallel text data, where the input and output sequences are already aligned, and the model learns to map the input sequence to the output sequence through the attention mechanism and linear layers.

Inference process of transformer

The inference process of a transformer typically includes the following steps:

1. Data pre-processing and Generating Positional Encoding of Input. It is noteworthy that during inference, we will not have a target sequence.

2. Passing through the encoder and decoder block. It is noteworthy that for decoder input, there is a slight difference during training and inference. During training, we pass the actual target to the first decoder block. whereas, during inference, instead of a target, we will pass tokens that are inferred till the current state. The reason is that we do not have a target sequence during inference.

Types of transformers and their applications

Until now, we explained the architecture of the transformer for machine translation. Nonetheless, there are many variations of the transformer. Let us review them.

Encoder only model

It only has the encoder layer of a transformer model. The attention layer can access all the words in the initial sentence. The encoder-only model often has bi-directional attention and is called an auto-encoding model. Let us look at examples and applications of the encoder-only model.

Some examples of encoder-only models that have been proposed include:

- **Bidirectional Encoder Representations from Transformers (BERT)**: BERT is a pre-trained transformer encoder-only model that has been trained on a large corpus of text and has been shown to be effective in a wide range of natural language processing tasks, including sentiment analysis, text classification, and question answering.

- **A Lite BERT (ALBERT)**: ALBERT is a lightweight version of BERT that has been shown to achieve similar performance as BERT while using less computational resources.

Applications:

- **Sentiment analysis**: The encoder can be trained to extract features from a given text and predict its sentiment (positive, negative, or neutral).

- **Text classification**: The encoder can be trained to classify a given text into different categories, such as news, sports, politics, and so on.

- **Named entity recognition**: The encoder can be trained to identify entities such as people, organizations, and locations in a given text.

- **Language modeling**: The encoder can be trained to predict the next token in a sequence of tokens.

Decoder-only model

It only uses the decoder layer of a Transformer architecture. The attention layer only has access to the sequence till the current token. This type of model is often called an autoregressive model because they are trained to predict the next token in a sequence based on the previous tokens in the same sequence:

Example:

- GPT from the OpenAI.

- A Conditional Transformer Language Model for Controllable Generation (CTRL) Model.

Applications:

- The decoder-only model has great usage in text generation and **Natural Language Generation (NLG)**.

Encoder-decoder model

Also called the sequence-to-sequence model, uses both an encoder and a decoder. The original paper proposing transformer is encoder-decoder model. The attention layer at the encoder has access to all tokens in the input sequence, whereas the attention layer of the decoder has a view of only the current and past tokens. The future tokens are masked to the attention layer of the decoder.

Example:

- BART (Denoising Autoencoder Pre-training for Sequence Generation Tasks).

Applications:

- Machine translation

Conclusion

In summary, this book chapter offers a thorough examination of the development and significant milestones of NLP models. We appreciate how the Transformer architecture incorporates the best aspects of preceding NLP models. Additionally, we have delved into the prominent features of the transformer, including the self-attention mechanism and positional encoding. lastly, we explored various transformer variations and their applications, recognizing the vast scope of its influence across multiple machine learning tasks.

In the next chapter will be implementing the fundamental architecture of the transformer model in PyTorch. This will give us a strong foundation in understanding how each component works, which will be crucial when we delve into applying the transformer in various fields such as NLP, computer vision, speech processing, and tabular data processing.

Quiz

1. **Which of the following is a key disadvantage of traditional RNNs?**

    a. They are computationally efficient for long sequences

    b. They are unable to model long-range dependencies

    c. They are easy to parallelize for faster training

    d. None of the above

2. **What is the primary advantage of using LSTM cells over traditional RNN cells?**

    a. LSTMs are faster to train

    b. LSTMs can better handle vanishing and exploding gradients

    c. LSTMs require less memory to store

    d. None of the above

3. **In an RNN Encoder-Decoder model, what is the role of the encoder?**

    a. To encode the input sequence into a fixed-length vector representation

    b. To decode the output sequence from the decoder

    c. To perform attention-based operations on the input sequence

    d. All of the above

4. **What are the primary advantages of using transformer architecture for natural language processing tasks?**

    a. Better ability to model long-range dependencies

    b. Lower computational requirements compared to RNNs

    c. Greater accuracy on low resource datasets

    d. None of these.

5. **Which of the following is an integral component of a transformer architecture?**

    a. Convolutional layers

    b. Recurrent layers

    c. Self-attention layers

    d. Fully connected layers.

6. **What is the purpose of the self-attention mechanism in a transformer architecture?**

    a. To enable selective focus on different parts of an input sequence

    b. Calculating the dot product between input and weight vectors

    c. Executing pooling operations on said input sequence

    d. None of the Above

7. **What role does the encoder layer in a transformer architecture plays?**

    a. Encoding input sequence into a vector representation

    b. Decoding the output sequence from the decoder

    c. Applying attention-based operations on this input sequence

    d. All of the above

8. **What role does the decoder play in a transformer architecture?**

    a. Encodes input sequence into a vector representation

    b. Decodes the output sequence from the encoder

    c. Performs attention-based operations on that output sequence

    d. None of the above.

9. **What is multi-head attention in the transformer architecture?**

    a. Multi-head attention refers to an attention mechanism that enables the model to attend simultaneously to multiple parts of an input sequence

    b. A mechanism for computing dot products between input and weight vectors

    c. A pooling operation which reduces the dimensionality of the input sequence

    d. None of the above

10. **What is the purpose of positional encoding in the transformer architecture?**

    a. To provide information about each token's position within an input sequence

    b. To add noise to the input sequence in order to improve model robustness

    c. To reduce its dimensionality

    d. None of the above

11. **What is the purpose of layer normalization in a transformer architecture?**

    a. To normalize each layer's output to improve model stability

    b. To randomly drop units out of the network to prevent overfitting

    c. Adjusting the learning rate during training

    d. None of the above.

12. **What are the consequences of increasing the number of encoder and decoder layers in a transformer architecture?**

    a. Improved model capacity with enhanced ability to capture complex patterns from input/output sequences.

    b. Decreased model capacity and ability to capture complex patterns in the input and output sequences

    c. No impact on model performance

    d. None of the above

13. **How is the output of the transformer architecture generated?**

    a. Applying a linear transformation to the final encoder state

    b. Passing through a linear layer followed by softmax activation

    c. Applying a fully connected layer to the final encoder state

    d. None of the above.

14. **What is the purpose of residual connections in a transformer architecture?**

   a. To allow gradients to flow more easily during training and improve model performance

   b. To reduce parameters in the model

   c. Adding noise into input sequence for improved robustness

   d. None of the above

15. **BERT is Decoder Only model**

   a. True

   b. False

16. **GPT from OpenAI is Decoder Only model**

   a. True

   b. False

Answers

1. b.

2. b.

3. a.

4. a.

5. c.

6. a.

7. a.

8. b.

9. a.

10. a.

11. a.

12. a.

13. b

14. a.

15. b.

16. a.

CHAPTER 2
Hugging Face Ecosystem

Introduction

In this chapter, we delve into the universe of the Hugging Face ecosystem, a pioneering machine learning platform for state-of-the-art ML models. Hugging Face has become the premier resource for practitioners and researchers alike, offering easy-to-use libraries, cutting-edge ML models, a convenient model sharing platform, and a robust community. Importantly, Hugging Face provides libraries for multiple frameworks (like TensorFlow, PyTorch, etc.). However, almost all features are supported for PyTorch. Through a comprehensive examination, this book chapter aims to provide a solid understanding of the Hugging Face ecosystem, its components, and how to leverage its capabilities to build PyTorch-based transformer models.

Structure

This chapter contains the following topics:

- System resources
- Overview of Hugging Face and its components
- Datasets
- Models

- Sharing your model on Hugging Face
- Models
- Spaces

Objectives

In this book chapter, we intend to provide a thorough understanding on the core functionalities and features of the Hugging Face ecosystem, specifically focusing on the transformers, datasets, and tokenizers libraries. You will learn those libraries with practical and real-world examples. The chapter will also guide you through the process of training and fine-tuning open-source models. You will learn how to share your fine-tuned models on the Hugging Face platform. Additionally, the chapter delves into the specifics of fine-tuning the stable-diffusion-based Dreambooth model. We will walk you through each step of this process, using practical examples to illustrate how to effectively share this model on Hugging Face. This journey will equip you with the skills and knowledge to leverage these advanced tools in your projects.

System resources

For detailed instructions on setting the environment, please follow instructions at **https://github.com/bpbpublications/Building-Transformer-Models-with-PyTorch/blob/main/General/SettingVirtualEnvironment.ipynb.**

Activate virtual environment:

```
conda activate transformer_learn
```

To proceed with the coding tasks outlined in this chapter, please install the necessary packages as follows:

```
pip3 install transformers
```

```
pip3 install datasets
```

```
pip3 install git+https://github.com/huggingface/diffusers
```

```
pip3 install accelerate
```

```
pip3 install ftfy
```

```
pip3 install tensorboard
```

```
pip3 install Jinja2
```

Overview of Hugging Face

The Hugging Face ecosystem (**https://huggingface.co/**) is a comprehensive suite of resources and tools that supports the development, implementation, and deployment of state-of-the-art deep learning models. It was founded in 2016 to democratize artificial intelligence by providing accessible and user-friendly tools to the border community. Specifically, Hugging Face is known for its open-source transformer library, which has become a de-facto package for transformer-based models like BERT, GPT, and the like. Additionally, HuggingFace.co is a vibrant community with over 150K models already uploaded by the community.

Figure 2.1 displays the Hugging Face user interface. It offers datasets and models for a broad spectrum of ML tasks, including multimodal, computer vision, audio, tabular, and reinforcement learning. Furthermore, the interface enables users to explore specific subfields in more detail.

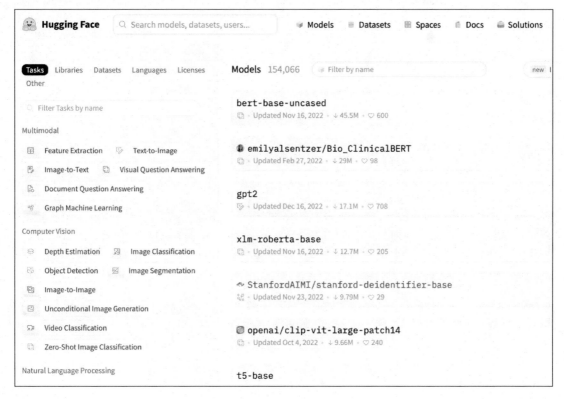

Figure 2.1: Hugging Face UI

Key component of Hugging Face

The Hugging Face ecosystem comprises six major components that together create a comprehensive machine learning platform. *Table 2.1* illustrates the key elements of the Hugging Face ecosystem:

Sl. No.	Name	Description
1	Transformer library	It open-source library offering a wide-range of pre-trained models (over 190).
2	Dataset library	It has over 24K ready-to-use datasets for ML.
3	Tokenizer library	Flexible library to handle pre-processing and tokenization of text data for NLP
4	ML integrations	It supports integration with multiple frameworks (PyTorch, TensorFlow, and JAX/Flax). PyTorch is supported by all models. Other frameworks have limited support.
5	Inference API	Enable user to deploy model from Hugging Face with just few lines of code. Overall, allows production-ready model deployment for small to large-scale project
6	Hugging Face Spaces	Users can build web applications, host demos, and collaborate with the community in a user-friendly environment.

Table 2.1: *Key components of Hugging Face*

Let us go over the major components in the next section.

Tokenizers

A tokenizer converts raw text into small units (character, word, sub-word) processed by NLP. *Table 2.2* shows the primary illustration of tokenization. HuggingFace Tokenizer provides several pre-trained tokenizer algorithms, as well as the mechanism to train your tokenizer algorithm.

The tokenizers		
Character Level	['T', 'h', 'e', ' ', 't', 'o', 'k', 'e', 'n', 'i', 'z', 'e', 'r', 's']	
Word Level	['The', 'Tokenizers']	
Sub-word Level	['the', 'token', '##izer', '##s']	

Table 2.2: *Tokenization process*

Create your custom Tokenizer

In certain situations, such as working in specialized fields like healthcare with unique jargon, you may need to develop a custom tokenizer; this section will guide you through the process of creating a tailor-made tokenizer to suit your specific needs.

Training

The following code demonstrates how:

1. Train a tokenizer with your dataset

2. Save the trained tokenizer as a JSON file,

3. Use it for inference.

Please modify line 4 by providing the file path of the text file on your computer. The accompanying documents contain the tokenizer_train.txt file; however, you can train the tokenizer with any text based on your use case. Additionally, modify line 13 by providing the location of your machine:

```
from tokenizers import Tokenizer, models, pre_tokenizers, trainers

'''Training'''

# Read the dataset from a file. The txt file is available in book's GitHub repo

with open("/Users/premtimsina/Documents/bpbbook/chapter2_huggingFace/datasets/tokenizer_train.txt", "r") as file:

    dataset = [line.strip() for line in file.readlines()]

# Initialize a BPE tokenizer. Byte Pair Encoding (BPE) is a sub-word tokenizer technique.

tokenizer = Tokenizer(models.BPE())

# Set the pre-tokenizer to split the input into words

tokenizer.pre_tokenizer = pre_tokenizers.Whitespace()

# Train the BPE tokenizer on the dataset

trainer = trainers.BpeTrainer(special_tokens=["[UNK]", "[CLS]", "[SEP]", "[PAD]", "[MASK]"])

tokenizer.train_from_iterator(dataset, trainer=trainer)

tokenizer.save("/Users/premtimsina/Documents/bpbbook/chapter2_huggingFace/model/tokenizer.json")
```

Inference

Let us employ our tailor-made tokenizer to perform inference. In the following code, **PreTrainedTokenizerFast** provides the mechanism to load the pre-trained tokenizers:

```
'''Inference'''

from transformers import PreTrainedTokenizerFast

fast_tokenizer = PreTrainedTokenizerFast(tokenizer_file="/Users/premtimsina/Documents/bpbbook/chapter2_huggingFace/model/tokenizer.json")
```

```
text = "The Tokenizers"
encoded = tokenizer.encode(text)
# Print the tokenized text
print(encoded.tokens)
```

Output:
```
['T', 'h', 'e', 'T', 'o', 'ken', 'iz', 'ers']
```

Visualization:
```
from tokenizers.tools import EncodingVisualizer
# Visualize the tokenization process
visualizer = EncodingVisualizer(fast_tokenizer._tokenizer)
visualizer(text="The Tokenizers")
```

Output:

Figure 2.2 displays the tokenization output for the phrase *The Tokenizers*. We can see that the tokenization process results in 8 tokens:

Figure 2.2: *Tokenization output*

Use pre-trained tokenizer from Hugging Face

In the following code, we utilize the pre-trained tokenizer **bert-base-uncased**. For general language purposes, a pre-trained tokenizer is typically more effective than a custom tokenizer:

```
from transformers import BertTokenizer
tokenizer = BertTokenizer.from_pretrained("bert-base-uncased")
print( tokenizer.tokenize("The tokenizers") )
```

Output:
```
['the', 'token', '##izer', '##s']
```

When we compare the tokenization done by our custom tokenizer (['T', 'h', 'e', 'T', 'o', 'ken', 'iz', 'ers']) with the pre-trained BertTokenizer (['the', 'token', '##izer', '##s']), it is evident that BertTokenizer performs much better. This is because we trained the custom tokenizer with only a few lines of code. To produce an optimal tokenizer, it is necessary to provide a sufficient amount of training data. However, creating a custom tokenizer is extremely useful when working in a specialized field that requires a lot of domain-specific vocabulary.

Datasets

[handwritten: Apache Arrow columnar in-memory]

Datasets is a powerful library that simplifies the process of downloading, pre-processing, and managing datasets for machine learning. Here are some salient features of the datasets:

- **Preloaded datasets**: It provides a vast array of datasets in multiple areas of ML tasks: computer vision, audio processing, NLP, reinforcement learning, and so on.

- **Efficient data handling and ease of use**: Under the hood, it uses Apache Arrow, a columnar in-memory data format that allows for efficient data processing and storage. Additionally, it has nice data versioning (good for reproducibility), and UI to review the dataset quickly.

- **Integration with Hugging Face Transformer and PyTorch**: The Datasets library is designed to be compatible with the Hugging Face Transformers library. Additionally, it has seamless integration with your PyTorch Framework.

Using Hugging Face dataset

Preparing the data: In the following example, we downloaded IMDb dataset and printed the sample row. As you can see in line 3, you can download the dataset just in one line:

```
from datasets import load_dataset
# Load the IMDb movie review dataset
imdb_dataset = load_dataset("imdb")
# Load the pre-trained model and tokenizer
# Select a sample text from the dataset
sample_text = imdb_dataset["test"][0]["text"]
print (sample_text)
```

Output:

I love sci-fi and am willing to put up with a lot. Sci-fi movies/TV are usually underfunded…..

Using the IMDB dataset for sentiment analysis, let us do the sentiment analysis with the IMDB dataset:

```
from transformers import  AutoModelForSequenceClassification, pipeline
from transformers import AutoTokenizer
model_name = "distilbert-base-uncased-finetuned-sst-2-english"
```

```
tokenizer = AutoTokenizer.from_pretrained(model_name)

model = AutoModelForSequenceClassification.from_pretrained(model_name)

sentiment_analysis_pipeline = pipeline("sentiment-analysis", model=model,
tokenizer=tokenizer)

# Select a sample text from the dataset

sample_text = imdb_dataset["test"][0]["text"]

# Perform sentiment analysis on the sample text

result = sentiment_analysis_pipeline(sample_text)

# Print the result

print("Sample Text:", sample_text)

print("Sentiment Analysis Result:", result)
```

Output:

Sentiment Analysis Result: [{'label': 'NEGATIVE', 'score': 0.999616265296936}]

Analysis:

This is an exciting development! With less than 20 lines of code, we were able to perform end-to-end sentiment analysis. You can customize the above code to suit your specific use case. In the above code, we use the pre-trained model **distilbert-base-uncased-finetuned-sst-2-english** for both tokenization and inference. This specific model is trained with an uncased English vocabulary and has been fine-tuned on the **Stanford Sentiment Treebank (SST-2)** dataset for sentiment analysis tasks. It is essential to understand that when using a pre-trained model for inference, it is advisable to use the same model for tokenization as well.

load_dataset(...).with_format("torch")

Using the Hugging Face dataset on PyTorch

Directly passing Hugging Face's dataset to DataLoader: In the following code, we are loading the dataset with **torch** format. This will convert the data into PyTorch Tensor:

```
from datasets import load_dataset

from torch.utils.data import DataLoader, Dataset

import torch

# Load the HuggingFace dataset (IMDb movie review dataset as an example)

imdb_dataset = load_dataset("imdb").with_format("torch")
```

Let us review the loaded dataset: We can review dataset using **DatasetInfo**:

```
from datasets import DatasetInfo

print(DatasetInfo(imdb_dataset))
```

Output:
```
DatasetInfo(description=DatasetDict({
    train: Dataset({
        features: ['text', 'label'],
        num_rows: 25000
    })
    test: Dataset({
        features: ['text', 'label'],
        num_rows: 25000
    })
    unsupervised: Dataset({
        features: ['text', 'label'],
        num_rows: 50000
    }))
```

Analysis:

The **imdb_dataset** has a train, test, and unsupervised components. Additionally, each row contains both text and label components. Now let us create the **DataLoader**:

```
from torch.utils.data import DataLoader, Dataset

train_loader = DataLoader(imdb_dataset['train'], batch_size=8, shuffle=True)

test_loader = DataLoader(imdb_dataset['test'], batch_size=8, shuffle=False)
```

The accompanying Notebook files contain an approach where we create **CustomDataset** class.

Models

There are over 150K models on Hugging Face for many machine-learning tasks. In the earlier example, we discussed the sentiment analysis on IMDB dataset using the pre-trained transformer model.

In this section, we will focus on the fine-tuning of the stable diffusion-based implementation of Dreambooth. Dreambooth is a text-to-image diffusion model that generates images based on the text input provided. Typically, a text-to-image model can generate an image based on a prompt like *man climbing Mount Everest*. However, if you want the model to generate an image of you climbing Mount Everest, Dreambooth can be used to fine-tune the model with a few images of yourself. Once the model is fine-tuned, it can generate any image that includes you doing something. This makes Dreambooth an effective tool for subject-driven image generation.

Environmental setup

Please activate your Conda environment and enter the following command in the terminal. Follow the prompts and input the necessary parameters accordingly.

```
accelerate config
```

The **accelerate config** command is typically used to set up the default parameters for the Accelerate library, such as the precision mode (for example mixed precision or full precision), the gradient accumulation settings, and other related parameters. This command must be run before any other code is executed in the PyTorch script to ensure the Accelerate library is configured correctly.

Training

Make sure to download train_dreambooth.py from the GitHub and place it on your computer. (**https://github.com/huggingface/diffusers/tree/main/examples/dreambooth**). Please run the following command on your Terminal. This will start training the Dreambooth model:

```
export MODEL_NAME="CompVis/stable-diffusion-v1-4"

export INSTANCE_DIR="/Users/premtimsina/Documents/bpbbook/chapter2_
huggingFace/datasets/dreambooth/photo"

export OUTPUT_DIR="/Users/premtimsina/Documents/bpbbook/chapter2_
huggingFace/datasets/dreambooth/model"


accelerate launch train_dreambooth.py \
  -pretrained_model_name_or_path=$MODEL_NAME   \
  -instance_data_dir=$INSTANCE_DIR \
  -output_dir=$OUTPUT_DIR \
  -instance_prompt="a photo of sks boy" \
  -resolution=512 \
  -train_batch_size=1 \
  -gradient_accumulation_steps=1 \
  -learning_rate=5e-6 \
  -lr_scheduler="constant" \
  -lr_warmup_steps=0 \
  -max_train_steps=1000
```

To provide a better understanding of the parameter mentioned above, let us explore its meaning in detail. To fine-tune the Dreambooth model, we need to export three variables in the command line interface:

The first variable is **MODEL_NAME**, which specifies the name of the base model. In this case, we are using the stable diffusion model.

The second variable is **INSTANCE_DIR**, which specifies the photo's location for fine-tuning the model. We recommend using 5-10 images in PNG format. I used these three photos in my fine-tuning. You could use any subject, including cat, flower, yourself, and so on. However, a photo with a clear face and transparent background seems to work better:

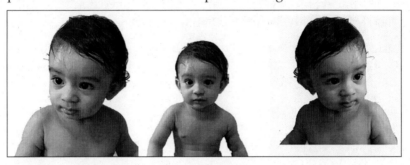

Figure 2.3: *Pictures used for training*

- The third variable is **OUTPUT_DIR**, which specifies the directory where the fine-tuned model will be saved. Please ensure that this directory is empty before running the code.

- The **instance_prompt** parameter is a crucial identifier that is required for inference. In the provided code, the **instance_prompt** is set as *a photo of sks bo*y. Please ensure that you provide an appropriate identifier for your training process, as this will be necessary for accurate inference.

The total training time for the model may vary based on the specifications of your computer and the configuration you have set for acceleration. It typically takes 30 minutes to 1 hour to complete the entire training process. As an example, I conducted the training on a Mac with an M2 Max processor and 32 GB of RAM, and it took me 45 minutes.

Inference

You have successfully created your Dreambooth model. Now, let us use that model to generate images by providing various prompts:

```
from diffusers import StableDiffusionPipeline

import torch

model_id = "/Users/premtimsina/Documents/bpbbook/chapter2_huggingFace/
datasets/dreambooth/model/"
```

```
pipe = StableDiffusionPipeline.from_pretrained(model_id, torch_dtype=torch.
float16).to("mps")
prompt = "a photo of sks boy riding horse"
image = pipe(prompt, num_inference_steps=500, guidance_scale=7.5).images[0]
image.save("/Users/premtimsina/Documents/bpbbook/chapter2_huggingFace/
datasets/dreambooth/photo/boy_ridding_horse.png")
```

Explanation:

- In line 4 of the code, we have converted the tensor to **mps** format as it is required to run the code on Mac systems. However, if you are running the code on a GPU, you need to convert the tensor to **cuda** format instead.

- It is crucial to ensure that the tensor is in the correct format to avoid any errors during code execution. If you encounter any issues, please double-check the format of the tensor and make the necessary adjustments accordingly.

- Additionally, please note that in line 6, the prompt starts with a photo of **sks** boy. We have given this identifier during training, and during inference, your identifier should always start with this identifier.

- *Figure 2.4* shows the image generated by the custom **DreamBooth** model. The image generated by our model appears decent. The facial features seem to match. If you want to generate high-quality images, you can experiment and optimize the training parameters.

Here are a few images on Inference:

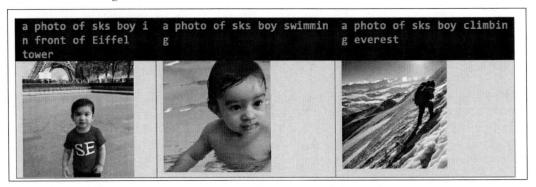

Figure 2.4: Image generated by custom DreamBooth model

This is awesome. With just a few lines of code—We create text to image generator with the subject we specified.

Sharing your model on Hugging Face

In this section, we will cover the process of sharing your model on Hugging Face and creating a space via Gradle. Detailed instructions for the process can be found in the accompanying notebook. Once the model is successfully shared, it will appear in your Hugging Face account as follows.

Model

The following figure displays the **dreambooth_boy** model on huggingface.co, where you can enter a prompt and, as depicted in the illustration, obtain a generated image corresponding to the given prompt:

Figure 2.5: *Shared model in Hugging Face*

Spaces

The following screenshot showcases the corresponding space for our Dreambooth-boy model. Hugging Face Spaces offer a straightforward approach to develop applications based on your model. Specifically, you can perform the following tasks:

- Deploy your model

    o   Host Jupyter notebooks

    o   Utilize Gradio to design user-friendly interfaces,

    o   Create interactive web applications using Streamlit

    o   Share your space with collaborators, enabling multiple individuals to work on the same app.

Figure 2.6: Your model space in Hugging Face

Conclusion

In this chapter, we have taken a detailed look at the Hugging Face ecosystem, a key player in the world of machine learning. Focusing on its core elements - the Transformers, Datasets, and Tokenizers libraries – we have shown you how to apply these tools in real-world scenarios. We also learned how to fine-tune models for specific tasks and share them on the Hugging Face platform, making them accessible to others. This journey has provided a practical understanding of how to use these advanced technologies in various projects, particularly highlighting the process of adapting the Dreambooth model for personalized use.

The Hugging Face ecosystem stands out as a versatile and comprehensive resource for anyone in the field of AI, specifically Transformer based model. It offers a range of functionalities, from creating custom tokenizers to leveraging pre-trained models. By exploring its capabilities, we have equipped you with the knowledge and skills to explore the vast possibilities of machine learning, using Hugging Face's innovative tools to enhance your work. With this chapter, you are now ready to dive deeper into the world of AI, using the Hugging Face ecosystem as a solid foundation for your future projects.

Quiz

1. **What is the purpose of the Tokenizers library in the Hugging Face ecosystem?**

    a. To split text into individual tokens

    b. To convert text to image data

    c. To preprocess audio data

2. **Which tokenizer algorithm is used in BERT?**

    a. Byte Pair Encoding (BPE)

    b. WordPiece

    c. SentencePiece

3. **What is the purpose of a subword tokenizer?**

    a. To split words into their component morphemes

    b. To split text into smaller pieces than words

    c. To remove stopwords from text

4. **How can you fine-tune a pre-trained model in Hugging Face?**

    a. By providing your own training data and labels

    b. By adjusting the hyperparameters in the model configuration

    c. By increasing the number of epochs during training

5. **What is the purpose of the Datasets library in the Hugging Face ecosystem?**

    a. To generate synthetic datasets for training

    b. To preprocess and transform raw data for machine learning

    c. To provide pre-labeled datasets for machine learning tasks

6. **What is mixed-precision training in Hugging Face?**

    a. A technique for optimizing model performance using multiple GPUs

    b. A technique for combining multiple pre-trained models into a single model

    c. A technique for reducing the memory usage of deep learning models during training

7. **Which of the following is correct if you are running your code in GPU?**

   a. pipe = StableDiffusionPipeline.from_pretrained(model_id, torch_dtype=torch.float16).to("mps")

   b. pipe = StableDiffusionPipeline.from_pretrained(model_id, torch_dtype=torch.float16).to("cuda")

8. **What is DreamBooth?**

   a. DreamBooth is a text-to-image generation implementation based on Stable Diffusion that allows users to generate personalized subject images.

   b. It is image to text model

Answers

1. a.

2. b.

3. b.

4. a.

5. c.

6. c.

7. b.

8. a.

Join our book's Discord space

Join the book's Discord Workspace for Latest updates, Offers, Tech happenings around the world, New Release and Sessions with the Authors:

https://discord.bpbonline.com

CHAPTER 3
Transformer Model in PyTorch

Introduction

Welcome to this chapter where we will be breaking down PyTorch's implementation of the transformer model. We will look at each part of how PyTorch runs transformer models, and go over different setups, such as encoder only, decoder only, and the core transformer layer. We will also go over two important ideas: Positional encoding and masking, which play a huge role in how transformer models work. To ensure everything is clear, we will discuss each component in detail, supplemented with practical examples. This chapter is all about getting you comfortable and confident with how transformer models work in PyTorch.

Structure

The chapter is organized in the following structure:

- System resources
- Transformer components in PyTorch
- Embedding
- Masking

- Encoder component of a transformer

- Decoder component of a transformer

- Transformer layer

Objectives

In this chapter, our objective is to dive deeply into the PyTorch implementation of the transformer architecture, thoroughly examining its various components. We will guide you through the process of developing end-to-end transformer models using PyTorch. This includes learning how to build models in different configurations, such as Encoder Only, Decoder Only, and the combined Encoder-Decoder setup. Our focus will be on providing a comprehensive understanding of each aspect of these models, ensuring you gain practical knowledge for implementing them effectively in your projects.

System resources

For detailed instructions on setting the environment, please follow instructions at **https://github.com/bpbpublications/Building-Transformer-Models-with-PyTorch/blob/main/General/SettingVirtualEnvironment.ipynb**.

Activate virtual environment:

```
conda activate transformer_learn
```

To proceed with the coding tasks outlined in this chapter, please install the necessary packages as follows:

```
pip3 install transformers
```

```
pip3 install datasets
```

```
pip3 install torch
```

```
pip3 install torchtext
```

Transformer components in PyTorch

Figure 3.1 illustrates the transformer architecture discussed in *Chapter 1, Transformer Architecture*:

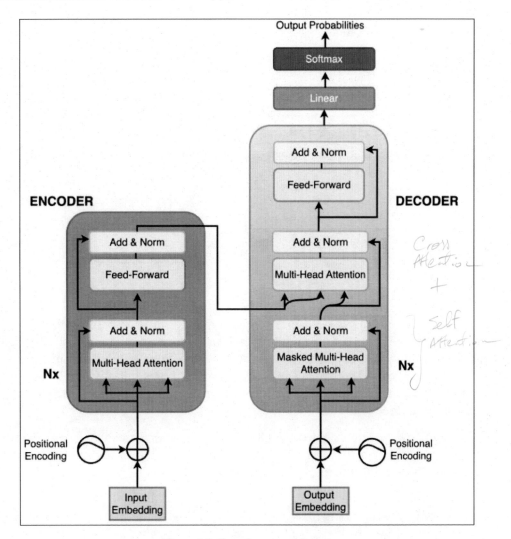

Figure 3.1: *Transformer architecture*

Table 3.1 displays the key components of the transformer in PyTorch. In the subsequent sections of this chapter, we will explore these components in greater detail.

Embedding	`torch.nn.Embedding`	Implements an embedding layer in neural networks. An embedding layer is used to convert discrete tokens (such as words, characters, or other discrete elements) into continuous vector representations.

Positional Encoding (PE)	Not Available	Pytorch does not has inbuilt implementation of PE

Transformer Encoder	`torch.nn.TransformerEncoder`
	
	`torch.nn.TransformerEncoderLayer`
		It consists of two main components: Multi-head attention, feed-forward layer

Transformer Decoder	`torch.nn.TransformerDecoder`
	
	`torch.nn.TransformerDecoderLayer`
		It consists of three main components: self-attn, multi-head-attn and feedforward network

Transformer	`Torch.nn.Transformer`	It consists of both an encoder and a decoder layer

Table 3.1: Major transformer components in PyTorch

Embedding

The **torch.nn.Embedding** is not a pre-trained embedding model. Instead, it learns the embedding vectors during the training process. It utilizes a lookup table (usually a matrix) to map each unique element (for example words or characters) onto an integer-valued continuous vector with fixed dimensions. The lookup table is initially filled with random values and learned by the model during training. Here is a simple explanation of the algorithm behind **torch.nn:Embedding**:

- Assign each unique element in the vocabulary an index. You could store this mapping using a dictionary-like structure; for instance, assign **{"apple": 0, "banana": 1, "orange": 2}**

- Create an embedding matrix (a lookup table) with the size **(number_of_unique_ elements, embedding_dimension).** Each row in this matrix corresponds to an element's index in the dictionary; **embedding_dimension** determines how large each element's continuous vector representation should be.

- Start the embedding matrix with random values; these will be adjusted during training.

- Embedding Matrix acts as a lookup table. When you need to convert an element into its embedding representation, look up the row in the embedding matrix.

- During training, the model adjusts the value of the embedding matrix so that the similar token has similar vector representation. This is achieved by minimizing the loss function and updating the embedding matrix using an optimizer (for example gradient descent).

Example

The following section presents an illustration of how the embedding layer is implemented in PyTorch:

```
import torch
import torch.nn as nn


# Define the parameters
num_embeddings = 10  # Size of the vocabulary
embedding_dim = 3  # Embedding vector size


# Create the embedding layer
embedding = nn.Embedding(num_embeddings=num_embeddings, embedding_
dim=embedding_dim)
input_tokens = torch.tensor([1, 5])
output_embeddings = embedding(input_tokens)
print(output_embeddings)
```

In line 9, num_embeddings represents the total number of unique tokens in our dataset, and **embedding_dim** refers to the dimension of the vector used to represent each token. The code above creates an embedding layer with 10 unique tokens, and each token is represented by a 3-dimensional vector. When we pass tensor ([1, 5]) for embedding, the output is:

```
tensor([[-1.3973, -1.9344,  0.8324],

        [-0.8258, -0.6737,  0.2057]], grad_fn=<EmbeddingBackward0>)
```

In the transformer model, the embedding layer will be the first layer of your neural nets. Also, in the default setting of the transformer model, the input to the embedding layer should be of shape **[max_seq_length, batch_size]**.

Positional encoding

PyTorch does not have an inbuilt positional encoding module. Thus, let us write a class to do positional encoding: The positional embedding excepts the embedding vector, and returns the positional encoding information attached to the embedding vector. Importantly, Encoder excepts the data in the form of **[sequence length, batch size, embedding dimension]**.Thus, the input and output of the PE should adhere to that dimension:

```
class PositionalEncoding(nn.Module):
```

```
def __init__(self, dim_embedding, dropout=0.1, max_seq_len=5000):
    super(PositionalEncoding, self).__init__()
    self.dropout = nn.Dropout(p=dropout)
    postional_encoding = torch.zeros(max_seq_len, dim_embedding)
    position = torch.arange(0, max_seq_len, dtype=torch.float).
unsqueeze(1)
    denom_term = torch.exp(torch.arange(0, dim_embedding, 2).float() *
(-math.log(10000.0) / dim_embedding))
    postional_encoding[:, 0::2] = torch.sin(position * denom_term)
    postional_encoding[:, 1::2] = torch.cos(position * denom_term)
    postional_encoding = postional_encoding.unsqueeze(0).transpose(0, 1)
    self.register_buffer('postional_encoding', postional_encoding)

def forward(self, x):
    x = x + self.postional_encoding[:x.size(0), :]
    return self.dropout(x)
```

Explanation:

- In line 7, we are doing unsqueeze so that the position tensor changes to the dimension of [**max_seq_len** **,1**]. This is required for matrix multiplication on lines 7 and 8.

- In line 11, the **unsqueeze(0).transpose(0, 1)** operation is used to change the shape of the positional encoding tensor to match the expected input shape of the transformer model.

- **unsqueeze(0)**: This operation adds an extra dimension at position 0. If the original shape of the positional encoding tensor **pe** is [**max_len, d_model]**, after **unsqueeze(0),** the shape becomes [**1, max_len, d_model]**. This operation essentially turns the 2D tensor into a 3D tensor with a batch dimension of size 1.

- **transpose(0, 1)**: This operation swaps the first two dimensions of the tensor. So, the shape [**1, max_len, d_model] becomes [max_len, 1, d_model]**. This transposition is done to make the positional encoding tensor compatible with the input shape that the transformer expects, which is [**sequence length, batch size, embedding dimension]**.

The examples of using a Positional Encoder are provided in the accompanying notebook.

Masking

Masking is a crucial concept in the transformer architecture, as it is used to hide or replace specific input tokens during processing. A thorough understanding of masking is essential to create an accurate transformer model. These masking parameters are present in all variations of transformer models, and it is important to have a good grasp of them before delving into actual model development:

- **tgt_mask**: An optional tensor of shape **(seq_len, seq_len)** representing the mask for the input sequence. It is used to prevent the decoder from attending to future tokens. The format should be:

  ```
  tensor([[0., -inf, -inf],
      [0., 0., -inf],
      [0., 0., 0.]], device='mps:0')
  ```

  o   In above example, seq_length=3

  o   where **-inf** signifies the tokens that need to be masked

- **memory_mask**: An optional tensor of shape (**seq_len, src_seq_len**) representing the mask for the encoder output sequence. It is used to prevent the decoder from attending future tokens in the encoder input sequence:

  ```
  tensor([[0., -inf, -inf],
      [0., 0., -inf],
      [0., 0., 0.]], device='mps:0')
  ```

  o   in the above example, seq_length=3

  o   where -inf signifies the tokens that need to be masked. Usually, you will not mask the memory: Thus, you will pass:

  ```
  tensor([[0., 0, 0],
     [0., 0., 0],
     [0., 0., 0.]], device='mps:0')
  ```

- **tgt_key_padding_mask**: An optional tensor of shape **(batch_size, seq_len)** representing the mask for padding tokens in the input sequence:

  ```
  tensor([[False, False, False],
      [False, False, False],
      [False, True, False],
      [True, True, False]], device='mps:0')
  ```

  o   In the above example, batch_size=4, seq_len=3. True signifies the particular token is a padded token and masks it. False signifies the particular token is not a padded token and do not masks it.

- **memory_key_padding_mask**: An optional tensor of shape **(batch_size, src_seq_len)** representing the mask for padding tokens in the encoder output sequence:

```
tensor([[False, False, False],
    [False, False, False],
    [False, True, False],
    [True, True, False]], device='mps:0')
```

  o   In the above example, batch_size=4, seq_len=3. True signifies the particular token is padded token. False signifies the particular token is not padded token.

Accompanying notebook illustrates how to implement masking while you create your PyTorch model.

Encoder component of a transformer

There are many use cases where you just need an encoder layer of the transformer. Some of the examples are sentiment analysis, text classification, NER, and the like. Thus, PyTorch provides us the flexibility of using just the encoder layer. Below is an example of a simple classification model using **TransformerEncoder** and **TransformerEncoderLayer**:

```
class TextClassifier(nn.Module):
    def __init__(self, vocab_size, embedding_dim, nhead, num_layers, num_
classes):
        super(TextClassifier, self).__init__()


        self.embedding = nn.Embedding(vocab_size, embedding_dim)
        self.positional_encoding = PositionalEncoding(embedding_dim)
        self.encoder_layer = nn.TransformerEncoderLayer(embedding_dim,
nhead)
        self.encoder = nn.TransformerEncoder(self.encoder_layer, num_
layers)
        self.fc = nn.Linear(embedding_dim, num_classes)
        self.embedding_dim=embedding_dim
        self.init_weights()

    def init_weights(self) -> None:
        initrange = 0.1
        self.embedding.weight.data.uniform_(-initrange, initrange)
        for layer in self.encoder.layers:
```

```python
            nn.init.xavier_uniform_(layer.self_attn.out_proj.weight)
            nn.init.zeros_(layer.self_attn.out_proj.bias)
            nn.init.xavier_uniform_(layer.linear1.weight)
            nn.init.zeros_(layer.linear1.bias)
            nn.init.xavier_uniform_(layer.linear2.weight)
            nn.init.zeros_(layer.linear2.bias)
        self.fc.bias.data.zero_()
        self.fc.weight.data.uniform_(-initrange, initrange)


    def forward(self, x, key_padding_mask=None):
        x = self.embedding(x)* math.sqrt(self.embedding_dim)
        x = self.positional_encoding(x)
        x = self.encoder(x, src_key_padding_mask=key_padding_mask)

        # Pooling the last dimension and use the first token representation
        x = x.mean(dim=0)

        # Fully connected layer for classification
        x = self.fc(x)
        x=torch.sigmoid(x)
        return x
```

Analysis:

- In lines 7 and 8, we are constructing a **TransformerEncoder** in two steps:

- First, we define a single encoder block using **TransformerEncoderLayer(embedding_dim, nhead)**. Important consideration while choosing **nhead**—the division (**embedding_dim // n_head**) should result in an integer (remainder should be zero).

- Second, we create the entire encoder by instantiating **TransformerEncoder** and passing the **TransformerEncoderLayer** along with the number of encoder blocks to be used.

- Line 13 illustrates the weight initialization ensuring efficient learning and improved convergence in neural networks. This is an essential component; otherwise, you may notice the **exploding gradient** or slow convergence.

- In Line 35, the output of the last block of the encoder is passed to the fully connected layer for classification.

- It is interesting to understand what we are doing on line 32. After passing the input through the embedding, positional encoding, and transformer encoder layers, the tensor x has a shape of **(sequence_length, batch_size, embedding_dim)**. We want to create a fixed-size representation of the entire sequence to feed into the **Fully Connected (FC)** layer for classification. One simple way to do this is to average the embeddings of all tokens in the sequence, which is called mean pooling. To perform mean pooling, we use the mean() function with the argument dim=0, which calculates the mean along the sequence dimension. This reduces the tensor shape from **(sequence_length, batch_size, embedding_dim) to (batch_size, embedding_dim)**.

The end-to-end implementation of text classification with IMDB dataset is provided in the accompanying notebook.

Decoder component of a transformer

There are also many use cases where you just need a decoder layer of transformer. Some examples are text generation, code generation, and music generation. Thus, PyTorch provides the functionality of just using the transformer's decoder. Below is an example of simple text generation model using just **TransformerDecoderLayer**, and **TransformerDecoder**:

```python
class TransformerDecoder(nn.Module):
    def __init__(self, vocab_size, embedding_dim, num_layers, dropout):
        super().__init__()


        self.memory_embedding = nn.Embedding(vocab_size, embedding_dim)
        self.memory_pos_encoder = PositionalEncoding(embedding_dim,
dropout)
        self.tgt_embedding = nn.Embedding(vocab_size, embedding_dim)
        self.tgt_pos_encoder = PositionalEncoding(embedding_dim, dropout)
        self.decoder = nn.TransformerDecoder(
            nn.TransformerDecoderLayer(d_model=embedding_dim, nhead=8, dim_
feedforward=2048, dropout=dropout),
            num_layers=num_layers)


        self.fc = nn.Linear(embedding_dim, vocab_size)
        self.d_model=embedding_dim
```

```
def forward(self, tgt,  memory=None, tgt_mask=None, memory_mask=None,
memory_key_padding_mask=None,tgt_key_padding_mask=None):
        tgt = self.tgt_embedding(tgt) * self.d_model ** 0.5
        tgt=self.tgt_pos_encoder(tgt)
        print(tgt)
        memory=self.memory_embedding(memory) * self.d_model ** 0.5
        memory=self.memory_pos_encoder(memory)
        print(memory)
        output = self.decoder(tgt=tgt, memory=memory, tgt_mask=tgt_mask,
memory_mask=memory_mask, memory_key_padding_mask=memory_key_padding_
mask,tgt_key_padding_mask=tgt_key_padding_mask)
        print(output)
        output = self.fc(output)
        return output
```

Let us now delve into a discussion of the code snippet provided above and examine its functionality:

- This model is a transformer-based decoder-only language model, which takes as input a target sequence (tgt) and an memory sequence (memory) and generates an output sequence of the same length as the input sequence.

- The input target sequence is first passed through an embedding layer and a positional encoding layer. Similarly, the input memory sequence is passed through an embedding layer and a positional encoding layer.

- During training:

  o **memory** is training data of shape (seq_len, batch_size)

  o **target:** During model training, the target sequence would be the input sequence shifted by one position.

- These processed input sequences are then fed into the transformer decoder, which consists of multiple transformer decoder layers. Each decoder layer processes the input sequences using multi-head self-attention and a feedforward neural network.

- Finally, the output of the transformer decoder is passed through a linear layer (fully-connected neural network) to generate the final output sequence, with each element of the sequence representing the probability distribution over the vocabulary of the target language.

Transformer layer in PyTorch

There are many situations where you will need a sequence-to-sequence model, such as for machine translation. In such a scenario, you will use the entire **torch.nn.Transformer**. Let us implement a Machine Translation Model using **torch.nn.Transformer**:

```
class TransformerModel(nn.Module):

    def __init__(self,num_encoder_layers, num_decoder_layers, d_model,
nhead, src_vocab_size=tokenizer_src.vocab_size, tgt_vocab_size=tokenizer_
tgt.vocab_size, dim_feedforward=512, dropout=0.1):

        super(TransformerModel, self).__init__()

        self.src_embedding = nn.Embedding(input_dim, d_model)

        self.trg_embedding = nn.Embedding(output_dim, d_model)

        self.src_pos_encoder = PositionalEncoding(d_model, dropout)

        self.trg_pos_encoder = PositionalEncoding(d_model, dropout)

        self.transformer = nn.Transformer(d_model=d_model, nhead=nhead,
num_encoder_layers=num_encoder_layers, num_decoder_layers=num_decoder_
layers,dim_feedforward=dim_feedforward, dropout=dropout)

        self.fc = nn.Linear(d_model, tgt_vocab_size)

        self.dropout = nn.Dropout(dropout)

        self.d_model = d_model


    def forward(self, src, trg, src_mask=None, src_padding_mask=None,trg_
mask=None, trg_padding_mask=None, memory_key_padding_mask=None):


        src = self.src_embedding(src) * (self.d_model ** 0.5)

        src = self.src_pos_encoder(src)

        trg = self.trg_embedding(trg) * (self.d_model ** 0.5)

        trg = self.trg_pos_encoder(trg)

        output = self.transformer(src, trg,src_mask, trg_mask, None,
                            src_padding_mask, trg_padding_mask, memory_
key_padding_mask)

        output = self.fc(self.dropout(output))

        return output
```

Let us now delve into a discussion of the code snippet provided above and examine its functionality:

- The major components of the model are Embedding, Positional Encoding, and transformer Layer. As shown in code snippet lines 4 and 5; make sure to have different Embedding for source and target sequence.

- Forward function: These are major operations in forward function.

  o The source and target sequences are embedded and scaled by the square root of the embedding dimension. This scaling helps mitigate the issue of gradients exploding or vanishing during the training process.

  o The positional encodings are added to the embeddings.

  o The transformer processes the source and target sequences, with masking:

    ▪ `src_mask, trg_mask`==> This is done to prevent the future flow of information.

    ▪ `src_padding_mask, trg_padding_mask` ==> This is done to mask padded data. We are doing this so that model do not attend to padded tokens.

- The output of the transformer is passed through a fully connected layer to get the predicted target sequence.

- The model predicts the next token in German, given all the tokens in English and tokens until the current step in German.

The end-to-end Machine Translation Model is provided in the accompanying notebook.

Conclusion

In this chapter, we delved into the core elements of the transformer Architecture using PyTorch. We examined the transformer's two critical components: the encoder layer and the decoder layer. These components can be combined in various configurations, such as utilizing only the encoder or decoder, or integrating both. This adaptability allows the transformer model to be applied to a wide range of tasks, from categorizing data to language translation.

Key concepts crucial to the transformer model were also explored: Positional Encoding and Masking. Positional encoding is vital for maintaining the sequential order of data elements, and we demonstrated how to implement this in PyTorch. Masking, another significant feature, enables the model to concentrate on relevant data while disregarding unnecessary parts. To help understand these concepts in practice, we provided real-world examples.

Furthermore, this chapter offered practical insights into creating positional encoding and masking, and constructing models with either encoder only, decoder only, or both (Encoder-Decoder) using PyTorch.

Quiz

1. **What is the purpose of masking in the Transformer architecture?**

   a. To selectively hide or replace certain input tokens during processing

   b. To shuffle the input tokens randomly

   c. To add noise to the input tokens

   d. None of the above

2. **What is the purpose of positional encoding in the Transformer architecture?**

   a. To learn the embedding of each input token

   b. To learn the relation between different input tokens

   c. To add the concept of position to the input sequence

   d. None of the above

3. **Which variation of Transformer is used when only the encoding of the input sequence is required?**

   a. Encoder Only

   b. Decoder Only

   c. Encoder-Decoder

   d. None of the above

4. **Which variation of Transformer is used when only the decoding of the input sequence is required?**

   a. Encoder Only

   b. Decoder Only

   c. Encoder-Decoder

   d. None of the above

5. **Which variation of Transformer is used when both encoding and decoding of the input sequence is required?**

   a. Encoder Only

   b. Decoder Only

   c. Encoder-Decoder

   d. None of the above

6. **What is the purpose of input masking in the Transformer architecture?**

   a. To prevent attention from being paid to certain input tokens

   b. To remove certain input tokens from the input sequence

   c. To add noise to the input sequence

   d. None of the above

7. **What is the purpose of padding masking in the Transformer architecture?**

   a. To prevent attention from being paid to padded tokens

   b. To remove padded tokens from the input sequence

   c. To add noise to the padded tokens

   d. None of the above

8. **What is the purpose of sequence masking in the Transformer architecture?**

   a. To prevent attention from being paid to future tokens in the input sequence

   b. To prevent attention from being paid to past tokens in the input sequence

   c. To remove future tokens from the input sequence

   d. None of the above

9. **What is the dimension of input to the Transformer?**

   a. (batch_size, seq_len)

   b. any dimension is fine

   c. (seq_len, batch_size)

10. **What is the dimension of src_mask?**

    a. (seq_len, seq_len)

    b. (batch_size, seq_len)

11. **In the src_mask, how would you signify the masking token?**

    a. 0

    b. True

    c. -inf

12. **In the tgt_key_padding_mask, how would you signify the masking token?**

    a. 0

    b. True

    c. -inf

Answers

1. a.

2. c.

3. a.

4. b.

5. c.

6. a.

7. a.

8. a.

9. c.

10. a.

11. c.

12. b.

Join our book's Discord space

Join the book's Discord Workspace for Latest updates, Offers, Tech happenings around the world, New Release and Sessions with the Authors:

https://discord.bpbonline.com

CHAPTER 4

Transfer Learning with PyTorch and Hugging Face

Introduction

You are a computer programmer who excels in back-end development. Over the years, you have perfected your skills in Python, mastered multi-threading and multi-processing, and deeply understood how complex back-end systems operate. One day, you decide to switch careers and venture into the world of machine learning, focusing on model development, deployment, and operations.

You will not wipe your memory clean or discard your years-earned expertise. In fact, your knowledge of developing and maintaining large, distributed systems is invaluable and ideally suited for your new career endeavor. Your primary focus will now be on learning machine learning algorithms and unique skills related to AI. The wealth of knowledge you have accumulated over the years can be applied to the exciting task of building next-generation AI systems. Before you know it, you will be developing incredible models, deploying them seamlessly, and ensuring their stability and scalability in production.

Transfer learning in the context of deep learning models operates on a similar principle. A pre-trained model has already acquired a wealth of knowledge from processing vast amounts of data. For instance, models like ResNet have been trained on millions of images to accurately extract image features. When you fine-tune this pre-trained model for a new, specific task (such as using ResNet to analyze chest X-rays and classify COVID positive or negative), it is akin to our back-end developer learning to create AI models. The model does not need to start from scratch; it can capitalize on its existing knowledge to rapidly adapt to the new task, resulting in superior performance and quicker training. This approach is a departure from traditional AI model development, where each use case requires building a model entirely from the scratch.

Structure

This chapter is organized into following sections:

- System requirements
- Need of transfer learning
- Using transfer learning
- Where can you get pre-trained model
- Popular pre-trained model
- Project: develop classifier by fine tuning BERT-base-uncased

Objectives

In this book chapter, we have a few main goals we want to achieve. First off, we want to make sure you get a complete picture of what transfer learning is, why it is useful, and where it can be used. We also want to introduce you to some pre-trained models that are very popular in fields like **natural language processing** (**NLP**), speech processing, and computer vision.

We will not just want to talk about them, but also want to show how they are used in real life. So, we will demonstrate how to use transfer learning with tools called Hugging Face and PyTorch. We will even walk you through a project where we develop a system that can tell the difference between real and fake news. To do this, we will use a pre-trained model known as the 'BERT-base-uncased' model as our starting point. This way, you will be able to see transfer learning in action.

System requirements

For detailed instructions on setting the environment, please follow instructions at **https://github.com/bpbpublications/Building-Transformer-Models-with-PyTorch/blob/main/General/SettingVirtualEnvironment.ipynb**.

Activate virtual environment:

```
conda activate transformer_learn
```

To proceed with the coding tasks outlined in this chapter, please install the necessary packages:

```
pip3 install transformers
```

```
pip3 install datasets
```

```
pip3 install torch
```

```
pip3 install torchtext
```

```
pip3 install accelerate
```

```
pip3 install sentencepiece
```

```
pip3 install sacremoses
```

Need of transfer learning

Suppose we want to build a deep learning model to diagnose pneumonia from chest X-ray images using a transformer-based architecture. Collecting hundreds of thousands of labeled chest X-ray images is practically very difficult, if not impossible. A single institution may not have access to such a vast number of pneumonia cases, and sharing data across multiple institutions faces hurdles due to HIPAA and other government regulations. Even if we somehow obtained thousands of labeled datasets, smaller institutions like hospitals might not be able to afford weeks of substantial GPU costs just for running experiments on model training. In this case, model training would become a costly endeavor.

This is where transfer learning comes into play, offering a practical solution. Instead of starting from scratch, our hospital can take a pre-trained vision transformer which has been trained on an enormous corpus of image data and has already learned to extract image features. The hospital can then adapt this model to the task of diagnosing pneumonia from chest X-ray images.

The following are some advantages of using transfer learning over developing model from scratch. Please go through the *Table 4.1:*

1.	Improve performance	The pre-trained **Vision Transformer (ViT)** model has already learned useful features and representations from its vast training dataset. This knowledge can be adapted to our specific task, potentially leading to better performance than a model trained from scratch on the limited chest X-ray dataset.
2.	**Reduce training time**	Fine-tuning the pre-trained ViT model on our target task takes significantly less time
3.	**Handling small dataset**	Transfer learning allows the hospital to make the most of their small dataset of chest X-ray images.

| 4 | **Adaptability** | We can also use transfer learning to adapt the pre-trained ViT model to various other medical imaging tasks, such as detecting tumors in MRI scans or identifying retinal diseases. |
| 5. | **Lower computational resources** | We can achieve good results with relatively less computational power, making the task more accessible to researchers with limited resources. |

Table 4.1: Benefits of transfer learning

Using transfer learning

Figure 4.1 illustrates the general structure of pre-trained ML models. As shown in *Figure 4.1*, the typical ML model has Feature Extractor Layers and Fully Connected Layers. Specifically, we will understand the architecture by explaining **distilbert-base-uncased-finetuned-sst-2-english**. It is a lightweight transformer-based model that has been fine-tuned on the SST-2 dataset for English sentiment analysis. It gives positive or negative as output. Let us delve into the components of a typical pre-trained model; refer to the following figure:

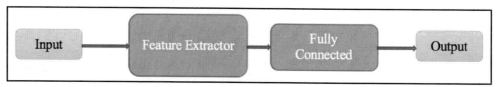

Figure 4.1: *General structure of pre-trained ml model*

Following is the detailed explanation of some key terms:

- **Feature extractor**: This component is responsible for taking raw input data, extracting relevant features, and generating vector representations of those features. In the case of **distilbert-base-uncased-finetuned-sst-2-english**, the feature extractor is the Transformer Encoder. The primary purpose of the feature extractor is to convert the raw input into a more meaningful representation that can be used for the target task.

- **Fully connected layer**: This is a linear layer where all neurons are connected to every neuron in the previous layer. In the **distilbert-base-uncased-finetuned-sst-2-english** model, for example, the last few fully connected layers provide the output by applying a softmax function. This component is used to make predictions based on the features extracted by the feature extractor.

  Let us understand what the paradigm is for using the pre-trained ML model:

- **Pre-trained ML model**: If your problem involves understanding the sentiment of regular English text, you can use **distilbert-base-uncased-finetuned-sst-2-english** as is for your new sentiment analysis task.

- **Fixed feature extractor:** In this approach, the feature extractor part of the pre-trained model's weights is not updated. You will freeze the weights of the Encoder part of `distilbert-base-uncased-finetuned-sst-2-english` and only retrain a few fully connected layers. Even with a small amount of data, you can develop a decently performing model.

- **Fine-tuning:** In this step, the pre-trained model is adapted to the target task by updating its weights for the specific task. You will update the weights of both the feature extractor and the fully connected layer. Fine-tuning can involve updating the weights of the entire model or just a subset of layers. The learning rate is typically set to a smaller value during fine-tuning to prevent the model from losing the previously learned features.

Now, the question is how do you decide which paradigm you should follow for Transfer Learning? The answer to our problem can be thought through two dimensions (2S: Size & Similarity):

- **Size:** The size of retraining data.

- **Similarity:** Similarity with the original dataset and problem on which the pre-trained model was trained.

Now, let us discuss when to use the above three paradigms from the *Table 4.2*:

Pre-trained model	A. The new problem is exactly the same as the original problem/dataset.
	B. For example, if your problem is to understand the sentiment of movie comments. You can use **distilbert-base-uncased-fine-tuned-sst-2-english** without finetuning it. This is because **distilbert-base-uncased-finetuned-sst-2-english** was trained on IMDB dataset
Fixed feature extractor	A. The new problem is similar to the original problem/dataset. OR/AND
	B. The size of new dataset is small
	C. For example, if your problem is to understand the sentiment of amazon review; you may want to use **distilbert-base-un-cased-finetuned-sst-2-english** as Fixed Feature Extractor.
Fine-tunning	A. The new problem is not similar to the original problem/dataset. OR/AND
	B. You have large amount of Dataset
	C. For example, if your problem is to understand the sentiment of clinical notes: you want to fine-tune the **distilbert-base-uncased-finetuned-sst-2-english**. The new problem is not similar to original dataset on which **distilbert-base-uncased-finetuned-sst-2-english** was trained.

Table 4.2: Transfer learning paradigm

Where can you get pre-trained model

Here is a list of reporitories where you can get pre-trained model:

- **Hugging Face**: A widely-used library that offers state-of-the-art pre-trained models for machine learning tasks, such as BERT, GPT-2, RoBERTa, T5, ViT, and many more (**https://huggingface.co/transformers/**).

- **Pytorch Hub**: A repository for pre-trained models provided by the PyTorch team, including models for image classification, object detection, and NLP tasks. (https://pytorch.org/hub/)

- **Torch Image Models (timm)**: A repository by *Ross Wightman* that contains a collection of pre-trained image classification models, including EfficientNet, ResNet, and many others. (**https://github.com/rwightman/pytorch-image-models**).

These repositories and libraries offer a wide range of pre-trained models that can be used for transfer learning, fine-tuning, or as feature extractors for various machine learning tasks.

Popular pre-trained model

In this section, we are going to explore a variety of transformer-based pre-trained models specifically used in the fields of **Natural Language Processing (NLP)**, computer vision, and speech processing. These models are a huge time-saver since they come pre-trained on massive amounts of data. This allows users to tweak them for specific tasks, saving time and computational power.

Each of these models is unique, both in terms of their strengths and the areas where they're most commonly used. This means they can be used in a wide variety of different projects. For instance, BERT was trained with a masked language modeling objective, while GPT was trained with a sequence modeling objective. There are also differences in each model's structure.

Our goal in exploring these models is to help you better understand and use these models in your own work. By the end of it, you should have a good grasp of how you can take advantage of these powerful tools to improve your own projects.

NLP

Here is a list of some widely-used NLP pre-trained models.

- **Bidirectional Encoder Representations from Transformers (BERT)**: A powerful pre-trained model for various NLP tasks, such as sentiment analysis, named entity recognition, and question-answering.

- **Generative pre-trained Transformer (GPT-2):** A large-scale language model known for its impressive text generation capabilities.

- **Text-to-Text Transfer Transformer (T5)**: A versatile pre-trained model designed to handle a wide range of NLP tasks using a unified text-to-text format.

- **BART**: This model incorporates a bi-directional encoder (similar to BERT) and an autoregressive decoder, establishing itself as an encoder-decoder framework

- **LLAMA2**: As of the writing of this book in September 2023, it is arguably the most popular open-source autoregressive model, holding its ground against GPT3.5 in numerous benchmarks. It features a range of models with varying parameters, spanning from 2 billion to 70 billion

- **Falcon**: It is created by Technology Innovation Institute in Abu Dhabi, and released under Apache 2.0 license. Falcon 180b is 2.5 times larger than Llama2 70b. The Falcon 180b surpasses the performance of Llama 2 70B and OpenAI's GPT-3.5 in the MMLU tests, and is comparable to Google's PaLM 2-Large in various benchmarks[1].

Computer vision

Here is a list of some widely-used computer vision pre-trained models:

- **ViT**: A transformer-based model that applies the transformer architecture to image classification tasks, dividing images into patches and treating them as sequences.

- **Data-efficient Image Transformer (DeiT)**: A variant of the Vision Transformer that is specifically designed for data-efficient training, requiring fewer labeled images for good performance.

- **Swin transformer**: A hierarchical transformer model for computer vision tasks, using shifted windows to capture local and global information efficiently.

- **Stable Diffusion**: It is arguably the most popular model for generating images from text. This model is grounded on latent diffusion principles and incorporates three primary components: 1) An Autoencoder, 2) U-Net, and 3) CLIP's Text Encoder.

Speech processing

Here is a list of some widely-used speech processing pre-trained models:

- **Wav2Vec 2.0**: A transformer-based model for self-supervised speech recognition that learns speech representations directly from raw audio data.

---

[1] **https://huggingface.co/blog/falcon-180b#what-is-falcon-180b**

→ Conv + Recurrent + SelfAttention !!

- **Conformer**: A hybrid model that combines convolutional, recurrent, and self-attention mechanisms, used for various speech processing tasks, such as automatic speech recognition and keyword spotting.

Project: Develop classifier by fine tuning BERT-base-uncased

We have covered the basics of transfer learning. Now, let us create a classifier fine-tuning the `BERT-uncased` model. We will build the real news vs. fake news detection engine. We want to demonstrate how this pipeline can be adapted to your organization's specific needs. Instead of using a pre-built dataset, we will download a dataset from Kaggle and utilize it in our fine-tuning process. This approach will help illustrate how the pipeline can be tailored to work with custom datasets in real-world applications. *Figure 4.2* shows an outline of the fine-tuning process:

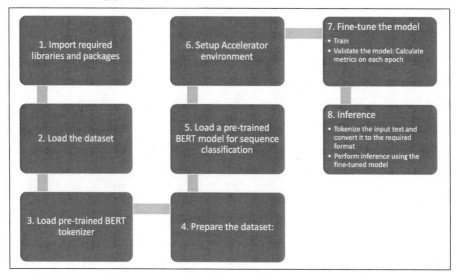

Figure 4.2: Outline for fine-tunning NLP classifier

The steps below guide you through the fine-tuning process.

1. Import required libraries and packages using the following code snippet for training a sequence classification model using the Hugging Face transformers library and PyTorch:

```
import pandas as pd
from sklearn.model_selection import train_test_split
from accelerate import Accelerator
import torch
```

```
from torch.utils.data import DataLoader, RandomSampler,
SequentialSampler
from tqdm import tqdm
from transformers import AutoTokenizer
from transformers import AutoModelForSequenceClassification
from transformers import AdamW
from transformers import get_scheduler
```

Now, let us set up device. The code defines a function **get_device()** that checks the available hardware (CUDA, Apple Metal Performance Shaders, or CPU) and returns the appropriate device for PyTorch tensor operations.

= mps: Apple Metal Performance Shaders (handwritten annotation)

```
def get_device():
  device="cpu"
  if torch.cuda.is_available():
    device="cuda"
  elif  torch.backends.mps.is_available():
    device='mps'
  else:
    device="cpu"
  return device
device = get_device()
print(device)
```

2. **Load dataset:** First, download the dataset from Kaggle (**https://www.kaggle.com/datasets/clmentbisaillon/fake-and-real-news-dataset).** Then perform the data cleaning. In the following code, we are conducting these operations:

   a. Reading data from two CSV files: True.csv (real news) and Fake.csv (fake news)

   b. Cleaning and preprocessing the data in each CSV file

   c. Concatenating both data frames into a single data frame

   d. The resulting data frame contains two columns: **text** for the news content and 'label' for its corresponding category (real or fake):

   ```
   real=pd.read_csv('/Users/premtimsina/Documents/bpbbook/chapter4/
   dataset/True.csv')
   
   fake=pd.read_csv('/Users/premtimsina/Documents/bpbbook/
   chapter4/dataset/Fake.csv')
   
   real = real.drop(['title','subject','date'], axis=1)
   ```

```
real['label']=1.0
fake = fake.drop(['title','subject','date'], axis=1)
fake['label']=0.0
dataframe=pd.concat([real, fake], axis=0, ignore_index=True)
df = dataframe.sample(frac=0.1).reset_index(drop=True)
```

3. **Load pre-trained tokenizer**: We will utilize the **bert-base-uncased** as our pre-trained model for fine-tuning. As a result, it is essential to use the corresponding tokenizer to ensure that the input data is properly processed and compatible with the model. If an incorrect tokenizer is used, the data fed into the model will be inadequate or incorrect, negatively affecting the training process and resulting in suboptimal performance.

```
tokenizer = AutoTokenizer.from_pretrained("bert-base-uncased")
```

4. **Prepare dataset**: The data preparation process for BERT-based uncased models involves tokenizing the text, mapping tokens to input_ids, creating attention masks (attention_mask), and preparing the tensor labels. Each item of the Dataset Class should be a dictionary of the following structure:

```
{'input_ids':          torch.Tensor(),'attention_mask':torch.Tensor(),
'labels': torch.Tensor()  }
```

Let us discuss the component of the above dictionary:

- **input_ids**: Each token from the tokenized text needs to be mapped to an ID using BERT's vocabulary. The resulting input IDs should be in the form of a tensor or array with specified shape (**batch_size**, **max_sequence_length**).

- **attention_mask**: The attention mask is used to differentiate between the actual tokens and padding tokens. It has the same shape as the **input_ids** tensor, that is, (**batch_size**, **max_sequence_length**). The mask has 1s for actual tokens and 0s for padding tokens.

- **labels**: The labels tensor contains the true class for each example in the dataset. It usually has a shape of (batch_size,). For classification tasks, these labels are one-hot-encoded labels.

The following code illustrates the data processing. The output of the following code is three lists: **input_ids**, **attention_mask**, and labels for both the training and the validation dataset:

```
# this is just creating a list of tuples. Each tuple has (text, label)
data=list(zip(df['text'].tolist(), df['label'].tolist()))


# This function takes two lists as Parameter
# This function return input_ids, attention_mask, and labels_out
```

```python
def tokenize_and_encode(texts, labels):
    input_ids, attention_masks, labels_out = [], [], []
    for text, label in zip(texts, labels):
        encoded = tokenizer.encode_plus(text, max_length=512, padding='max_
length', truncation=True)
        input_ids.append(encoded['input_ids'])
        attention_masks.append(encoded['attention_mask'])
        labels_out.append(label)
    return torch.tensor(input_ids), torch.tensor(attention_masks), torch.
tensor(labels_out)

# seprate the tuples
# generate two lists: a) containing texts, b) containing labels
texts, labels = zip(*data)

# train, validation split
train_texts, val_texts, train_labels, val_labels = train_test_split(texts,
labels, test_size=0.2)

# tokenization
train_input_ids, train_attention_masks, train_labels = tokenize_and_
encode(train_texts, train_labels)
val_input_ids, val_attention_masks, val_labels = tokenize_and_encode(val_
texts, val_labels)
```

Custom dataset class

Let us write custom dataset class:

```python
class TextClassificationDataset(torch.utils.data.Dataset):
    def __init__(self, input_ids, attention_masks, labels, num_classes=2):
        self.input_ids = input_ids
        self.attention_masks = attention_masks
        self.labels = labels
        self.num_classes = num_classes
        self.one_hot_labels = self.one_hot_encode(labels, num_classes)

    def __len__(self):
```

```python
        return len(self.input_ids)

    def __getitem__(self, idx):
        return {
            'input_ids': self.input_ids[idx],
            'attention_mask': self.attention_masks[idx],
            'labels': self.one_hot_labels[idx]
        }



    @staticmethod
    def one_hot_encode(targets, num_classes):
        targets = targets.long()
        one_hot_targets = torch.zeros(targets.size(0), num_classes)
        one_hot_targets.scatter_(1, targets.unsqueeze(1), 1.0)
        return one_hot_targets

train_dataset = TextClassificationDataset(train_input_ids, train_attention_
masks, train_labels)
val_dataset = TextClassificationDataset(val_input_ids, val_attention_masks,
val_labels)
```

Let us discuss what the above code is doing.

- **For tunning BERT-based-uncased:** Each item of dataset must be of type dictionary with at least following keys:

  o   input_ids

  o   attention_mask

  o   labels

  The **__getitem__** should return a dictionary of the following structure:

  ```python
  {
          'input_ids': self.input_ids[idx],
          'attention_mask': self.attention_masks[idx],
          'labels': self.one_hot_labels[idx]
  }
  ```

- **one_hot_encode method:** A static method that takes in targets (labels) and **num_ classes** as arguments. It converts the given targets into one-hot encoded tensors.

The method first converts the targets to long tensors and then initializes a zero tensor of shape (number of samples, **num_classes**). The scatter_ function is used to place 1.0 in the appropriate position for each sample's label, resulting in a one-hot encoded tensor.

DataLoader

Now, let us create dataloader that we can feed to our fine tunning task:

```
train_dataloader = DataLoader(train_dataset, batch_size=8, shuffle=True)
eval_dataloader = DataLoader(val_dataset, batch_size=8)
```

Revisiting dimension requirements for Transformers in Pytorch from *Chapter 3, Transformer Model in PyTorch*. The encoder expects data with dimensions (**seq_len**, **batch_size**). However, Hugging Face's BERT-based-uncased model requires data with dimensions (**batch_size**, **seq_len**). As a result, the output from the **train_dataloader** has dimensions of (**batch_size**, **seq_len**). We can execute below code to review the dimension of dataloader:

```
item=next(iter(train_dataloader))
item_ids,item_mask,item_labels=item['input_ids'],item['attention_mask'],item['labels']
print ('item_ids, ',item_ids.shape, '\n',
       'item_mask, ',item_mask.shape, '\n',
       'item_labels, ',item_labels.shape, '\n',)
```

Output:

```
 item_ids,  torch.Size([8, 512])

 item_mask,  torch.Size([8, 512])

 item_labels,  torch.Size([8, 2])
```

This is aligned with the shape requirement for fine-tuning `BERT-based-uncased`

- **Load pre-trained BERT-based-uncased:** There are two important concepts in below code:

  o In this step, we are loading the BERT-base-uncased model using the **AutoModelForSequenceClassification** class, which is a convenient way to add a final fully connected layer to the Transformer architecture for the classification task. By doing so, we adapt the pre-trained model to handle our specific classification problem.

  o Additionally, we are initializing the AdamW optimizer, which is a popular optimization algorithm for training deep learning models, specifically designed for training Transformer models.

```
model = AutoModelForSequenceClassification.from_pretrained("bert-
base-uncased", num_labels=2)

optimizer = AdamW(model.parameters(), lr=5e-5)
```

- **Prepare accelerator**: Let us take a moment to discuss the accelerator and the benefits it offers when training deep learning models. The accelerator delivers a user-friendly API for training various deep learning models with ease. It offers two main advantages that make it a valuable tool for the training process.

  o **Flexibility** to conduct training on various hardware accelerators, such as GPUs, TPUs, and Apple's **Metal Performance Shaders** (**MPS**). In our example, during training, we do not specifically select 'mps' device. The accelerator automatically detects it and uses **mps** for training.

  o The **accelerator library** is particularly useful for distributed training and mixed-precision training.

The following code is a general syntax for preparing the accelerator:

```
# Declare accelerator

accelerator = Accelerator()

model, optimizer, train_dataloader, eval_dataloader = accelerator.prepare(
    model, optimizer, train_dataloader, eval_dataloader
)
```

- **Fine tune the model:** The following code describes the fine-tuning process:

```
num_epochs = 1

num_training_steps = num_epochs * len(train_dataloader)

lr_scheduler = get_scheduler(
        "linear",
        optimizer=optimizer,
        num_warmup_steps=0,
        num_training_steps=num_training_steps
    )

progress_bar = tqdm(range(num_training_steps))

for epoch in range(num_epochs):
    for batch in train_dataloader:
        outputs = model(**batch)
        loss = outputs.loss
        accelerator.backward(loss)
```

```
        optimizer.step()
        lr_scheduler.step()
        optimizer.zero_grad()
        progress_bar.update(1)
    model.eval()
    device = 'mps'
    preds = []
    out_label_ids = []

    for batch in eval_dataloader:
        with torch.no_grad():
            inputs = {k: v.to(device) for k, v in batch.items()}
            outputs = model(**inputs)
            logits = outputs.logits

            preds.extend(torch.argmax(logits.detach().cpu(), dim=1).
numpy())
            out_label_ids.extend(torch.argmax(inputs["labels"].detach().
cpu(),dim=1).numpy())
    accuracy = accuracy_score(out_label_ids, preds)
    f1 = f1_score(out_label_ids, preds, average='weighted')
    recall = recall_score(out_label_ids, preds, average='weighted')
  precision = precision_score(out_label_ids, preds, average='weighted')

    print(f"Epoch {epoch + 1}/{num_epochs} Evaluation Results:")
    print(f"Accuracy: {accuracy}")
    print(f"F1 Score: {f1}")
    print(f"Recall: {recall}")
    print(f"Precision: {precision}")
```

Now, let us discuss what we are doing in the above code:

- `lr_scheduler` in the provided code is an instance of a learning rate scheduler, which is responsible for adjusting the learning rate during the training process. The learning rate scheduler helps improve the training process by dynamically adjusting the learning rate based on the number of training steps. In this code, the learning rate starts with the initial value set in the optimizer and decreases linearly to 0 as the training progresses. Some benefits of **lr_scheduler** over optimizer alone are:

- **Avoid overshooting:** When using a fixed learning rate, the optimizer might overshoot the optimal solution, especially in the later stages of training. By decreasing the learning rate over time, the model can make smaller updates and fine-tune its weights.

- `progress_bar` is just a utility to show the progress of training.

The following code block is the standard syntax for finetuning:

```
outputs = model(**batch)
loss = outputs.loss
accelerator.backward(loss)
optimizer.step()
lr_scheduler.step()
optimizer.zero_grad()
progress_bar.update(1)
```

You can notice that during training, we are not explicitly converting `tensor` into the device. `accelerator` is automatically identifying the `device` and converts `tensor` into the appropriate format.

After each epoch, we are also printing the evaluation metrics over the evaluation dataset.

The following output demonstrates the results of fine-tuning our classifier. We have successfully created a capable classifier for distinguishing between real and fake news. However, it is worth noting that the dataset contains news provider names (for example ABC, CBS) for real news articles. This might lead the model to rely on such information, resulting in exceptionally high performance.

```
100%|████████████████████████████████████████████
Accuracy: 0.9977728285077951
F1 Score: 0.9977724507291988
Recall: 0.9977728285077951
Precision: 0.9977820316957794
```

Figure 4.3: The output of fine-tuning process

Inference

We have developed a machine-learning model to distinguish between real and fake news. Now it is time to create an inference pipeline that allows us to input any text passage, and the model will return a result indicating whether the given text block belongs to real news or fake news.

Let us discuss some crucial points in the below code:

- **tokenizer = BertTokenizer.from_pretrained('bert-base-uncased')**:
  You need to use the same tokenizer that was used for fine-tunning

- **logits.detach().cpu()**:

  o **detach** is done to prevent unintentional back-propagation

  o **cpu** is done so that the output is compatible with scikit-learn libraries for further computation:

```python
from transformers import BertTokenizer
import torch
tokenizer = BertTokenizer.from_pretrained('bert-base-uncased')

def inference(text, model,  label, device='mps'):
    # Load the tokenizer

    # Tokenize the input text
    inputs = tokenizer(text, return_tensors='pt', padding=True,
truncation=True)
    # Move input tensors to the specified device (default: 'cpu')
    inputs = {k: v.to(device) for k, v in inputs.items()}

    # Set the model to evaluation mode and perform inference
    model.eval()
    with torch.no_grad():
        outputs = model(**inputs)
        logits = outputs.logits

    # Get the index of the predicted label
    pred_label_idx = torch.argmax(logits.detach().cpu(), dim=1).
item()

    print(f"Predicted label index: {pred_label_idx}, actual label
{label}")
    return pred_label_idx
```

Now let us use the inference pipeline:

```python
# Example usage
text="CNN (Washington) General Motors plans to phase out widely used Apple
(AAPL) CarPlay and Android Auto technologies that allow drivers to bypass
a vehicle's infotainment system, shifting instead to built-in infotainment
```

```
systems developed with Google (GOOG) for future electric vehicles."

pred_label_idx = inference(text, model, 1.0)
```

Output:

Predicted label index: 1, actual label 1.0

This is the correct output, as the news article was retrieved from CNN.

Conclusion

In this chapter, we highlighted the significance of transfer learning in efficiently training models for various tasks. We explored the fine-tuning process, using pre-trained models as a base and adjusting their weights for target tasks.

We introduced Hugging Face Transformers library as a popular resource for pre-trained models and discussed popular models for NLP, Speech Processing, and computer vision. Each model has its strengths and weaknesses, making them suitable for different tasks.

The chapter concluded with a practical example, demonstrating how to fine-tune the **bert-base-uncased** model using Hugging Face Transformers library to create a real-news vs. fake-news classifier.

Quiz

1. **What is transfer learning?**

    a. A technique that trains models from scratch

    b. Using a pre-trained model as a starting point for a new task

    c. Training models on unrelated tasks

    d. None of the above

2. **What is the purpose of using `AutoModelForSequenceClassification` for loading bert-based-uncased?**

    a. It adds classification head

    b. No particular purpose

3. **What is the purpose of the AdamW optimizer?**

    a. To adjust model weights during training

    b. To tokenize input text

    c. To compute loss values

    d. None of the above

4. **What is the dimension requirement for input tensors in BERT-based models?**

   a. (seq_len, batch_size)

   b. (batch_size, seq_len)

   c. (batch_size, seq_len, num_classes)

   d. None of the above

5. **What is the purpose of the "logits" variable in the code?**

   a. To store tokenized input text

   b. To store the output probabilities for each class

   c. To store model weights

   d. None of the above

6. **Why is it important to use the corresponding tokenizer for the chosen pre-trained model?**

   a. To ensure compatibility with the pre-trained model

   b. To prevent training with incorrect data

   c. Both A and B

   d. None of the above

7. **Which of the following is an advantage of using Hugging Face Accelerator?**

   a. Flexibility to conduct training on various hardware accelerators

   b. Distributed training and mixed-precision training

   c. Both a and b

   d. None of the above

8. **Which of the following is NOT an advantage of transfer learning?**

   a. Reduces training time

   b. Requires fewer labeled examples

   c. Always outperforms models trained from scratch

   d. Leveraging pre-trained models for new tasks

9. **In our project, which method was used to compute gradients for the model parameters?**

    a. optimizer.step()

    b. optimizer.zero_grad()

    c. accelerator.backward()

    d. None of the above

10. **In the book chapter, what is the purpose of using torch.backends.mps as a device?**

    a. To utilize Apple GPU acceleration if available

    b. To make the code compatible with Hugging Face Accelerator

    c. To store model weights

    d. None of the above

11. **In the Dataset class, what is the purpose of the one_hot_encode function?**

    a. To convert label indices into one-hot encoded vectors

    b. To tokenize input text

    c. To pad input sequences

    d. None of the above

12. **What does the __getitem__ method in the Dataset class return?**

    a. A single training example with its corresponding input_ids, attention_mask, and one-hot encoded labels

    b. A batch of training examples

    c. A single training example without any preprocessing

    d. None of the above

13. **What is the primary function of a tokenizer in the context of fine-tuning a pre-trained model?**

    a. To optimize model weights

    b. To convert input text into a format compatible with the model

    c. To compute loss values

    d. None of the above

Answers

1. b.

2. a.

3. a.

4. b.

5. b.

6. c.

7. c.

8. c.

9. c.

10. a.

11. a.

12. a.

13. b.

Join our book's Discord space

Join the book's Discord Workspace for Latest updates, Offers, Tech happenings around the world, New Release and Sessions with the Authors:

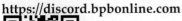

https://discord.bpbonline.com

## CHAPTER 5

Large Language Models: BERT, GPT-3, and BART

Introduction

Over the past few years, transformer models have emerged as the undisputed champions of NLP, consistently outperforming traditional methods and setting new benchmarks in various tasks. From classification to sentiment analysis, and from question-answering to text summarization, these models have become the go-to choice for researchers and practitioners.

Not only limited to traditional machine learning tasks, but transformers are also involved in more exciting developments. NLP research has already started moving toward **Artificial General Intelligence (AGI)**. AGI represents the quest for creating machines that possess the ability to understand, learn, and reason across a wide range of tasks and domains, much like human beings. As we progress in our pursuit of AGI, transformer models have emerged as a promising stepping stone in this direction. We already have some promising results, with the development of large-scale language models like GPT-4 and Codex, which exhibit remarkable performance and capabilities.

In this chapter, we will discuss the various variant of transformer models for NLP, and we will also discuss creating your own language model to capture your organizational context.

Structure

The book is organized into the following sections:

- Large language model

- Key determinants of performance

- Pioneering LLMs and their impact

- Creating your own LLM

Objectives

This chapter aims to provide an understanding of **Large Language Models (LLMs)**. The discussion begins by exploring the concept of LLMs and delving into their significance in NLP. It subsequently explores the diverse variants of LLMs, explaining their architectures and highlighting their relevance in different NLP applications. The chapter also delves into transformer models, distinguishing between pre-trained and task-specific models. Lastly, it an explanation of the process involved in creating a language model tailored to capture an organization's unique context, offering insights into the practical implementation of custom LLMs.

Large language model

A **LLM** is a computer program originally designed to understand and generate text like humans. You can think of ChatGPT as an example of an LLM: it can write poems like Shakespeare, pass pre-med exams, help you find bugs in your code, and explain complex code in simple terms. It is as if a human expert is helping you complete your tasks. In general, LLM can understand and comprehend your questions and generate responses as if a human expert is providing them. Let us understand how LLMs are created. Creating an LLM involves several steps helping the model to learn from vast amounts of data and apply that knowledge to various language tasks. Here are the simplified steps of creating LLM:

1. **Collect data**: The first step is to gather a huge dataset containing text from diverse sources, such as websites, books, articles, and social media posts. This dataset provides the raw material that the model will learn from, helping it understand language structure, grammar, and context. For example, GPT-2 was trained on a dataset of 8 million web pages.

2. **Pre-process the data**: Before training the model, the text data needs to be pre-processed and cleaned. After that, the data are prepared in a shape required by model architecture.

3. **Define the model architecture**: We can develop the model architecture by following the given steps:

   a. It involves defining structure of model and choosing the transformer variant (Encoder Only, Decoder Only, Encoder-Decoder)

   b. Defining number of layers and neurons

   c. Defining how model learns and process the data. For example, in GPT-2 model learns to predict the next word.

4. **Pre-train**: With the model architecture and dataset ready, the pre-training phase begins. Normally, it is an unsupervised approach—the model is exposed to the text data and learns to generate coherent text. A typical pre-training approach is to predict the next word. Thus, the data consists of a sequence of text, and the "labels" are essentially the input texts shifted by one position. For example:

   ```
   Data = ['I', 'live', 'in', 'New York']
   Label = ['live', 'in', 'New York']
   ```

   The core idea at the pre-training stage is to make the model understand the general structure of language. An example of pre-trained LLM is ` DistilBERT-base-uncased`

5. **Fine tune the model**: Once the model has learned the general structure and nuances of language during pre-training, it is time to fine-tune it for specific tasks, such as sentiment analysis, question-answering, or text summarization. This is normally supervised learning. This involves training the model on a smaller, task-specific dataset, allowing it to specialize in that particular task. An example of fine-tunned model is **distilbert-base-uncased-finetuned-sst-2-english**. It is ` DistilBERT-base-uncased` fine-tunned on **SST-2** dataset to predict the sentiment of given text.

6. **Evaluate and test the model**: After fine-tuning, it is essential to evaluate the model's performance. One of the gold-standard of evaluating your LLM is via. **Super General Language Understanding Evaluation (SuperGLUE)** benchmark. It is a benchmark designed to evaluate performance on a diverse set of tasks.

7. **Deploy the model**: After pre-training and fine-tuning your model on a task-specific dataset, it is time to deploy it. If you fine-tuned the model for question-answering, you could integrate it into a chatbot. If you fine-tuned for classification, you could deploy it to solve classification problems, and so on. The deployment will vary depending on the specific task the model has been fine-tuned for.

In the later sections of this chapter, we will embark on an exciting journey to create our own LLM. This will enable us to optimize our organization's AI capabilities by developing an LLM that captures the unique context and problems of our organization.

Key determinants of performance

The performance of large language models is determined by various factors related to their scale and complexity. In this section we will discuss these factors in detail:

Size of network: Number of encoder and decoder layers

The depth of a neural network, represented by the number of encoder and decoder layers, plays a crucial role in its ability to model complex patterns and relationships in language. For instance, **Bidirectional Encoder Representations from Transformers (BERT)** is a transformer-based model with different configurations, such as BERT-Base and BERT-Large, which have 12 and 24 encoder layers, respectively. Deeper networks can capture higher-level abstractions and learn more sophisticated representations of input data, which results in better performance.

Number of model parameters

In a neural network, parameters refer to the weights and biases associated with the connections between neurons. Weights determine the strength of the connection between neurons, while biases help adjust the output of a neuron. The total number of parameters in a neural network is an indicator of its complexity and capacity to learn intricate relationships in the data. There are different LLMs with various parameters. For example, Bert-base has 110 million parameters; whereas GPT-4 has 170 trillion parameters. This allows GPT-4 to process the wider range of text with higher accuracy compared to Bert-based.

Max-sequence length

The maximum sequence length of a model refers to the longest input text it can process in a single pass. For BERT, the default max sequence length is 512 tokens; whereas Longformer has a max sequence length of 4096. This length can impact the model's ability to capture long-range dependencies and process longer documents.

Size of embedding dimension

It is a fixed-length vector to represent each input token. BERT-Base has an embedding dimension of 768, while BERT-Large has an embedding dimension of 1024. Larger embedding dimensions can help the model capture more information about the input tokens, leading to better performance in NLP tasks.

Pre-training dataset size and types

A crucial aspect of model performance is the size and variety of pre-training datasets used. Many pre-trained language models are trained on vast amounts of data from diverse sources. For instance, GPT-3 was trained on a dataset containing 489 billion tokens, which includes data from web crawls, books, and Wikipedia. In contrast, BERT was trained on a smaller dataset comprising BooksCorpus (800 million words) and English Wikipedia (2,500 million words). The quality and diversity of these datasets play a significant role in shaping the model's understanding of language patterns and its performance on various tasks.

Pioneering LLMs and their impact

In the following section, we will discuss three majors pioneering LLMS.

a Encoder, a way to remember it's Encoder-only, unlike BART (Enc + Dec)

BERT and its variants

BERT is a powerful pre-trained language model developed by Google in 2018. It is encoder-only model. In the following section, we will discuss the BERT, pre-training, fine-tunning, and different variations.

BERT pre-training

The model is trained on a large text corpus using **Masked Language Modeling (MLM),** and **Next Sentence Prediction** (**NSP**). *Figure 5.1* shows the BERT Pre-training Process. During the pre-training phase, BERT processes input sequences that are prepared to include both masked words for the **Masked Language Model** (**MLM**) task and sentence pairs for the **Next Sentence Prediction** (**NSP**) task:

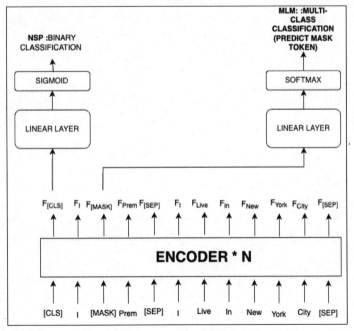

Figure 5.1: BERT pre-training process

Here is how to input sequences are created for pre-training:

- **Collecting sentence pairs**: From the input corpus, consecutive pairs of sentences (Sentence A and Sentence B) are extracted. Sentence Pairs are Created in such a way that 50% of Pairs are consecutive sentences and 50% of pairs are random pairs. As shown in *Figure 5.1*, during pre-training, the input sequence is the sentence pairs.

- **Tokenization**: The sentence pairs are tokenized.

- **Add special tokens**: Special tokens are added to the tokenized sequences. [CLS] is added at the beginning of each sequence, and [SEP] is added between Sentence A and Sentence B, as well as at the end of Sentence B. For example:

  `[CLS] I Am Prem [SEP] I Live In New York City [SEP]`

- **Masking for MLM**: A certain percentage of tokens (e.g., 15%) in the input sequence are randomly selected to be masked. These tokens are replaced with the [MASK] token. The following is the input sequence after adding a special token and Masking token

  `[CLS] I [MASK] Prem [SEP] I Live In New York City [SEP]`

- **Creating input labels for MLM and NSP**: For MLM, the labels are the unmasked tokens corresponding to masked positions. For the NSP task, the labels are binary 1 if Sentence B is the actual next sentence of Sentence A, and 0 otherwise.

- **Optimization**: As illustrated in *Figure 5.1*, during pre-training, BERT utilizes two separate linear layers for MLM and NSP tasks. For MLM, the number of the output node of the linear layer is vocabulary size. This is because we are identifying the masked token among all the tokens in the vocabulary. Whereas for NSP, the number of output nodes in the linear layer is 2. This is because it is a binary classification problem. The model is optimized by jointly considering both tasks, where the total loss is computed as the average of the MLM loss and the NSP loss. This combined optimization approach allows BERT to learn a rich understanding of language through both masked language modeling and next-sentence prediction tasks.

You can find the pre-trained Bert in Hugging Face: **bert-base-uncased**.

BERT fine-tunning

Following the pre-training of BERT, the subsequent step is to fine-tune the model on a specific task or dataset. Fine-tuning involves training the pre-trained model for a few additional epochs on a labeled dataset designed for the target task.

For instance, if you aim to distinguish between satisfied and unsatisfied customers, you could use customer chat logs from help-center interactions as input texts. After manually creating labels for these interactions, you can train the **bert-base-uncased** model with this labeled dataset to tackle your classification problem. This fine-tuning process allows

BERT to adapt to the nuances of your specific task while leveraging the general language understanding acquired during pre-training.

BERT Variations

Table 5.1 presents the primary variants of BERT. All these models share an encoder-only architecture but differ in their pre-training objectives and specific architectural designs.

	Release Date	Para (base)	Architecture	Salient feature
BERT	2018	110M	12 Encoder Layers	Standard Feature
RoBERTa (Robustly Optimized BERT Approach)	2019	125M	Use just MLM It is dynamic masking. The masked token change on each epoch	Use large text corpus for training Improved Performance compared to BERT
ALBERT (A Lite BERT)	2019	12M	Factorized embedding parameterization (separates the size of the word embeddings (E) from the hidden layer size (H) in the model). Sentence Order Prediction (SOP) task instead of NSP	Cross-layer parameter sharing
DistilBERT (Distilled BERT)	2019	66 M	6 Encoder layers	
LONGFORMER	2020	148 M	Use sliding window attention. Thus reducing complexity from $O(2n)$ to $O(n)$	Max-seq length= 4096 compared to 512 in BERT

Table 5.1: *Variants of BERT*

Applications

BERT is generally better suited for tasks requiring bidirectional context understanding. Some of the NLP tasks where BERT excels are:

- Text classification
- **Named Entity Recognition (NER)**

- **Question-Answering (QA)**

- Sentiment analysis

- Paraphrase detection

Generative pre-trained Transformer

It is a transformer decoder Only model developed by OpenAI for natural language processing tasks. It is autoregressive, meaning it generates texts by predicting one token at a time using the previously generated tokens as context for the next predictions. *Figure 5.2* shows the GPT architecture. You can see in the diagram that gives prompt (Describe First Law of Robotics) and previously generated tokens (<s>, A), the GPT predicts the next token which is `Robot`:

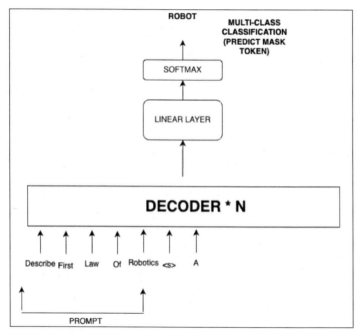

Figure 5.2: GPT Architecture

Pre-training of GPT

Let us discuss the pre-training process of GPT:

- **Data collection and processing**: GPT-2 is pre-trained on a large corpus of text data collected from various sources, such as web pages, books, and Wikipedia articles. The first step involves gathering and cleaning this data to ensure it is suitable for training the model. The data is tokenized, which means this process converts the text into a sequence of tokens that can be processed by the model.

- **Input data preparation**: The tokenized texts are chunked into fixed lengths. For example, in GPT-2 max-sequence length is 512. Thus, each input should consist of a sequence of length 512. If the certain sequence is less than 512, you can pad it with special padding tokens.

- **Label preparation**: The input sequence is the original chunk, and the label sequence is the same chunk shifted by one position to the left. For example, if you have the following sequence chunk:

```
Text Chunk=[ 'A', 'robot', 'may', 'not', 'injure', 'a', 'human',
'being', 'or',',', 'through',' inaction',',', 'allow', 'a','human','
being',' to',' come',' to',' harm','.']
```

The input sequence will be:

```
Input=[ 'A', 'robot', 'may', 'not', 'injure', 'a', 'human', 'being',
'or',',', 'through',' inaction',',', 'allow', 'a','human',' being','
to',' come',' to',' harm','.']
```

And the corresponding label sequence will be:

```
Label=[ 'robot', 'may', 'not', 'injure', 'a', 'human', 'being',
'or',',', 'through',' inaction',',', 'allow', 'a','human',' being','
to',' come',' to',' harm','.',' <end>']
```

- **Batching**: Create batches of input-label sequence pairs for training. Each batch should have a specified batch size (e.g., 16, 32, or 64)

- **Model architecture**: the GPT-2 model architecture is chosen, which defines the number of layers, attention heads, and hidden dimensions. There are several variants of GPT-2 with different sizes, such as small (12 layers), medium (24 layers), large (36 layers), and extra-large (48 layers). The size of the model affects its performance and computational requirements.

- **Training the model**: Finally, you can pre-train the model

- **Fine-tunning model**: Now, you can fine-tune the pre-trained model with the task in your hand.

Table 5.2 illustrates the various iterations of the GPT architecture. It is essential to note that GPT-2 is the latest open-source version of the generative pre-trained model:

Version	Description
GPT-2	**Architecture:** Decoder-only model that comes in multiple versions with different layer counts. The various model sizes have 12, 24, 36, or 48 layers
	Dataset: 40Gb Raw Text
	Parameters: GPT-2 comes in four sizes with varying numbers of parameters: 117 million (small), 345 million (medium), 774 million (large), and 1.5 billion (extra-large)

Version	Description
GPT-3	**Architecture:** Similar to GPT-2 and comes up with 96, 192, or 384 layers in various model sizes **Pre-training Dataset:** 45 TB **Parameters:** 125 million (small), 350 million (medium), 760 million (large), 1.3 billion, 2.7 billion, 6.7 billion, 13 billion, and the largest model with 175 billion parameters
GPT-4	Not Publicly Declared.

Table 5.2: *GPT Versions*

Applications

GPT is an autoregressive model; thus, is better suited for tasks involving text generation or completion such as:

- Text completion or continuation

- Content generation (for example stories, articles, or poems)

- Code completion or generation

- Conversational AI and chatbots

Bidirectional and Auto-Regressive Transformers

Bidirectional and Auto-Regressive Transformers (BART) combines the strength of both BERT and GPT architectures. It has a bidirectional encoder and an autoregressive decoder, which allows the advantages of both BERT and GPT pre-training methods. The encoder and decoder architecture of BART is similar to the original transformer architecture. However, the pre-training objective of BART is unique compared to other models. In the following section, we will delve into the details of BART.

Pre-training

The pre-training objective is to reconstruct the original input text after it has been corrupted, which helps to learn the structure and semantics of the language. Let us describe the process in detail:

- **Data collection and pre-processing**: Collect, clean, and pre-process the data. This process is similar to what you would do for pre-training with the BERT model.

- **Text corruption**: Create a noise function that will be applied to the input text. This function should introduce various types of corruptions to the text, such as token masking, token deletion, token replacement, and text shuffling.

- **Corrupting input text**: Apply the noise function to the pre-processed text to generate corrupted versions of the input text.

- **Model architecture**: The BART-base model consists of 6 encoders and 6 decoders, while the BART-large model is equipped with 12 encoders and 12 decoders.

- **Label:** The true label for BART is the input sequence without corruption.

- **Pre-training**: BART's pre-training objective is to minimize the difference between the reconstructed text generated by the decoder and the original, uncorrupted text. This is achieved by using a cross-entropy loss function that compares the predicted token probabilities at each position with the actual tokens in the original text.

Application

While BERT excels at tasks requiring bidirectional context understanding, and GPT is better suited for text generation tasks due to its auto-regressive nature, BART bridges the gap between these two models by combining their strengths. BART has been found to perform particularly well in the following application areas:

- Text summarization

- Machine translation

- Text generation

- Sentiment analysis

- Conversational AI

- Question-answering

In summary, if you require a large language model that excels in tasks involving both auto-regression and bidirectional context understanding, BART is an optimal choice.

Creating your own LLM

Imagine you are building a house. You could head to Home Depot, purchase all the pre-made kitchens, doors, and quickly assemble your home. However, would it not be fantastic if your house design could cater to your unique needs and desires? Additionally, you should consider cost overruns; thus, not building all the materials from scratch. That is where creating your own **Language Model** (**LM**) comes in.

Off-the-shelf LLMs are impressive, but they might not capture your organization's specific data, industry jargon, and contextual information. This challenge is intensified if you work in a specialized industry. Let us discuss the healthcare domain. Real clinical notes, for example, are not available for general LLMs during pre-training due to HIPAA and government regulations. As a result, `bert-based-uncased`, which was trained with internet datasets and book datasets, does not capture the way doctors write clinical notes. By creating your own LLM, you can optimize your organization's language understanding. Moreover, you will not have to start from scratch. Creating an LLM from scratch requires hundreds of thousands of dollars (just for GPU costs). Instead, you can take a pre-trained model and further pre-train it with your organization's dataset. Let us highlight some of the major benefits of creating LLMs tailored to your organization.

- **Customized knowledge**: An in-house LLM can be further trained on your organization's specific data, industry jargon, and contextual information. This means it'll understand your organization's lingo like a seasoned employee, ensuring better performance and more accurate results.

- **Adaptability**: You can continuously pre-train it based on the latest trends, emerging technologies, and shifting priorities, ensuring it stays relevant and effective.

- **Privacy and security:** You can maintain control over sensitive data while not sacrificing the performance of NLP.

- **Competitive advantage**: The LLM tailored to your organization and industry can deliver insights and understanding that generic LLMs cannot. You will have a competitive advantage compared to industry peers.

In the following section, we will create Clinical BERT by further pre-training the **bert-based-uncased** model using healthcare data.

Clinical-Bert

Our goal is to further pre-train the **bert-based-uncased** model using a clinical notes dataset. Here is the plan for this chapter:

- Import necessary packages.

- Obtain the dataset from Kaggle:

  o We will use the **akashadesai/clinical-notes** dataset.

  o Save the dataset on your computer.

- Clean and organize the data:

  o Create a pandas dataframe, placing each sentence in a new row.

  o Ensure consecutive sentences are in consecutive rows (for example Sentence A in row i and Sentence B in row i+1).

- Develop a custom Dataset class:

  o For BERT training, format each item as: Sentence A + [SEP] + Sentence B.

  o The **getitem** method should return the tokenization of (Sentence A + [SEP] + Sentence B).

- Create a **DataCollatorForPreTraining** class for the DataLoader:

  o This class should inherit from **DataCollatorForLanguageModeling**

  o Mask a few tokens from Sentence A

- Set up a DataLoader:

  o Pass the **DataCollatorForPreTraining** object as **collate_fn** to DataLoader

- Choose the model, loss function, and optimizer.

- Get the accelerator ready for GPU and multi-device training.

- Train the BERT-based-uncased model further, and you will have a Clinical BERT model!

The accompanying notebook provides a comprehensive end-to-end implementation of the plan outlined above. You can follow the approach demonstrated in the notebook to create an LLM for your organization. Keep in mind these key points before creating your LLM:

- Choose the appropriate model architecture based on:

  o The task you are solving, which determines the variant of the model (encoder only, decoder only, encoder-decoder)

  o The size of the pre-training data

  o The availability of computational resources

- Prepare the dataset based on the pre-training objective:

- Data cleaning is a crucial step – even with the finest model architecture, a sub-optimal pre-training dataset will yield sub-optimal results.

Conclusion

In this book chapter, we explored LLMs and delved into the pioneering language models that have shaped the field. We then demonstrated how to create a customized language model for an organization by further pre-training the **bert-based-uncased** model, resulting in a tailored solution that addresses specific needs and requirements.

In the next chapter, we will discuss various NLP tasks and how transformers can be used to solve them. Additionally, we will devolve deeper into classification, text generation and question-answer tasks.

Quiz

1. **Which of the following is a encoder only language model?**

   a. BERT

   b. GPT-3

   c. BART

   d. LSTM

2. **Which language model is decoder only language model?**

   a. BERT

   b. GPT-3

   c. BART

   d. LSTM

3. **Which language model is encoder-decoder language model?**

   a. BERT

   b. GPT-3

   c. BART

   d. LSTM

4. **What is the purpose of pre-training in the context of LLMs?**

   a. Training the model on a specific task

   b. Learning general language understanding

   c. Fine-tuning the model on task-specific data

5. **What is the purpose of fine-tuning in the context of LLMs?**

   a. Reducing over-fitting

   b. Learning general language understanding

   c. Adapting the model to a new task

   d. Reducing overfitting

6. **What is the main advantage of using bidirectional context in BERT?**

   a. For text generation

   b. Better understanding of context

   c. Faster training

   d. Reduced overfitting

7. **Which language model uses a "MLM" and "NSP" objective during pre-training?**

   a. BERT

   b. GPT-3

   c. BART

   d. LSTM

8. **What is the primary pre-training objective of GPT-3?**

   a. Masked language modeling

   b. Denoising autoencoding

   c. Autoregressive language modeling

   d. Sequence-to-sequence modeling

9. **What pre-training technique does BART use?**

   a. Masked language modeling

   b. Denoising autoencoding

   c. Autoregressive language modeling

   d. Next Sentence Prediction

10. **What is the main benefit of creating a custom LLM for your organization?**

    a. Faster training

    b. Lower computational cost

    c. Tailored knowledge and understanding

    d. Easier implementation

11. **What is the key difference between BERT and GPT-3?**

    a. Bidirectional context vs. autoregressive generation

    b. Denoising vs. autoregressive generation

    c. MLM vs. Denoising

12. **Which of these models is more suitable for text Classification?**

    a. BERT

    b. GPT-3

13. **What is the primary purpose of a custom Dataset class when creating an Large Language Model?**

    a. To define the pre-processing steps

    b. To define the model architecture

    c. To prepare the input data for training

14. **What objective function `BertForPreTraining` provides?**

    a. NSP and MLM

    b. NSP

    c. MLM

15. **What is the primary goal of DataCollatorForPreTraining class in the context of LLMs?**

    a. To define the model architecture

    b. To create masked tokens for pre-training

16. **Which of the following best describes the difference between pre-training and fine-tuning?**

    a. Pre-training focuses on general language understanding, fine-tuning adapts model for specific task

    b. Both are same

    c. None of the above

Answers

1. a.

2. b.

3. c.

4. d.

5. c.

6. b.

7. a.

8. c.

9. b.

10. c.

11. a.

12. a.

13. c.

14. a.

15. d.

16. a.

## CHAPTER 6

NLP Tasks with Transformers

Introduction

The ultimate goal of **Natural Language Processing (NLP)** is to enable computers to understand, interpret, and generate human-like language in a manner that is both meaningful and useful. With the introduction of transformer models such as T5, GPT, and BERT, NLP has seen a significant leap in capabilities and performance, leading to state-of-the-art results in various NLP tasks. In this chapter, we will discuss various NLP tasks and how transformers can be used to solve them.

Structure

The chapter is organized in following structure:

- System requirement
- NLP Tasks
- Text classification
- Text generation
- ChatBot with transformer
- Training with PEFR and LORA

Objectives

By the end of this chapter, the reader will learn how to comprehend key NLP tasks and their resolution using transformers, understand the utilization of transformers for text classification, with an emphasis on handling long sequences, and fine-tune transformers for text generation. The readers will also be able to fine-tune transformers for creating instruction following models, as well as understand how we can fine-tune the transformer on commodity hardware.

System requirements

For detailed instructions on setting the environment, please follow instructions at **https://github.com/bpbpublications/Building-Transformer-Models-with-PyTorch/blob/main/General/SettingVirtualEnvironment.ipynb.**

Activate virtual environment:

```
conda activate transformer_learn
```

To proceed with the coding tasks outlined in this chapter, please install the necessary packages detailed as following:

```
pip install transformers
pip install datasets
pip install accelerate
pip install peft
pip install bitsandbytes
pip install sentencePiece
```

NLP tasks

Natural language processing is a diverse and expansive domain that encompasses a multitude of tasks aimed at enabling machines to comprehend and interact with textual data more effectively. In this section, we will delve into various NLP tasks, showcasing how they are specifically designed to facilitate machine understanding and interaction with textual information. *Table 6.1* shows the major NLP tasks. You can search for and retrieve the model mentioned in the table from the Hugging Face Models repository at **https://huggingface.co/models**:

Tasks	Summary	Popular models
Text classification	Assign predefined classes/ categories to a given Text. Example, Sentiment Analysis, Spam Detection, Topic categorization	BERT, RoBERTa, DistilBERT, cardiffnlp/twitter-roberta-base-sentiment, distilbert-base-uncased-finetuned-sst-2-english
Token classification	Labeling individual tokens within the text with specific categories. Example, NER, POS tagging	BERT, BioBERT, Davlan/distilbert-base-multilingual-cased-ner-hrl
Table question answering	Extracting answers from structured data.	tapas-base, tabex-base
Question answering	Giving answer to the natural language questions based on the context	Roberta-base-squad2
Zero shot classification	Ability of a model to classify instances into categories it has never seen before	GPT3, bart-large-mnli
Summarization	Create concise representation of given text	facebook/bart-large-cnn, google/pegasus-cnn_dailymail
Text generation	Generate coherent text based on the prompt	gpt2, distilgpt2, Llama
Text2Text generation	Transforming one-form of text into another. Example, paraphrasing	T5, prithivida/parrot_paraphraser_on_T5
Fill mask	predicting the missing word(s) in a given sentence with appropriate contextual information.	BERT, GPT, xlm-roberta-base
Sentence similarly	measuring the semantic similarity between two sentences.	SBERT, USE (Universal Sentence Encoder), sentence-transformers/all-MiniLM-L6-v2
Translation	Converting text from one language to another.	t5-base, BART,
Conversational	Creating human like conversation. Example, chatbot	GPT, microsoft/DialoGPT-medium, PygmalionAI/pygmalion-6b

***Table 6.1**: Major NLP tasks*

In the following section, we will devolve deeper into some of the most important NLP tasks.

Text classification

Text classification is one of the most common NLP tasks you encounter in any industry. Some of the use cases of text classification are sentiment analysis, topic identification, spam detection, language identification, intent recognition, emotion detection, and so on.

Most appropriate architecture for text classification

Generally, encoder-only models or BERT variations are most appropriate for text classification for the following reasons:

- **Focus on understanding input text:** BERT variations are designed to understand input tokens by creating contextualized embeddings for each token.

- **Bidirectional context:** BERT and its variations are pre-trained to understand bidirectional context, as opposed to autoregressive models such as GPT. This helps to understand the context of language from both directions.

- **Efficiency:** Encoder-only models can be used for text classification by simply adding a fully connected layer, whereas decoder-only models may require more complex adaptations.

Text classification via fine-tunning transformer

Figure 6.1 shows the outline of text classification by fine tuning the existing language model:

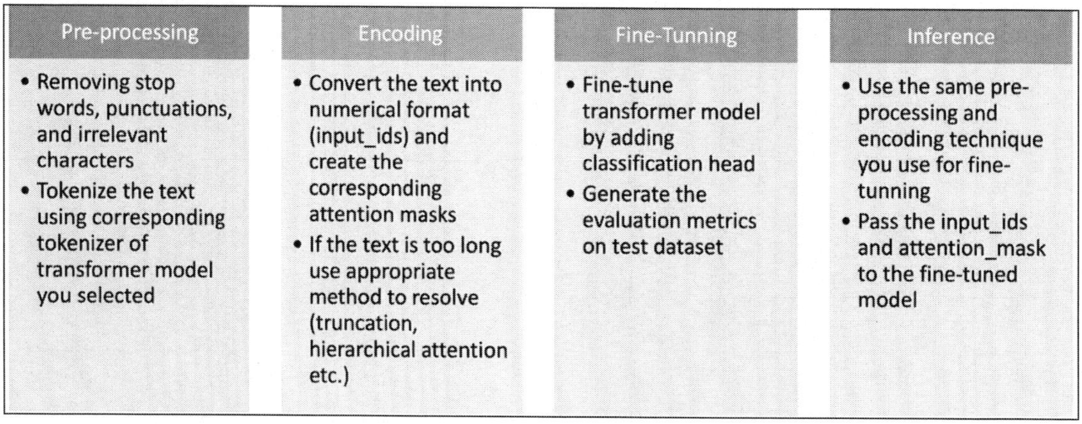

Pre-processing	Encoding	Fine-Tunning	Inference
• Removing stop words, punctuations, and irrelevant characters • Tokenize the text using corresponding tokenizer of transformer model you selected	• Convert the text into numerical format (input_ids) and create the corresponding attention masks • If the text is too long use appropriate method to resolve (truncation, hierarchical attention etc.)	• Fine-tune transformer model by adding classification head • Generate the evaluation metrics on test dataset	• Use the same pre-processing and encoding technique you use for fine-tunning • Pass the input_ids and attention_mask to the fine-tuned model

Figure 6.1: Text classification process

Handling long sequence

The majority of transformer architectures have a maximum limit on the sequence length they can handle. For example, the max sequence length for BERT is 512 tokens. Transformers have a low maximum sequence length because of the quadratic complexity of self-attention computation. Nevertheless, the real-world text data that you find in your company can often be longer than the maximum sequence length that a transformer model can handle. Thus, we need to find effective strategies to handle the max sequence length. In the following sections, we enlist a few of them:

- **Truncate:** If a sequence is longer than the model's maximum sequence length, you can simply truncate it. This is the easiest approach but may result in a loss of information and poor performance for tasks that require understanding the entire context.

- **Chunking:** Divide the long sequences into non-overlapping chunks and process the self-attention individually. You can combine the outputs using various strategies such as mean, max pooling, or concatenation. This approach may lose information related to context between the chunks.

- **Hierarchical approach:** Create a hierarchical structure by dividing long sequences into sentences or paragraphs. Then, encode each sentence or paragraph into a fixed-size encoding. Afterward, perform attention on sentence or paragraph representations. This allows the model to capture both local and global attention.

- **Custom architecture:** Some transformers, like LongFormer (max-seq_len=4096) and BigBird(max-seq_len=4096), are specifically designed to handle long sequences. These architectures use a combination of local and global attention so that the overall complexity of attention computation is not quadratic.

In the real world, you will experiment with various approaches and also consider the importance of capturing the entire context and resource availability to choose the appropriate approach. Here, we will do two projects where we will explore the mechanism to handle long sequence via document chunking and Hierarchal Attention.

Project 1: Document chunking

In this project, we will fine-tune the BERT-base-uncased model to predict sentiment in the IMDB dataset. The following steps provide an overview of the model architecture:

1. **Divide long text into smaller chunks:** The code splits extensive text data into smaller, more manageable chunks or sentences. This step is crucial for handling long sequences effectively.

2. **Process each chunk with BERT:** Each of these smaller chunks is then individually processed through the BERT model. This processing generates a vector representation for each sentence, capturing its essential features and meaning.

3. **Create a composite representation:** Finally, the code averages these vector representations from all chunks to form a single, comprehensive representation of the entire long text. This average representation encapsulates the overall context or sentiment of the text.

The complete end-to-end project implementation is provided in the accompanying notebook.

Project 2: Hierarchical attention

Similar to the previous project, we will calculate the sentiment score on IMDB dataset. However, instead of document chunking, we will use the **Hierarchical attention mechanism**:

- **Hierarchical attention:** This model uses a two-level hierarchical attention mechanism:

  o **Local attention:** Applied to individual sentences in a document to create sentence representations.

  o **Global attention:** Applied to sentence representations to create a document representation.

- **Sentence representation:**

  o Reshape the data to have dimensions (**batch_size * num_sentences**, **hidden_size**) Pass **input_ids** and **attention_mask** to the ALBERT model to get hidden states (**outputs.last_hidden_state**).

  o Apply the attention layer (**self.attention**) to the hidden states, followed by **softmax** function to compute attention weights (**attention_weights**). The **attention_weights** gives the weight of each token

  o Calculate the sentence representation by multiplying hidden states with their corresponding attention weights and summing along the sequence dimension (**torch.sum(attention_weights * hidden_states, dim=1)**).

  o Reshape the **sentence_representation** tensor to have dimensions (**batch_size**, **num_sentences**, **hidden_size**).

- **Document representation:**

  o Apply the attention layer (**self.attention**) to the sentence representations, followed by a **softmax** function to compute document-level attention weights (**doc_attention_weights**).

  o Follow the same method to create document representation.

The complete end-to-end project implementation is provided in the accompanying notebook.

Text generation

In this section, we will outline the text generation using the transformer-based models. Typical steps for creating a text generation model involve:

1. **Acquire** and pre-process the data.

2. **Choose a transformer** model and fine tune it. Select an appropriate pre-trained model. Typically, an autoregressive model such as GPT works best for the text generation task.

3. **Generate text:** Utilize the trained model to generate new text by providing an initial prompt or seed text, which the model will use as a starting point.

4. **Post-process:** Clean up and format the generated text to make it more human-readable or appropriate for your use case.

Project 3: Shakespeare like text generation

In this project, we will generate Shakespeare-like text using the GPT-2 model fine-tuned on the Tiny Shakespeare dataset.

Data preparation

Lines 14-16 in the following code block illustrate that the dataset is a long sequence of text (**num_rows=1**). At the end of data preparation, this is what each item of the dataset class looks like:

- **input_ids:** Tokenized input text chunk. We will divide the whole text into chunks of text (for example, **1** tokens).

- **attention_mask:** A binary mask indicating which tokens should be attended to by the model during the forward pass.

- **labels**: **Input_ids** shifted by 1 position. This is crucial for text generation fine-tuning, as the training objective is to train the model to predict the next word given the tokens at the current position.

Let us examine the most important aspect of the following code. Lines 31-37 split the entire text into chunks, with each chunk consisting of 100 tokens. Refer to the following code:

```
import torch
from torch.utils.data import DataLoader, Dataset
from datasets import load_dataset
from transformers import GPT2Tokenizer
tokenizer = GPT2Tokenizer.from_pretrained("gpt2")
```

```
# Set the padding token
tokenizer.pad_token = tokenizer.eos_token

# Load the dataset
dataset = load_dataset("tiny_shakespeare")
'''
DatasetDict({
    train: Dataset({
        features: ['text'],
        num_rows: 1
    })
    validation: Dataset({
        features: ['text'],
        num_rows: 1
    })
    test: Dataset({
        features: ['text'],
        num_rows: 1
    })
})
'''


# Split the continuous text into smaller chunks
def split_text(text, max_length=100):
    return [text[i:i+max_length] for i in range(0, len(text), max_length)]


# Apply the split_text function to the dataset


split_texts = split_text(dataset["train"]["text"][0])


# Tokenize the split_texts
tokenized_texts = tokenizer(split_texts, return_tensors="pt", padding=True,
truncation=True)
```

Let us take a closer look at the key aspect of the next code block. The **ShiftedDataset** class demonstrates the custom dataset preparation process. Our primary objective in fine-tuning is to provide text and predict the next token. As a result, the **input_ids** consist of tokenized text chunks, and the labels represent the input text shifted by one position. Additionally, we append an **eos_token_id** at the end of the labels:

```python
class ShiftedDataset(Dataset):
    def __init__(self, encodings):
        self.encodings = encodings

    def __getitem__(self, idx):
        input_ids = self.encodings["input_ids"][idx]
        attention_mask = self.encodings["attention_mask"][idx]
        labels = input_ids[1:].tolist() + [tokenizer.eos_token_id]
        return {"input_ids": input_ids, "attention_mask": attention_mask,
"labels": torch.tensor(labels)}

    def __len__(self):
        return len(self.encodings["input_ids"])


# Create a DataLoader
train_dataset = ShiftedDataset(tokenized_texts)
train_dataloader = DataLoader(train_dataset, shuffle=True, batch_size=4)
```

Training

In the following code block, we are just preparing the data loader, model, and optimizer for the accelerator. Another important thing is that we use the **LMHeadModel** variant (in this case, **GPT2LMHeadModel**) when fine-tuning GPT-2 for text generation tasks for the following reasons:

- The **LMHeadModel** is designed explicitly for language modeling tasks, which involve predicting the next token in a sequence of tokens. In the case of GPT-2, GPT2LMHeadModel is tailored for such tasks, making it suitable for text generation where the model needs to generate coherent sequences of text.

- The **GPT2LMHeadModel** adds the linear layer on top of transformer for the next word prediction.

Refer to the following code:

```
from accelerate import Accelerator
from transformers import GPT2LMHeadModel


# Initialize the Accelerator
accelerator = Accelerator()


# Configure the training arguments
num_epochs = 20
learning_rate = 5e-5


# Initialize the GPT-2 model and optimizer
model = GPT2LMHeadModel.from_pretrained("gpt2")
optimizer = torch.optim.Adam(model.parameters(), lr=learning_rate)


# Prepare the model and optimizer for training with Accelerator
model, optimizer, train_dataloader = accelerator.prepare(model, optimizer,
train_dataloader)
```

The important aspect of the following code is that we are saving the model every five epochs. The reasons are:

- **Checkpointing:** Saving the model periodically creates checkpoints, allowing you to resume training from the latest saved epoch.

- **Early stopping:** If the performance on validation sets starts degrading, we can implement the early stopping technique.

Refer to the following code:

```
from transformers import AdamW
from tqdm import tqdm


# Fine-tuning loop
for epoch in range(num_epochs):
    epoch_iterator = tqdm(train_dataloader, desc=f"Epoch {epoch + 1}")
    for step, batch in enumerate(epoch_iterator):
        optimizer.zero_grad()
        input_ids = batch["input_ids"]
```

```
        attention_mask = batch["attention_mask"]
        labels = batch["labels"]

        outputs = model(input_ids=input_ids, attention_mask=attention_mask,
labels=labels)
        loss = outputs.loss

        accelerator.backward(loss)
        optimizer.step()

        if step % 500 == 0:
            epoch_iterator.set_postfix({"Loss": loss.item()}, refresh=True)

    # Save the model every 5 epochs
    if (epoch + 1) % 5 == 0:
        model_save_path = f"/Users/premtimsina/Documents/bpbbook/chapter6/
model/tiny_shakespeare/model_checkpoint_epoch_{epoch + 1}"
        model.save_pretrained(model_save_path)
        print(f"Model saved at epoch {epoch + 1}")
```

The model is ready; now, you can use it to write a poem as if it was written by Shakespeare. The end-to-end implementation of the model with the inference pipeline is included in the accompanying notebook.

ChatBot with transformer

In this section, we will develop a tool similar to ChatGPT for your organization. This type of model is known as an instruction following model, and we will delve into the reasons why it is essential for your organization.

An instruction following model is designed to comprehend and carry out tasks based on natural language instructions. These models often form the foundation for chatbots, as they allow the systems to understand and respond to user instructions in a human-like manner.

Let us explore why incorporating an instruction following model is crucial for your organization's competitive advantage:

- **Customized chatbot:** You can create a transformer model tailored to your organization's data. Systems like ChatGPT do not possess your organizational data and context.

- **Security and Privacy**: Your organization's chatbot will remain within your firewall, ensuring that no data leaves your organization's network.

Under the hood, instruction following models encompass various types of transformer models, such as QA, TAPAS, Summarization, and more. Nevertheless, we will implement the instruction following model using only a transformer fine-tuned for QA tasks. You can build upon this concept to include other types of transformers.

Project 4: Clinical question answering transformer

Let us now go over the various stages in this project.

Data preparation

Loading Data: We use the **Medical Question Answering Dataset (MedQuAD)** which includes 47,457 medical question-answer pairs. The dataset can be downloaded from **https://github.com/abachaa/MedQuAD**. The dataset is 1000s of XML files. We will do the data cleaning and produce a single JSON file three keys ['Instruction', 'Input', 'Output'] for each document.

The JSON files look like:

```
[{'instruction':'How Can you treat my diabetes?','input': 'I have
uncontrolled diabetes. MY A1C is above 7.5','output': 'You can treat in
following ways:\n 1. Get physical\n 2. take medication as prescribed by
your doctor \n3. check your blood sugar regularly' }]
```

Model declaration

We will utilize the lama-7b-hf model created by Meta. LlaMA 7b is trained with 1Trillion tokens with next word prediction as pre-training objective. LLaMA outperformed GPT-3 in several natural language processing tasks, such as sentiment analysis. This could be attributed to LLaMA's extensive training dataset, which gives it an advantage over GPT-3. LlaMA is released under non-commercial license; thus, you need to be cognizant on using this model. To obtain the model weights from Meta, you must submit a request through **https://ai.facebook.com/blog/large-language-model-llama-meta-ai/**. However, the Llama model's weights were inadvertently leaked and incorporated into Hugging Face's decapoda-research/llama-7b-hf. As a result, we will employ the Llama model from decapoda-research rather than requesting the weights from Meta which takes longer time.

Creating prompt and tokenization

Prior to tokenization, we must construct the prompt. Here is the structure of the prompt:[1]:
```
def generate_prompt(data_point):
```

---

[1] **https://github.com/tloen/alpaca-lora**

```
    if data_point["input"]:
        return f"""Below is an instruction that describes a task, paired
with an input that provides further context. Write a response that
appropriately completes the request.


### Instruction:
{data_point["instruction"]}


### Input:
{data_point["input"]}


### Response:
{data_point["output"]}"""
    else:
        return f"""Below is an instruction that describes a task. Write a
response that appropriately completes the request.


### Instruction:
{data_point["instruction"]}


### Response:
{data_point["output"]}"""
```

We tokenize the prompt and create the training and validation dataset with the following format:

```
Dataset({
 features: ['instruction', 'input', 'output', 'input_ids', 'attention_
mask'],
 num_rows: 14762
})
```

Training with PEFT and LORA

The general approach to using large language models involves two steps:

1. Pre-training the LLM with a huge amount of data (such as GPT, BERT, T5)

2. Fine-tuning it for downstream tasks to improve performance.

However, as LLMs become larger, fine-tuning becomes computationally expensive, making it impossible to fine-tune many LLMs on commodity hardware. Additionally, storing task-specific fine-tuned models also becomes a challenge as a single fine-tuned model can be in the range of hundreds of gigabytes. To address these issues, **Parameter-Efficient Fine-Tuning (PEFT)** was introduced.

PEFT freezes most of the parameters from the original pre-trained model and only trains a small number of extra model parameters, which avoids the problem of catastrophic forgetting behavior as most of the parameters from the original model are kept fixed. Another important benefit of PEFT is that it reduces the size of the task-specific fine-tuned models, making them more portable. PEFT offers various methods such as **Low Rank Adaptation of Large Language Models (LORA)**[2], Prefix Tuning, P-Tuning, Prompt Tuning, and AdaLoRA.

For the AI doctor project, LORA was chosen. LORA freezes all parameters of the pre-trained model and injects trainable rank decomposition matrices into each layer of the Transformer architecture, greatly reducing the number of trainable parameters needed for downstream tasks. For the AI doctor project, only 0.06% of the original parameters of LlaMA needed to be trained, thanks to LORA.

The complete end-to-end code for model development, inference, and sharing on hugging face are provided in the accompanying notebook.

Let us see few examples of inference done by AI doctor:

```
print(ask_ai_doctor('What are symptoms of Cirrhosis?', model))
```

Output:

```
The following list of signs and symptoms may be associated with
cirrhosis.  Some people with cirrhosis do not have any of these
symptoms.  If you are concerned about how your general health is
affected by cirrhosis, talk to your doctor or nurse practitioner.
Signs and Symptoms of Cirrhosis  -------------------  Abdominal
swelling (ascites)  Bleeding problems  Blurred vision  Breath odor
Confusion  Constipation  Difficulty concentrating  Dizziness
Fatigue  Fluid retention  Gallstones  Gout  Hair loss  Headache
Itching  Jaundice  Liver cancer  Memory loss  Muscle weakness
Nausea  Neuropathy  Night sweats  Pain in the upper right abdomen
Poor appetite  Skin itching  Sleepiness  Stomach pain  Swollen
legs and feet  Tiredness  Weight gain  Yellow skin and eyes
```

---

[2] **https://huggingface.co/docs/peft/conceptual_guides/lora**

It is incredible that we have developed an AI Doctor capable of answering a diverse set of questions. What is even more fascinating is that we were able to complete fine-tuning in just 30 minutes using a single GPU machine with 32 GB of RAM. Moreover, the cost of training was just a few dollars.

Conclusion

Through this chapter, we have explored the major NLP tasks and how transformers can be effectively used to solve them. Additionally, we have discussed how transformers can be fine-tuned for text classification, text generation, and instruction following models. Finally, we discussed how we can fine-tune transformers in commodity hardware.

Quiz

1. **Which layer of transformer is responsible for processing the input text?**

    a. Attention Layer

    b. Feedforward Layer

    c. Encoding Layer

    d. Decoding Layer

2. **What is the main challenge in handling long sequences in natural language processing?**

    a. The computational complexity of seq_len is quadratic.

    b. Insufficient training data

    c. Poor quality of data

    d. None of the above

3. **What is the standard approach to handle long sequences in transformers?**

    a. Truncation

    b. Chunking

    c. Padding

    d. All of the above

4. **What is the primary disadvantage of truncation?**

    a. Loss of information

    b. Increase in training time

    c. Decrease in accuracy

    d. None of the above

5. **What is the typial structure of Dataset before feeding into classification model?**

    a. {'input_ids': input_ids_tensor, 'attention_mask': attention_masks_tensor, 'label': labels_tensor}

    b. {'input_ids': input_ids_tensor, 'attention_mask': attention_masks_tensor}

6. **What does the 'pooler_output' represent in the BERT model?**

    a. Sequence Embedding

    b. First Token Embedding

7. **Which of the following accelerators is supported by the Hugging Face library?**

    a. GPU

    b. TPU

    c. MPS

    d. All of the above

8. **Which type of transformer is used for text generation?**

    a. Unidirectional Transformer

    b. Bidirectional Transformer

    c. Autoregressive Transformer

    d. None of the above

9. **Which pre-trained transformer model is widely used for text generation?**

    a. GPT-2

    b. BERT

    c. RoBERTa

    d. XLNet

10. **What is the difference between GPT and BERT transformers?**

    a. BERT is bidirectional while GPT is unidirectional

    b. GPT is bidirectional while BERT is unidirectional

    c. Both are bidirectional transformers

    d. Both are unidirectional transformers

11. **Which transformer model is most commonly used for instruction following tasks?**

    a. BERT

    b. GPT-2

    c. LlaMA

    d. XLNet

12. **What is the function of PEFT?**

    a. Enabling training of LLMs on commodity hardware.

    b. Reducing the size of fine-tuned models for better portability.

    c. Both A and B.

13. **What is the purpose of LORA?**

    a. Freezes the parameters of pre-trained model and adds few trainable parameters.

    b. Increases training time.

Answers

1. c.

2. a.

3. a.

4. a.

5. a.

6. d.

7. c.

8. a.

9. a.

10. c.

11. c.

12. a.

13. a.

Join our book's Discord space

Join the book's Discord Workspace for Latest updates, Offers, Tech happenings around the world, New Release and Sessions with the Authors:

https://discord.bpbonline.com

CHAPTER 7

CV Model Anatomy: ViT, DETR, and DeiT

Introduction

This chapter presents an in-depth exploration of the **Vision Transformer (ViT)**, a novel approach in computer vision that leverages the transformer architecture, which is traditionally associated with breakthroughs in natural language processing. ViT is crucial in the field of computer vision as it introduces a method for processing images as sequences of patches, applying self-attention across these patches to understand the global context of the image, enhancing performance on complex tasks like image classification.

Alongside ViT, we will delve into image pre-processing—an indispensable stage that involves resizing, normalizing, and augmenting images to make them compatible with transformer models. This process ensures that our models are fed high-quality, standardized data, which is crucial for effective learning and accurate results. The chapter also covers the **Distilled Vision Transformer (DeiT)** and the **Detection Transformer (DETR)**, two advanced iterations of transformer-based models. DeiT refines the training process through knowledge distillation, leading to more efficient learning when data is scarce, while DETR revolutionizes object detection by interpreting images as a set of objects, eliminating the need for the complex region proposal networks used in traditional methods.

As we navigate through this chapter, we will not only dissect the theoretical underpinnings of these models but also engage with practical applications, using them to tackle real-world computer vision problems. This hands-on approach will provide readers with a comprehensive toolkit to understand and implement these cutting-edge technologies in their own projects, signifying the broadening horizon of AI in visual understanding.

Structure

The chapter is organized in the following structure:

- System requirement
- Image pre-processing
- Vision transformer architecture
- Distillation transformer
- Detection transformer

Objectives

This chapter will provide a foundational understanding of image pre-processing techniques and their significance in computer vision tasks. It will also delve into the architecture and workings of the **ViT** and its role in image classification, explore the **DeiT** architecture, focusing on its unique characteristics and advantages over ViT, as well as examine the architecture of the **DETR** and its application in object detection tasks. Lastly, it will help the reader understand ViT, DeiT, and DETR through practical examples.

System requirements

For detailed instructions on setting the environment, please follow instructions at **https:// github.com/bpbpublications/Building-Transformer-Models-with-PyTorch/blob/main/ General/SettingVirtualEnvironment.ipynb**.

Activate virtual environment:

```
conda activate transformer_learn
```

To proceed with the coding tasks outlined in this chapter, please install the necessary packages detailed as follows:

```
pip install transformers
pip install datasets
pip install accelerate
pip install torch
pip install torchvision
pip install scikit-learn
```

Image pre-processing

Image pre-processing is an essential step in computer vision. Similar to NLP, where raw text is converted into embeddings, certain steps must be conducted before feeding images into any machine learning model. The essential steps of image pre-processing are:

1. **Image resizing**: Most ML models require fixed image dimensions. Thus, based on the model requirement, you need to resize the image. For example, if you are using **vit_base_patch16_224**, the model requires your image to be of 224*224 dimensions. This is an essential step.

2. **Image normalization**: This is the process of scaling pixel values to a specific range, usually between 0 and 1, or -1 and 1. It helps stabilize the learning process, making it easier for the model to converge and learn optimal weights. There are many techniques, such as min-max scaling, mean-standard deviation scaling, and dividing pixel values by 255. Although it is an optional step, it is highly recommended.

3. **Data augmentation**: This involves applying random transformations to the original images. It helps improve the model's generalization capabilities by exposing it to a diverse set of examples. Additionally, data augmentation techniques can be used to create new samples by transforming original samples. This is an optional step. The following *Table 7.1* illustrates basic data augmentation techniques:

Methods	Description
Rotation	Rotating the image by a random angle.
Translation	Shifting the image horizontally or vertically.
Flipping	Mirroring the image horizontally or vertically.
Zooming	Scaling the image while preserving its aspect ratio
Color perturbation	Adjusting the brightness, contrast, or saturation of the image

Table 7.1: Data augmentation techniques

4. **Grayscale conversion**: This involves converting color images into grayscale with a single channel. It is useful when color information is not relevant to the task at hand. This reduces the image size, thus decreasing the computation requirements for training and inference. It is an optional step.

5. **RGB conversion**: Sometimes, color images may have additional channels, like an alpha channel. In such cases, you need to convert the images into RGB format. This is an optional step.

Example of image pre-processing

Now, let us have a demo of the image pre-processing technique.

Load the image using the following code:

```
import torch
import torchvision.transforms as T
from PIL import Image
import requests
from io import BytesIO


# Load an example image
url = " https://github.com/bpbpublications/Building-Transformer-Models-
with-PyTorch/blob/main/chapter7_ComputerVisionArch/tulip_field.png"
response = requests.get(url)
img = Image.open(BytesIO(response.content))
# convert to RGB
img = img.convert("RGB")
```

Display original image using the following code:

```
from IPython.display import display


display(img)
```

Refer to the following *Figure 7.1*:

Figure 7.1: *Example image before pre-processing*

Performing pre-processing

The transformation does the following things:

- **RandomRotation**: Randomly rotates the image between -15 and 15 degrees. Fills vacant pixels with zero.

- **RandomResizedCrop**: Resizes the image to a size of 224 x 224 pixels. Additionally, scales the image randomly between 80% and 100% of its original size.

- **RandomHorizontalFlip**: Applies a horizontal flip to the image with a 50% probability.

- **RandomVerticalFlip**: Applies a vertical flip to the image with a 50% probability.

- **ColorJitter**: Adjusts the image's brightness, contrast, and saturation.

- **ToTensor**: Converts the image to a PyTorch tensor.

- **Normalize**: Normalizes the image using the specified mean and standard deviation values.

Refer to the following code:

```
# Define the resizing, data augmentation, and normalization  pipeline
transforms = T.Compose([
    T.RandomRotation(degrees=(-15, 15), fill=0),
    T.RandomResizedCrop(size=(224, 224), scale=(0.8, 1.0)),
    T.RandomHorizontalFlip(p=0.5),
    T.RandomVerticalFlip(p=0.5),
    T.ColorJitter(brightness=0.2, contrast=0.2, saturation=0.2, hue=0.1),
    T.ToTensor(),
    T.Normalize(mean=[0.485, 0.456, 0.406], std=[0.229, 0.224, 0.225]),
])


# Apply the data augmentation pipeline to the image
augmented_img = transforms(img)


# To visualize the augmented image, you can convert it back to a PIL image
# Don't forget to undo the normalization before converting it
unnormalized_img = T.Compose([
    T.Normalize(mean=[-0.485/0.229, -0.456/0.224, -0.406/0.225],
std=[1/0.229, 1/0.224, 1/0.225]),
```

```
    T.ToPILImage(),
])(augmented_img)
```

Display the transformed Image using the following code:

```
from IPython.display import display


display(unnormalized_img)
```

Refer to the following *Figure 7.2*:

Figure 7.2: *Example image after image pre-processing*

Vision transformer architecture

Dosovitskiy[1] *et al.* proposed the **vision transformer architecture (ViT)**, which is an adaptation of the original transformer architecture for image classification tasks. The idea behind the ViT is to treat an image as a sequence of fixed-sized non-overlapping patches. This is similar to how a transformer treats natural language as a sequence of tokens.

---

[1] Dosovitskiy, A., Beyer, L., Kolesnikov, A., Weissenborn, D., Zhai, X., Unterthiner, T., ... &Houlsby, N. (2020). An image is worth 16x16 words: Transformers for image recognition at scale. *arXiv preprint arXiv:2010.11929*.

The following *Figure 7.3* depicts the architecture of ViT:

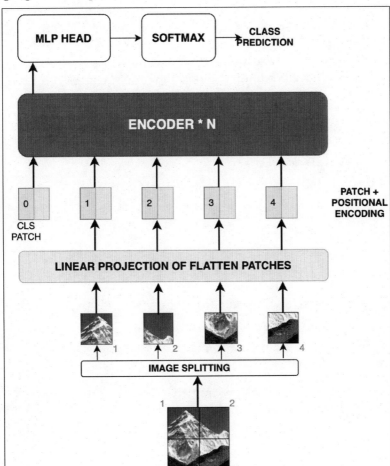

Figure 7.3: *ViT architecture*

The key components of ViT are as follows:

- **Image pre-processing**: Resize the image and split it into non-overlapping patches (for example, 16x16 pixels).

- **Patch embedding**: Flatten each patch into a 1D vector and linearly embed it into a high-dimensional representation. This is similar to token embedding in NLP.

- **Positional encoding**: Add location information to each patch.

- **Transformer layers**: Pass the patch embedding through the Transformer layers.

- **Classification**: Pass the output of Transformer layers to the fully connected layers and perform a softmax function to calculate the probability for classification.

The original ViT model was pre-trained on the ImageNet-21k dataset, which comprises 14 million images and 21K classes. Its pre-training objective was to minimize the cross-entropy loss between predicted class probabilities and true labels. You can obtain the ViT model through the **timm** or **huggingface** libraries. Various ViT model variations exist, based on factors such as patch size, image size, and more. As of April 30, 2023, there are 143 models available in the **timm** library. To list all models available in **timm**, you can run the following code:

```
import timm


all_models = timm.list_models()
vit_models = [model for model in all_models if 'vit' in model]


print("Available ViT models in timm:")
for model in vit_models:
    print(model)
```

Let us see how we can declare ViT model from timm:

```
import timm
model = timm.create_model("vit_base_patch16_224", in_chans=3, num_
classes=4, pretrained=True)
```

What the above code does is: it uses pre-trained ViT image with 12 layers, a hidden size of 768, 12 heads, and a patch size of 16x16 pixels. The input image size is 224x224 pixels. Additionally, it also add classification head with 4 classes on the output.

Project 1: AI eye doctor

Carry out the following project:

- Obtain the cataract dataset from Kaggle: **https://www.kaggle.com/datasets/jr2ngb/cataractdataset**.

- This dataset contains eye images and is categorized into four classes: normal, cataract, glaucoma, and **retina_diseases**.

- The objective is to develop a classifier capable of automatically identifying the type of eye disease present in the images.

To aid you in this task, a complete end-to-end implementation provided in the notebook located in the chapter's directory on GitHub.

Distillation transformer

Distillation transformer (DeiT)[2] is an extension of ViT. DeiT differs from ViT only during the pre-training phase. During fine-tuning and inference, the underlying architecture is exactly the same. *Figure 7.4* depicts the architecture diagram for the pre-training phase. Let us dig deeper into the pre-training process of DeiT:

- **Teacher model:** Choose a pre-trained teacher model, usually a CNN, like ResNet-50. The teacher model is not updated during the training process. Let us understand the concept behind this. The concept is called *knowledge distillation*. The basic idea is that you have two networks, one pre-trained larger network called the teacher, and a second, randomly initialized student network. During the pre-training phase, the student network tries to learn and behave like the teacher.

- **Process** the image.

- **Model training**: As shown in *Figure 7.4*, during the pre-training phase, models are optimized across two losses:

  o **Classification loss**: This optimizes the difference between the predicted probability and the true label. As shown in the diagram, LossCE is attached to the first token of the last layer of the transformer.

  o **Teacher loss/distillation loss**: Measures the difference between the student model's (DeiT) output and the teacher model's output. The student model is trained to minimize this difference, effectively learning from the teacher model.

- There are different variations of knowledge distillation. DeiT uses hard distillation. In hard distillation, the objective function aims to reduce the cross-entropy loss between the teacher's labels and the student's logits predictions.

- Thus, the overall pre-training loss function becomes:

```
1/2 * CrossEntropy(true label, prediction logits)) + (1/2 *
CrossEntropy(teacher label, prediction logits)
```

Refer to the following *Figure 7.4*:

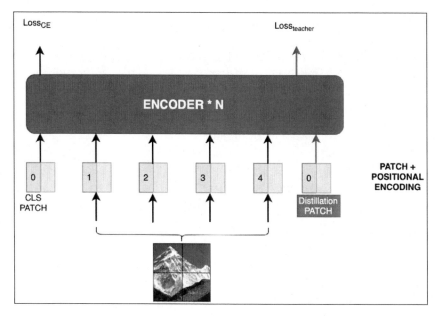

Figure 7.4: *Architecture of DeiT*

Advantages of DeiT

The primary advantage of DeiT over ViT is in scenarios where pre-training or fine-tuning datasets are limited.

Another advantage is knowledge distillation. DeiT learns to mimic the teacher model by minimizing the distillation loss. Due to knowledge distillation, DeiT achieves faster convergence than ViT.

Exercise

For fine-tuning AI eye doctor, we had a small dataset. The hypothesis is that DeiT should perform better than ViT. Please re-implement AI eye doctor using the DeiT model.

Detection transformer

Figure 7.5 depicts the typical **Detection transformer (DETR)**[3] architecture. It has three main components:

- CNN Backbone to extract image features
- Transformer encoder and decoder
- Two output heads for class prediction and bounding box prediction.

Refer to the following figure for DETR architecture:

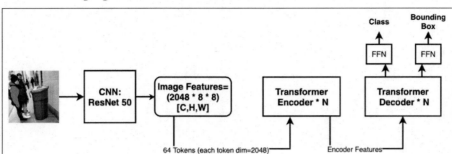

Figure 7.5: DETR architecture

Let us understand architecture in detail:

- **Image feature extraction**: A CNN model like ResNet-50 generates the feature map. This feature map is used as input to the transformer. Let us illustrate with an example. Suppose you have an image of size 256x256, and ResNet-50 generates a feature map of 8x8 with 2048 channels. Each 8x8 cell represents the spatial information about the input image, and the 2048 channels represent the high-level features.

- **Transformer encoder**: The extracted feature (for example, [2048, 8, 8]) is flattened and transformed into a sequence of 1D vectors that are fed into the transformer encoder. The encoder applies positional encoding and self-attention to capture both local and global contextual information. In our example, to feed the 2048x8x8 feature map into the transformer encoder, you need to reshape the feature map to be 64x2048 (8x8=64). Now, you have 64 vectors, each with a dimension of 2048, representing the spatial locations in the image. Each of these 64 vectors is considered a token for the transformer encoder. The sequence of 64 tokens (1D vectors of size 2048) is then fed to the transformer encoder.

- **Transformer decoder**: The transformer decoder takes in the output of the transformer encoder and object queries. The object queries represent potential object detections. In a typical example, there could be 100 object queries, each with 256 dimensions. This means in a single image, a maximum of 100 objects could be identified.

- **Output**: The output of the transformer decoder is a set of predicted bounding boxes and class probabilities for each object query. A loss function like bi-partite matching loss is used, which matches the predicted boxes with the ground truth boxes. For each object query, the output head produces two predictions. During pre-training of DETR, 100 object queries with 80 + 1 object categories were used (an additional 1 for "no object"):

- **Bounding box coordinates**: These are the coordinates (x, y, width, height) that define the predicted bounding box for the image. The output head will have four neurons dedicated to predicting the bounding box coordinates for each object query.

- **Class Probabilities**: These are the probabilities for each of the object categories.

Project 2: Object detection model

Let us create a program for object detection[2].

Import necessary packages using the following code:

```
import torch
import torchvision.transforms as T
from PIL import Image
import requests
from io import BytesIO
import matplotlib.pyplot as plt
from transformers import DetrForObjectDetection, DetrImageProcessor
```

Perform data pre-processing using the following code:

```
url = "https://raw.githubusercontent.com/pytorch/ios-demo-app/master/HelloWorld/HelloWorld/HelloWorld/image.png"
response = requests.get(url)
img = Image.open(BytesIO(response.content))
# Convert the image to RGB format
img = img.convert("RGB")
transform = T.Compose([
    T.Resize(800),
    T.ToTensor(),
    T.Normalize([0.485, 0.456, 0.406], [0.229, 0.224, 0.225]),
 ])
img_tensor = transform(img).unsqueeze(0)
```

Load model and make prediction using the following code:

```
processor = DetrImageProcessor.from_pretrained("facebook/detr-resnet-50")
```

---

[2] **https://huggingface.co/facebook/detr-resnet-50**

```
model = DetrForObjectDetection.from_pretrained("facebook/detr-resnet-50",
config=config)

model.eval()

with torch.no_grad():

    outputs = model(img_tensor)

target_sizes = torch.tensor([img.size[::-1]])

results = processor.post_process_object_detection(outputs, target_
sizes=target_sizes, threshold=0.9)[0]
```

Visualize the prediction using the following code:

```
fig, ax = plt.subplots(1, 1, figsize=(10, 10))

ax.imshow(img)


# get_cmap("tab20b")`is a qualitative colormap containing 20 distinct
colors.

# These colors are then used in the visualization code to assign

# unique colors to different object categories detected in the image.

colors = plt.get_cmap("tab20b").colors


# results["scores"] is prediction

# results["labels"] is true label

# results["boxes"] is the bounding box of object

for score, label, box in zip(results["scores"], results["labels"],
results["boxes"]):

    x, y, w, h = box

    w = w - x

    h = h - y

    rect = plt.Rectangle((x, y), w, h, linewidth=1, edgecolor=colors[label
% 20], facecolor="none")

    ax.add_patch(rect)

    ax.text(x, y, f"{model.config.id2label[label.item()]} {round(score.
item(), 3)}", fontsize=15, color=colors[label % 20])


plt.show()
```

Figure 7.6 shows the prediction. It is incredible, it is even able to identify the blurry and far behind car with 97% accuracy.

Figure 7.6: Outcome of object detection

Conclusion

This chapter has provided a fundamental overview of image pre-processing techniques and their importance in computer vision tasks. Following this, we explored the architectures of **ViT**, **DeiT**, and **DETR**.

We began by discussing essential image pre-processing steps, including resizing, normalization, and data augmentation. These steps are crucial for preparing images for machine learning models and optimizing computer vision performance. Subsequently, we delved into the architectural design of three major transformer-based computer vision models.

Through practical examples from two projects, we demonstrated how these transformer models can be applied to real-world scenarios, highlighting their effectiveness and versatility. By understanding the transformer architecture in computer vision, readers are equipped with the knowledge of how the transformer architecture has become a versatile method, converging various machine learning approaches.

The insights gained from this chapter will enable readers to appreciate the power and flexibility of transformer models in computer vision applications and motivate them to harness these advanced techniques in their own projects.

Quiz

1. **What is the primary benefit of data augmentation in image pre-processing?**

    a. Reducing the file size of images

    b. Improving model generalization

    c. Converting images to grayscale

    d. Reducing overfitting

2. **What does following Normalization does?**

    ```
    transforms = T.Compose([
    T.ToTensor(),
    T.Normalize(mean=[0.485, 0.456, 0.406], std=[0.229, 0.224, 0.225]),
    ])
    ```

    a. convert to tensor, normalize with mean=[0.485, 0.456, 0.406], std=[0.229, 0.224, 0.225]

    b. normalize to 0 and 1

3. **How can you Horizontally flip the image?**

    a. RandomRotation(degrees=(-15, 15), fill=0)

    b. RandomHorizontalFlip(p=0.5)

    c. RandomVerticalFlip(p=0.5)

4. **What is the primary purpose of image normalization in pre-processing?**

    a. To create visually appealing images

    b. To convert images to grayscale

    c. To stabilize the learning process and help the model converge

    d. To reduce the size of the dataset

5. **What are architectural component of ViT?**

    a. dividing an image into non-overlapping patches, convert to 1-D array and Positional Encoding, transformer encoder, output head

    b. CNN, Encoder

6. **In the below code: what should be size of input image**

    ```
    model = timm.create_model("vit_base_patch16_224", in_chans=3,
    num_classes=4, pretrained=True)
    ```

    a. Any size

    b. 224 * 224

7. **In ViT, what is the purpose of dividing an image into non-overlapping patches?**

    a. To reduce the size of the dataset

    b. To create visually appealing images

    c. To convert images into a sequence of tokens

    d. To apply data augmentation techniques

8. **What is the primary advantage of DeiT over ViT?**

    a. DeiT uses a convolutional neural network

    b. DeiT performs better with a smaller fine-tuning dataset

    c. DeiT has a larger architecture

    d. DeiT requires fewer patches

9. **How does DeiT use knowledge distillation to improve performance compared to ViT?**

    a. By mimicking the teacher model and minimizing the distillation loss

    b. By using a larger architecture

    c. By applying data augmentation techniques

    d. By increasing the number of patches

10. **In the DETR model, what is the purpose of the ResNet-50 backbone architecture?**

    a. To generate feature maps from the input image

    b. To perform data augmentation

    c. To convert images into grayscale

    d. To reduce the size of the dataset

11. **In the DETR model, what are two losses?**

    a. Prediction Loss, Teacher Loss

    b. Prediction Loss, Student Loss

Answers

  1. b.

  2. a.

  3. b.

  4. c.

  5. a.

  6. b.

  7. c.

  8. b.

  9. a.

10. a.

11. a.

Join our book's Discord space

Join the book's Discord Workspace for Latest updates, Offers, Tech happenings around the world, New Release and Sessions with the Authors:

https://discord.bpbonline.com

CHAPTER 8

Computer Vision Tasks with Transformers

Introduction

In this chapter, we will delve into teaching machines to see and interpret the world around us, recognize images, decipher emotions, and even generate visual data. By the time you reach the end of this chapter, you will comprehend the fundamental computer vision tasks and learn how to apply transformers to achieve these objectives. Additionally, we will also discuss the ground-breaking concept of stable diffusion, which has taken the field of image generation by storm.

Structure

The chapter is organized as follows:

- Computer vision task

- Image classification and comparison of DeiT, ViT and Resnet-50

- Image segmentation

- Diffusion model: Unconditional image generation

Objectives

This chapter will provide a comprehensive understanding of various computer vision tasks and their applications in real-world scenarios, and explore image classification techniques, comparing the performance of DeiT with well-established models such as ResNet-50 and ViT, demonstrating their effectiveness in solving classification problems.

The chapter will also offer an understanding of image segmentation and its practical applications, focusing on food image segmentation. We will implement an end-to-end food image segmentation model, demonstrating the process of training and evaluation. Lastly, the chapter will explain the principles behind diffusion models and their use in unconditional image generation. We will showcase the capabilities of these models by creating unique dog artwork, highlighting their potential in creative applications.

System requirements

For detailed instructions on setting the environment, please follow instructions at **https:// github.com/bpbpublications/Building-Transformer-Models-with-PyTorch/blob/main/ General/SettingVirtualEnvironment.ipynb**.

Activate virtual environment:

```
conda activate transformer_learn
```

To proceed with the coding tasks outlined in this chapter, please install the necessary packages detailed as follows:

```
pip install transformers
```

```
pip install datasets
```

```
pip install accelerate
```

```
pip install torch
```

```
pip install torchvision
```

```
pip install scikit-learn
```

```
pip install diffusers
```

Computer vision task

Table 8.1 illustrates the major tasks in computer vision. The model listed on the table can be searched and retrieved from **https://huggingface.co/models**:

Tasks	Summary	Popular models
Image classification	Classify images into categories	google/vit-base-patch16-224, microsoft/resnet-50*

Tasks	Summary	Popular models
Image segmentation	Partitioning image into different segments. It is pixel level partitioning.	facebook/detr-resnet-50-panoptic, nvidia/segformer-b0-finetuned-ade-512-512
Unconditional image generation	Generate coherent image without constraint or guidance. For example, create images of landscape, animals and so on, create painting in Picasso style based on its knowledge.	**Denoising Diffusion Probabilistic Models (DDPM)**
Zero-shot image classification	Classify images into categories which were not seen during training. For example, clip-vit was trained large dataset of image and its captions. The model learns to map text and images into shared high dimensional space. During inference, unseen image is processed by the encoder and the transformer tries identifying the class embedding that has highest match to image embedding.	openai/clip-vit-large-patch14
Depth estimation	Determine distance between objects in image.	Intel/dpt-large
Object detection	Identify different objects in an image.	DETR, facebook/detr-resnet-50
Image-to-image	Example, style transfer, colorization and so on.	ControlNet,
Video classification	Classify video on categories.	microsoft/xclip-base-patch32, facebook/timesformer-base-finetuned-k400

Table 8.1: Major tasks in computer vision

In the following section, we will delve deeper into the important computer vision tasks we enlisted in *Table 8.1*.

Image classification

In *Chapter 7, CV Model Anatomy: ViT, DETR, and DeiT* (`ViT.ipynb`), we conducted a cataract image classification project using ViT. In the accompanying notebook of this chapter (`deit_and_resnet_comparison.ipynb`), we performed the same experiment with DeiT and ResNet50. Here are the accuracy results after 5 epochs:

- **ViT:** 61.16%

- **DeiT:** 66.12%

- **ResNet50:** 29.75%

This experiment demonstrates that DeiT outperforms both ResNet50 and ViT. Prior research has also shown transformers to outperform ResNet50 in many fine-tuning tasks. Here are a few benefits of using transformers for image classification:

- **Complexity and transfer learning**: Both ViT and DeiT have higher complexity due to the self-attention mechanism. Pre-trained transformers have been shown to generalize better across a wide variety of tasks. If you are using transfer learning, then transformers could be more beneficial than ResNet50.

- **Multi-modal tasks**: Transformers can handle multi-modal data, such as images and text or images and audio, more naturally than CNNs. Thus, if your task involves multi-modal data, ViT and DeiT might be more suitable.

Exercise

Our implementation of the cataract image classifier is relatively basic. There are a couple of issues:

- Our fine-tuning dataset was quite small

- We performed minimal image pre-processing

To further improve the performance of the cataract dataset, consider experimenting with various data augmentation techniques. One option might be to double the dataset size using data augmentation.

Image segmentation

Image segmentation involves dividing the image into segments or regions, where each segment represents a specific object or area of interest. It might seem that object detection and image segmentation are similar; however, there is a significant difference. The primary goal of object detection is to identify the presence of objects and provide a rough estimate of their location using bounding boxes. On the other hand, image segmentation offers a more detailed representation of objects by assigning a class label to every pixel in the image, resulting in pixel-wise classification. This allows for the identification of not only the presence of objects but also their precise shape and boundaries.

Consider the following examples to understand when to use object detection and when to use image segmentation:

- **Object detection - autonomous vehicles**: Object detection is used to identify the presence of various objects, such as traffic lights, pedestrians, and other vehicles. Object detection can quickly determine the presence of these objects and their approximate locations, which is crucial for real-time decision-making in autonomous driving.

- **Image segmentation - medical imaging**: In medical imaging, such as CT scans or X-rays, it is essential to identify the exact structure of organs or tumors. Image segmentation can assign pixel-level classification, resulting in a fine-grained representation of the object. For instance, using object detection on the liver would only produce a rectangular bounding box, which is not helpful. In contrast, image segmentation provides the precise structure of the liver, which is crucial for accurate diagnosis and treatment planning.

Project 1: Image segmentation for our diet calculator

Problem statement: We are developing a calorie estimation app that calculates the caloric content of food, based on a picture. The first step in this process is to capture an image of the meal, then identify different food categories through image segmentation. By analyzing the segmentation results, we can estimate the quantities of various food items and ultimately determine the total calorie count. In this project, we will create a machine-learning model capable of performing image segmentation on food items.

Approach:

We can approach it in two steps:

1. Use FoodSeg103-BenchMark-V1 (**https://github.com/LARC-CMU-SMU/ FoodSeg103-Benchmark-v1**) dataset. It has 7118 images of different food categories.

2. Use **nvidia/mit-b0** as pre-trained model from huggingface.

Solution:

The end-to-end implementation is provided in the accompanying notebook. *Figure 8.1* shows the result of the inference:

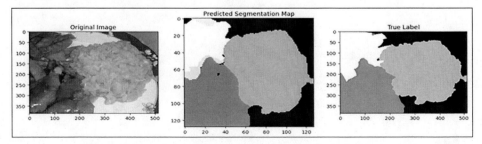

Figure 8.1: *Inference example of image segmentation*

Diffusion model: Unconditional image generation

Unconditional image generation is the process of generating realistic images without providing any conditional information as input. Over the past few years, numerous generative models have been proposed to address this problem, with diffusion models demonstrating some of the most promising results. In this section, we will explore the principles behind diffusion models and present a project that showcases end-to-end techniques for training a model specifically tailored for unconditional image generation.

The following *Figure 8.2* depicts the diffusion model, while the code block corresponds to the model definition. The general principle behind the diffusion model is to simulate a process that gradually transforms an original image into random noise and then reverses the process to reconstruct the image from noise. In the context of image generation, diffusion models consist of two main steps.

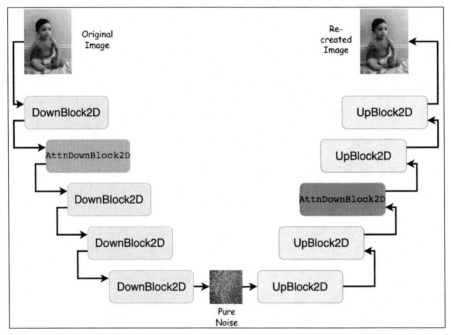

Figure 8.2: Unet architecture

Refer to the following code:

```
from diffusers import UNet2DModel

model = UNet2DModel(
    sample_size=config.image_size,
```

```
    in_channels=3,
    out_channels=3,
    layers_per_block=3,
    block_out_channels=(64, 128, 256, 512, 1024),
    down_block_types=(
        "DownBlock2D",
        "AttnDownBlock2D",
        "DownBlock2D",
        "DownBlock2D",
        "DownBlock2D",
    ),
    up_block_types=(
        "UpBlock2D",
        "UpBlock2D",
        "AttnUpBlock2D",
        "UpBlock2D",
        "UpBlock2D",
    ),
)
```

Forward diffusion

In this step, the model introduces noise into an image in a controlled manner, making it more like random noise. At each iteration, a new noisy image is generated based on the previous one and some predefined set of noise. The process goes through a series of steps, ultimately transforming the original image into pure noise. There are two major building blocks of forward diffusion:

- **DownBlock2D**: This block is responsible for downsampling the input feature maps while increasing the number of channels. In the preceding code example, we increased the channels in each subsequent block **(64, 128, 256, 512, 1024).** Typically, it consists of a series of convolutional layers followed by batch normalization and activation functions (for example, ReLU) and a downsampling operation, such as max-pooling or strided convolution.

- **AttnDownBlock2D:** In addition to the functionality of **DownBlock2D**, it includes an attention mechanism, such as self-attention or spatial attention, within the block.

Backward diffusion

The model starts from pure noise and attempts to reverse the process and reconstruct the original image. At each step, the model predicts the noise that was added to the image and subtracts the noise from the image, gradually reconstructing the image. There are two major building blocks of backward diffusion:

- **UpBlock2D**: This block is responsible for up-sampling the input feature maps while decreasing the number of channels.

- **AttnUpBlock2D**: Similar to **AttnDownBlock2D**, this block performs the same up-sampling operation as **UpBlock2D**, but includes an attention mechanism within the block.

Inference process

Figure 8.3 illustrates the inference process in a diffusion model. As depicted, the model starts with pure noise as its input. In each subsequent step, the model attempts to remove the noise, gradually reconstructing a new image. The process follows these main steps:

- **Input pure noise**: At the beginning of the inference process, the model takes a pure noise image. This noise image serves as the starting point for the model to reconstruct the target image.

- **Denoising steps**: In each denoising step, the model tries to estimate the amount of noise that was added during the forward diffusion process. The model then subtracts the estimated noise from the current image, refining the image's appearance. These denoising steps are performed for a predefined number of steps, with the model continually refining the image at each step.

- **Final image reconstruction**: At the end of the inference process, after going through all the denoising steps, the model generates a new image. This image is the result of the model's attempt to reverse the forward diffusion process, transforming the pure noise input into a realistic image. As you can see in *Figure 8.3*, our diffusion model was able to create the picture of baby at the final step.

In summary, the inference process in a diffusion model involves starting with pure noise and, through a series of denoising steps, reconstructing a new image. *Figure 8.3* provides a visual representation of this process, highlighting the gradual refinement of the image as noise is removed over multiple steps:

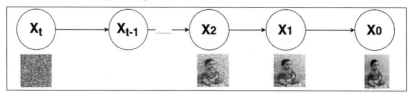

Figure 8.3: Inference process diffusion model

Learnable parameters

The main learnable parameters are found in the denoising model, which is used in both the forward and backward passes. The denoising model typically consists of neural networks like U-net, transformers, and so on. The learnable parameters in the denoising model include biases and weights of various layers, including CNN layers, attention mechanisms, and linear layers, depending on the specific architecture.

During forward diffusion, the denoising model is used to simulate the process of introducing noise. During the backward diffusion, the same denoising model is used, but the process is reversed. The model tries to predict the amount of noise added in each step.

Project 2: DogGenDiffusion

You are part of a creative art company and want to develop unique dog artwork for inspiration. Your task is to create a diffusion model that performs unconditional image generation of dogs.

Project name: DogGenDiffusion

Dataset: We will utilize the BirdL/DALL-E-Dogs dataset from HuggingFace, which contains 1,104 unique dog images.

Data transformation: All images will be resized to 128 x 128 pixels, and we will experiment with various data transformation techniques.

Model: The UNet2DModel from HuggingFace's Diffusers library will be employed for this task.

A comprehensive pipeline for model development and inference can be found in the accompanying notebook.

Conclusion

This book chapter provides a comprehensive overview of various computer vision tasks, including image classification, segmentation, and unconditional image generation. It delves into the comparison of DeiT with established models like ResNet-50 and ViT for image classification, demonstrating their effectiveness in solving real-world problems. The chapter also covers the implementation of an end-to-end food image segmentation model, showcasing the process of training and evaluation. Lastly, it explores the principles behind diffusion models for unconditional image generation, highlighting their potential in creative applications through the creation of unique dog artwork.

Quiz

1. **What type of model is DeiT?**

    a. Image classification model

    b. Image segmentation model

    c. Unconditional image generation model

    d. None of the above

2. **Which makes DeiT Unique compared to ViT?**

    a. teacher-student training strategy

    b. DeiT is transformer where ViT is not

    c. DeiT is GANs

3. **How does the performance of DeiT compare to ResNet-50 and ViT?**

    a. DeiT performs worse than both ResNet-50 and ViT

    b. DeiT performs better than ResNet-50 but worse than ViT

    c. DeiT performs worse than ResNet-50 but better than ViT

    d. DeiT performs better than both ResNet-50 and ViT

4. **What is the primary goal of image segmentation?**

    a. Classify images into categories

    b. Generate new images based on input images

    c. Assign each pixel into diffrent semantic categories

5. **Which of the following is NOT a component of a U-Net architecture?**

    a. DownBlock2D

    b. UpBlock2D

    c. AttnDownBlock2D

    d. Adversarial loss

6. **In the context of image generation, what is the primary purpose of diffusion models?**

    a. Classify images into categories

    b. Generate new images from noise

    c. Perform image segmentation

    d. Retrieve similar images from a database

7. **Which of the following models is NOT a variation of diffusion models?**

   a. DDPMPipeline

   b. DDIMPipeline

   c. PNDMPipeline

   d. GANPipeline

8. **What is the main learnable component in a diffusion model?**

   a. Denoising model

   b. Attention mechanism

   c. Pooling layer

   d. Loss function

9. **Which of the following is a typical building block of the forward diffusion process in a diffusion model?**

   a. DownBlock2D

   b. UpBlock2D

   c. AttnUpBlock2D

   d. None of the above

10. **What is the primary difference between AttnDownBlock2D and DownBlock2D?**

    a. AttnDownBlock2D includes an attention mechanism

    b. AttnDownBlock2D performs upsampling instead of downsampling

    c. AttnDownBlock2D has fewer layers than DownBlock2D

    d. None of the above

11. **Which library provides the UNet2DModel used in the diffusion model implementation?**

    a. TensorFlow

    b. PyTorch

    c. HuggingFace's Diffusers

    d. OpenCV

12. **Which of the following tasks can be accomplished using computer vision techniques?**

    a. Identifying objects in images

    b. Generating new images based on input images

    c. Dividing an image into semantically meaningful regions

    d. All of the above

13. In the context of diffusion models, which building block is responsible for upsampling the input feature maps while decreasing the number of channels?

    a. DownBlock2D

    b. AttnDownBlock2D

    c. UpBlock2D

    d. AttnUpBlock2D

14. What evaluation metrics we used in this chapter for image segmentation?

    a. IOU

    b. Sensitivity, Specificity

    c. Accuracy

15. What is the SegFormer used for?

    a. Image Generation

    b. Image Segmentation

    c. Text to Image

Answers

1. a.
2. a.
3. d.
4. c.
5. d.
6. b.
7. d.
8. a.
9. a.
10. a.
11. c.
12. d.
13. c.
14. a.
15. c.

## CHAPTER 9

Speech Processing Model Anatomy: Whisper, SpeechT5, and Wav2Vec

Introduction

Welcome to the exploration of speech processing using the transformer. It is one of the less mature yet rapidly growing fields of artificial intelligence, boasting a wide range of applications, including automated transcription, automated voice translation, speaker identification, and audio generation. Recently, transformer architectures, like Whisper, have outperformed traditional speech processing techniques. In this chapter, we will delve into the three most important speech processing transformer architectures and illustrate those with practical examples.

Structure

The chapter is organized in the following structure:

- System requirements
- Speech pre-processing
- Whisper
- Wav2Vec
- Speech T5
- Comparison of Whisper, Wav2Vec 2.0 and Speech T5

Objectives

The objective of this chapter is three-fold. By the end of it, the reader will have a foundational understanding of speech pre-processing, and a detailed analysis of Whisper, SpeechT5, and Wav2Vec Architecture. Finally, the chapter will also illustrate practical demonstrations. It aims to complement the theoretical understanding with practical demonstrations of fine-tuning Whisper with small dataset for new language transcription.

System requirements

For detailed instructions on setting the environment, please follow instructions at **https:// github.com/bpbpublications/Building-Transformer-Models-with-PyTorch/blob/main/ General/SettingVirtualEnvironment.ipynb**.

Activate virtual environment:

```
conda activate transformer_learn
```

To proceed with the coding tasks outlined in this chapter, please install the necessary packages detailed as follows:

```
pip install transformers
```

```
pip install datasets
```

```
pip install accelerate
```

```
pip install torch
```

```
pip install torchaudio
```

```
pip install scikit-learn
```

Speech processing

The preparation of raw audio signals for machine learning tasks includes several critical pre-processing steps. These steps convert the raw audio data into a format suitable for training and inference with transformers. Here are the pre-processing steps for audio signals:

1. **Pre-processing:** A crucial step for most transformer models is resampling. Transformers require an audio signal of a predefined sample rate. For instance, Whisper needs a sampling rate of 16KHz. Additional pre-processing, such as normalization or noise reduction, can be done to ensure consistency and faster convergence.

2. **Frame extraction**: The audio signal is split into overlapping frames of a fixed duration, typically between 20 to 40 milliseconds. Each frame corresponds to a short segment of the audio waveform. A standard principle is a 50% overlap,

meaning that adjacent frames share half of their samples. Overlapping ensures a smoother transition between adjacent frames and reduces the impact of frame boundaries on the extracted features.

3. **Windowing**: A windowing function, such as a hamming window, is applied to mitigate artifacts at the start and end of the frame by reducing the amplitude of the signal at these points.

4. **Feature extraction**: A feature extraction technique is applied to each frame. Common techniques include log-mel spectrograms, **Mel-frequency cepstral coefficients (MFCC)**, or other time-frequency representations.

5. **Sequence generation**: The extracted frames are arranged into sequences, each sequence representing a series of consecutive frames.

6. **Padding**: Padding is applied to the sequences to ensure that all sequences have the same length.

Example of speech pre-processing

In the following section, we will demo the speech pre-processing through practical example:

```
import torch

import torchaudio

from torchaudio.transforms import MFCC

from torchaudio.utils import download_asset


# Load the audio waveform
SAMPLE_SPEECH = download_asset("tutorial-assets/Lab41-SRI-VOiCES-src-
sp0307-ch127535-sg0042.wav")

waveform, sample_rate = torchaudio.load(SAMPLE_SPEECH)


# Get the duration of the waveform
waveform_duration = waveform.numel() / sample_rate


print("Waveform duration:", waveform_duration, "seconds")


# Define the frame length and frame shift in seconds
frame_length = 0.025  # 25 milliseconds
frame_shift = 0.01  # 10 milliseconds
```

```
# Define the desired sequence length and number of MFCC coefficients
sequence_length = 40
num_mfcc = 40

# Initialize the MFCC transform
mfcc_transform = MFCC(
    sample_rate=sample_rate,
    n_mfcc=num_mfcc,
    melkwargs={'hop_length': int(frame_shift * sample_rate)}
)

# Perform feature extraction
frames = torchaudio.transforms.Resample(sample_rate, 16000)(waveform)

print('number of frames',frames.shape[1])
print (frames.shape)

mfcc = mfcc_transform(frames)
# Reshape the MFCC features into sequences
sequences = mfcc.unfold(1, sequence_length, int(frame_shift * sample_rate))

# Perform padding if necessary
num_sequences = sequences.shape[2]
if num_sequences < sequence_length:
    pad_frames = torch.zeros(mfcc.shape[0], num_mfcc, sequence_length -
num_sequences)
    sequences = torch.cat([sequences, pad_frames], dim=1)

# Print the shapes of the extracted features and sequences
print("MFCC shape:", mfcc.shape)
print("Sequences shape:", sequences.shape)
```

Output:

Waveform duration: 3.4 seconds

torch.Size([1, 54400])

MFCC shape: torch.Size([1, 40, 341])

Sequences shape: torch.Size([1, 1, 341, 40])

Analysis

Let us delve into the details of the aforementioned code snippet to understand its operation:

- `torch.Size([1, 54400])`: This represents the shape of the waveform tensor, which has a size of 1 along the first dimension (batch dimension) and 54,400 along the second dimension (number of samples in the waveform).

- `MFCC shape: torch.Size([1, 40, 341])`: This indicates the shape of the MFCC tensor obtained from the feature extraction process. It has a size of 1 along the first dimension (batch dimension), 40 along the second dimension (number of MFCC coefficients), and 341 along the third dimension (number of frames).

- `Sequences shape: torch.Size([1, 1, 341, 40])`: This represents the shape of the sequences tensor after unfolding the MFCC features.

In summary, the output shows that the waveform has a duration of 3.4 seconds, the MFCC features have a shape of **(1, 40, 341)**, and the sequences have a shape of **(1, 1, 341, 40)**.

Whisper

Whisper[1] is a powerful **automated speech recognition (ASR)** system, designed for multilingual and multitasking applications. It supports transcriptions in multiple languages and facilitates translations from different languages into English. *Figure 9.1* illustrates the architecture of Whisper, which we will now explore in detail:

- **Input:** The raw waveform of the audio is divided into 30-second segments, along with corresponding subsets of the transcript that occur within that time frame. The raw audio signals are then transformed into spectrograms using Log-mel spectrogram techniques. Spectrograms provide a time-frequency representation of the audio, capturing both temporal and spectral information. Next, two consecutive Conv1D layers are applied to the spectrogram input. These Conv1D layers help capture local temporal patterns present in the spectrogram. Additionally, a Gaussian Error Linear Unit activation function is applied to introduce non-linearity. To preserve positional information, sinusoidal positional encoding is added to each input token.

- **Encoder:** The encoder block in Whisper follows the standard transformer encoder architecture. It captures contextual information from the input spectrogram, enabling the model to understand the underlying acoustic features.

- **Decoder block:** The decoder block in Whisper is similar to the standard transformer decoder, with one crucial difference. While the attention mechanism in the standard transformer decoder focuses on the decoder's own input tokens, in Whisper, attention is directed towards the encoder's feature sequence. This cross-attention mechanism allows the decoder to leverage the encoded acoustic information from the encoder, facilitating better alignment between input and output sequences.

- **Multi-task training:** Whisper serves as an entire speech processing pipeline and involves multi-task training. The model is trained to perform various tasks, such as language detection, transcription, translation, and voice activity detection. If we examine the decoder input, it consists of multiple components:

  o The first item is the **Start of Token (SOT)**

  o The second item represents the language (for example, **EN** for English)

  o The third item indicates the task (for example, **Transcription** in this example)

  o The fourth input determines whether to predict timestamps. With these inputs, the task and desired format are fully specified, and the model begins generating the corresponding output.

In summary, Whisper is a versatile ASR system that excels in multilingual and multitask scenarios. It leverages advanced techniques, such as Conv1D layers, cross-attention, and multi-task training, to deliver accurate transcriptions, translations, and more. Refer to the following *Figure 9.1*:

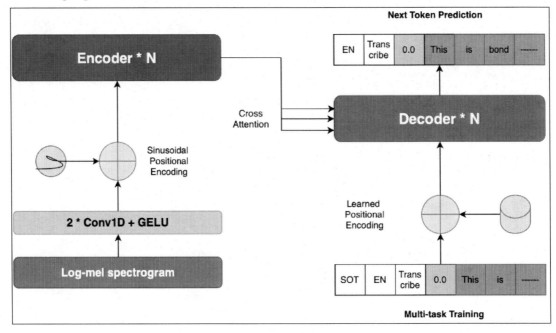

Figure 9.1: *Whisper architecture*

Project 1: Whisper_Nep

Develop a model named `Whisper_Nep` that is capable of transcribing lesser known languages.

Task

Construct a pipeline for fine-tuning the Whisper model for **Automatic Speech Recognition (ASR)** in any language.

Approach

The approach will be as follows:

- **The dataset:** The primary resource for this project is the mozilla-foundation/common_voice_13_0 dataset[1]. This extensive dataset includes MP3 audio files and their respective textual transcriptions. It boasts an impressive collection covering 17,689 validated hours of audio content across 108 different languages.

- **Methodology:** Devise a pipeline for fine-tuning the Whisper model, based on the specific language input.

- **Outcome:** After the completion of the training process, the model should be capable of performing ASR for the specified language.

Wav2Vec

Wav2Vec[2] is a self-supervised learning framework used for speech-processing tasks. The model undergoes two main stages: pre-training and fine-tuning. In pre-training, the model is trained on a large amount of unlabeled audio data. *Figure 9.2* illustrates the architecture of Wav2Vec. Let us explore its components:

---

[1] https://huggingface.co/datasets/mozilla-foundation/common_voice_13_0

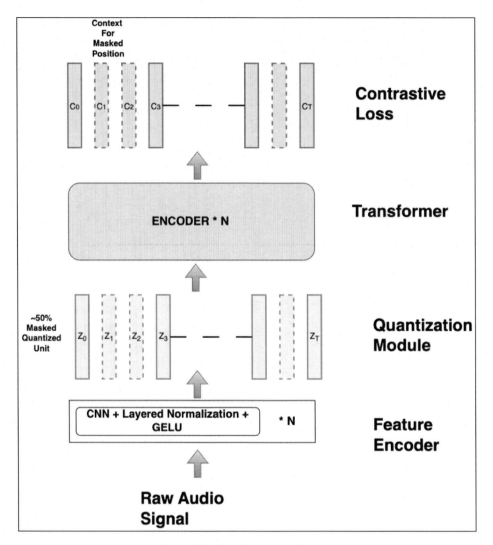

Figure 9.2: *Wav2Vec 2.0 architecture*

Pre-processing of raw audio

The steps for pre-processing raw audio are as follows:

1. The raw audio is divided into short segments called **context windows**, typically spanning a few seconds (~25 sec).

2. Within each context window, the audio is further divided into smaller chunks known as **input sequences**, usually a few milliseconds long.

3. A feature extractor is applied to each input sequence, transforming the audio into a fixed-dimensional representation that captures important spectral and temporal information.

Encoder

The steps to be followed by the encoder are as follows:

1. The encoder comprises multiple blocks, each consisting of a **Convolutional Neural Network (CNN)** followed by layer normalization and the GELU activation function.

2. The GELU activation function smoothens the transition for negative values, addressing the **dying ReLU** problem and ensuring better gradient flow during training.

3. The CNN processes the input sequences, extracting low-level acoustic features.

Quantization module

Follow the given steps:

1. For self-supervised pre-training, the output of the feature encoder is discretized into a finite set of speech representations using product quantization.

2. **Contextualized representation with transformer:** Relative positional encoding information is added to the quantized feature representation.

3. The quantized features are then passed through a transformer, which generates contextualized representations.

Pre-training

Follow the given steps:

1. During pre-training, Wav2Vec employs self-supervised learning. The model is trained to predict masked or corrupted speech representations within each context window. This is very similar to BERT pre-training.

2. As shown in *Figure 9.2*, 50% of the latent representations are masked before feeding to the transformer.

3. By reconstructing the masked or corrupted parts, the model learns to capture important speech features without explicit labels.

4. The loss function used in pre-training involves comparing the predicted representations with the original unmasked or uncorrupted representations.

Fine-tuning

Follow the given steps:

1. After pre-training, Wav2Vec can be fine-tuned on specific downstream tasks, such as speech recognition or speaker identification.

2. Fine-tuning involves training the model on labeled data specific to the target task, enabling it to adapt to the task's requirements.

Applications of Wav2Vec

Wav2Vec has found successful applications in various speech processing tasks, including speech recognition, speaker identification, speech synthesis, and keyword spotting.

SpeechT5

SpeechT5[3] is an adaptation of the **T5 architecture**, adapted for speech-focused tasks, encompassing ASR, text-to-speech synthesis, language comprehension, among others. The architecture of SpeechT5 is elucidated in *Figure 9.3* and *Figure 9.4*.

Depicted in *Figure 9.3* is the encoder-decoder structure of the model, which is composed of six modal-specific pre/post components. Let us dig deeper into these components:

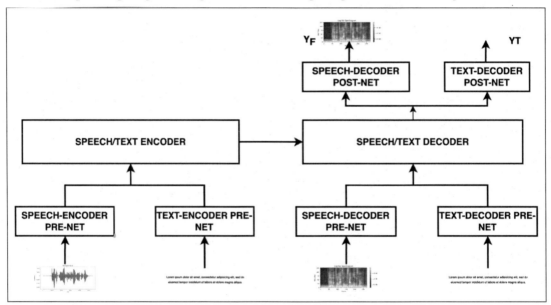

Figure 9.3: Speech T5 architecture

Input/Output representation

In SpeechT5, the problem is framed as converting speech/text into speech/text:

- **Text Pre/Post-net:** Here, we divide the text into units known as tokens, which are typically characters. When the tokens enter the system or the pre-net, they are transformed into embedding vectors. Later, the post-net takes these vectors and calculates the probability of each token being the right output, based on the learned information.

- **Speech Pre/Post-net:** For handling speech data, the system uses a component from Wav2Vec 2.0, known as a CNN feature extractor, as the encoder pre-net. This helps break down the speech into a more understandable format for the system. The decoder pre-net uses a feature of the audio input known as a Log-melfilter bank. This decoder pre-net comprises three fully connected layers followed by the RELU activation function. It also incorporates speaker embedding, which is a way of differentiating between different speakers' voices.

- Finally, the decoder post-net does two things:

  o It predicts the processed sounds of the output (referred to as the log Melfilterbank),

  o It converts the processed data (decoder output) into a single number, known as a scalar.

This scalar helps determine when to conclude the processing often referred to as predicting the stop token.

Refer to the following *Figure 9.4*:

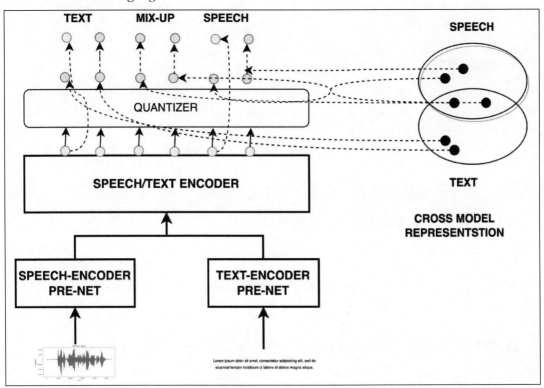

Figure 9.4: *Speech T5 architecture*

Cross-modal representation

In *Figure 9.4*, we see how SpeechT5 connects speech and text representations. It takes both speech and text inputs and changes them into cross modal vector representations. To align these two different types of data (speech and text), SpeechT5 uses something called vector quantized embeddings.

This process takes the continuous embeddings (the mathematically represented speech and text data) and splits them into a fixed set of distinct symbols, or codewords. It uses a shared **codebook** to categorize these codewords. Each mathematical representation of speech and text is matched with the closest matching codeword in this shared codebook. This way, SpeechT5 creates a common area where both speech and text inputs can be aligned and compared, making tasks like speech recognition or text-to-speech synthesis possible.

Encoder-decoder architecture

SpeechT5 is built around the transformer encoder-decoder structure. Interestingly, it adds relative positional encoding information, unlike the original architecture which uses absolute positional encoding.

Pre-training

Before being used, the T5 model was trained with a large amount of unlabeled speech and text data. This initial training or pre-training aimed to align text and speech information in the same feature dimension. Two goals guided the speech pre-training: bidirectional masked prediction and sequence-to-sequence generation. For text pre-training, about 30% of text spans were masked, with their span length following a Poisson distribution. The goal was to predict these masked text spans.

Fine-tuning and applications

After pre-training, the model was fine-tuned with the specific goal of minimizing the loss for a particular task. Specifically, it was fine-tuned for tasks like ASR, **Text to Speech (TTS)**, **Speech Translation (ST)**, **Voice Conversion (VC)**, **Speech Enhancement (SE)**, and **Speaker Identification (SID)**.

Comparing Whisper, Wav2Vec 2.0 and Speech T5

Refer to the following *Table 9.1*:

	Whisper	Wav2Vec 2.0	SpeechT5
Released year	Whisper 2021	Sep 2020	Oct 2021
Architecture	Encoder-decoder	Encoder only	Encoder decoder
Tasks	ASR, and ST	ASR, SI	ASR, TTS, ST, VC, SE, SID
Accuracy	Whisper performed better than Speech T5 and Wav2Vec on ASR and ST		
Salient features	**Entire speech processing pipeline:** voice activity detection, speaker diarization, and inverse text normalization.	**Contrastive loss:** representation of a particular times-stamp should be similar to nearby segments; and different from the representations of randomly sampled time steps	Combined pre-training of speech and text
Pre-training objective	Supervised training on 680K hours of audio and corresponding transcription	**Unsupervised:** predict masked latent feature representation	**Unsupervised:** unified modal representation of text and speech

Table 9.1: Comparison of Whisper, Wav2Vec 2.0 and Speech T5

Conclusion

In this chapter, we have examined the use of transformers, including Whisper, SpeechT5, and Wav2Vec, in the realm of speech processing. We have also delved into the intricate details of these three distinct transformer architectures. Additionally, we have demonstrated how to refine, or fine-tune, the Whisper model for use in multi-lingual **ASR** tasks.

Quiz

1. **In audio signal pre-processing, what does windowing help mitigate?**

    a. Artifacts at the start and end of the frame

    b. Overlapping frames

    c. High frequency components

    d. Low frequency components

2. **Which feature extraction technique is common for processing frames in audio signal pre-processing?**

    a. Log-mel spectrograms

    b. Fourier transforms

    c. Principal Component Analysis (PCA)

3. **Which of these is not a commonly used feature extraction technique applied to each frame?**

    a. Log-mel spectrograms

    b. Mel-frequency cepstral coefficients (MFCCs)

    c. Fast Fourier Transform (FFT)

    d. Time-frequency representations

4. **Why is padding applied to the sequences in audio signal preprocessing?**

    a. To reduce the size of the sequences

    b. To ensure that all sequences have the same length

    c. To add additional information to the sequences

    d. To make the sequences easier to read

5. **What does SpeechT5 aim to achieve?**

    a. Automated speech recognition

    b. Text-to-speech synthesis

    c. Unified-modal pre-training for spoken language processing

    d. Speaker Identification

6. **In SpeechT5, what is vector quantization used for?**

    a. Improving the efficiency of the model

    b. Aligning speech and text representations

    c. Reducing the size of the model

    d. Increasing the speed of the model

7. **What does the pre-net in SpeechT5 do with text tokens?**

    a. Transforms them into embedding vectors

    b. None

8. **Which model uses a contrastive loss during pre-training?**

    a. Whisper

    b. Wav2Vec 2.0

    c. SpeechT5

    d. BERT

9. **What is the purpose of dividing raw audio into short segments called "context windows" in the Wav2Vec model?**

    a. To facilitate faster training

    b. To capture important spectral and temporal information

    c. To allow for parallel processing of audio data

    d. All of the above

10. **In the Wav2Vec model, what is the role of the GELU activation function?**

    a. To discretize the output of the feature encoder

    b. To smooth the transition for negative values and ensure better gradient flow during training

    c. To add relative positional encoding information

    d. To perform self-supervised learning

11. **After pre-training, how is Wav2Vec fine-tuned for specific downstream tasks?**

    a. By predicting masked or corrupted speech representations within each context window

    b. By training the model on labeled data specific to the target task

    c. By comparing the predicted representations with the original unmasked or uncorrupted representations

    d. None of the above

12. **Which process involves discretizing continuous embeddings into a finite set of discrete symbols or codewords?**

    a. Padding

    b. Vector quantization

    c. Sequence generation

    d. Windowing

13. **What is the sampling rate required by the Whisper model?**

    a. 8 KHz

    b. 16 KHz

    c. 24 KHz

    d. 32 KHz

14. **What is the function of the Conv1D layers in the Whisper architecture?**

    a. To capture local temporal patterns present in the spectrogram

    b. To divide the audio into segments

    c. To create the spectrogram

    d. To add positional encoding

15. **What distinguishes the Whisper's decoder block from the standard transformer decoder?**

    a. Its use of sinusoidal positional encoding

    b. Its cross-attention mechanism focusing on the encoder's feature sequence

    c. Its use of Conv1D layers

    d. Its ability to handle multiple languages

16. **What type of training does the Whisper model use?**

    a. Single-task training

    b. Binary-task training

    c. Multi-task training

Answers

1. a.
2. a.
3. c.
4. b.
5. c.
6. b.
7. a.
8. b.
9. d.
10. b.
11. b.
12. d.
13. b.
14. a.
15. b.
16. c.

CHAPTER 10

Speech Tasks with Transformers

Introduction

In this chapter, we embark on a detailed exploration of speech processing, a field that encompasses a variety of tasks aimed at facilitating and improving human-computer audio interactions. Speech processing tasks such as **Automatic Speech Recognition (ASR)**, **Text-to-Speech (TTS)**, and audio-to-audio transformations are critical for developing applications that range from virtual assistants to automated transcription services, underlining their significance in both daily convenience and accessibility. We will investigate how these tasks are approached using transformer-based models, which have revolutionized the field with their ability to handle sequential data and capture the nuances of human language.

As we progress through the chapter, we will focus on practical applications by undertaking projects that demonstrate the power and versatility of these models. We will utilize cutting-edge tools like Whisper for ASR, delve into the intricacies of TTS with custom speaker embeddings to personalize synthetic voices, and employ sophisticated techniques for enhancing audio quality, particularly through noise reduction. These hands-on examples will not only solidify the theoretical knowledge of speech processing tasks but also provide a clear illustration of their applications, importance, and the transformative role of transformer models in pushing the boundaries of what's possible in speech processing technology.

Structure

This chapter includes the following topics:

- System requirements
- Speech processing tasks
- Text to speech
- Audio to audio

Objectives

This chapter aims to provide a comprehensive understanding of various speech processing tasks and their applications in real-world scenarios, as well as discuss how **TTS** works. It will also discuss what **ASR** is and how it functions, the process of transforming audio-to-audio, focusing specifically on improving speech quality and lastly, show examples of these tasks in action, to help readers understand better.

System requirements

For detailed instructions on setting the environment, please follow instructions at **https://github.com/bpbpublications/Building-Transformer-Models-with-PyTorch/blob/main/General/SettingVirtualEnvironment.ipynb**.

Activate virtual environment:

```
conda activate transformer learn
```

To proceed with the coding tasks outlined in this chapter, please install the necessary packages detailed as follows:

```
pip install transformers
pip install datasets
pip install ipywebrtc
pip install soundfile
pip install pydub
pip install ffmpeg-python
pip install accelerate
pip install bitsandbytes
pip install sentencePiece
pip install speechbrain
```

Speech processing tasks

Table 10.1 illustrates the major tasks in speech processing:

Tasks	Summary	Popular models
Speech to text (Automatic speech recognition)	Convert spoken language into text	Whisper
Text to speech	Convert text to spoken language/audio	microsoft/speecht5_tts, espnet/kan-bayashi_ljspeech_vits
Audio to audio	Transforming input audio into output audio: speech enhancement, noise removal, voice conversion	speechbrain/metricgan-plus-voicebank, microsoft/speecht5_vc
Audio classification	Classify audio into different categories	facebook/wav2vec2-base, harshit345/xlsr-wav2vec-speech-emotion-recognition,
Voice activity detection	Detect presence or absence of voice	pyannote/segmentation
Voice translation	Translate voice in one language into another language	Whisper

Table 10.1: *Major tasks in speech processing*

In the following section, we will delve deeper into the important computer vision tasks we enlisted in *Table 10.1*.

Speech to text

ASR stands as a crucial process in the realm of speech processing. A comprehensive ASR system entails several components, including voice activity detection, speaker diarization, and inverse text normalization. Historically, these tasks relied on an array of complex components, each carrying out a specific function. However, the advent of Transformer models such as Whisper has revolutionized this field. Whisper operates directly on raw audio signals, effectively delivering high-performing ASR outputs. In the subsequent section, we will embark on a project showcasing this technology. We will record our own voice and utilize Whisper for transcription, thereby demonstrating its practical application and effectiveness.

Project 1: Custom audio transcription with ASR using Whisper

In this demonstration, we will illustrate how Whisper can be utilized to transcribe any audio, regardless of its source. We will specifically be recording our own voices and then employ Whisper to carry out the transcription process. This will give us an opportunity to see how this powerful transformer model operates in a real-world application.

Perform necessary import using the following code:

```
import torch

from transformers import pipeline

from datasets import load_dataset

import torchaudio
```

Record audio

We will use **ipywebrtc** library to record the audio. You could use any library; or use external dedicated audio system (like Mac's QuickTime Player) to record high-quality audio. Refer to the following code:

```
from ipywebrtc import CameraStream, AudioRecorder

# Create camera stream

camera = CameraStream(constraints={'audio': True, 'video': False})

# Create audio recorder

recorder = AudioRecorder(stream=camera)

# Display recorder

display(recorder)
```

Save the audio to disk

TorchAudio works with a finite set of audio file formats, such as WAV, MP3, and others. In this project, we will be converting the audio files into the WAV format. However, if your audio is already in a format supported by TorchAudio, you will not need to perform this step. Refer to the following code:

```
import ffmpeg

# Save the recording to a file

recorder.save('output.webm')

# Convert webm to wav

ffmpeg.input('output.webm').output('output.wav').run()
```

Pre-process the audio

Whisper requires the audio signal to be in monochrome format and sampled at 16kHz. Additionally, Hugging Face's ASR pipeline expects the audio signal to be in the form of a numpy array. This preprocessing step is crucial to ensure accurate transcription. The following code demonstrates how to pre-process the data to meet these requirements:

```
import torchaudio
import torchaudio.transforms as T


waveform, sample_rate = torchaudio.load('output.wav')


# If audio is stereo, convert to mono
if waveform.shape[0] > 1:
    waveform = waveform.mean(dim=0)


# Resample the waveform to 16kHz
resampler = T.Resample(orig_freq=sample_rate, new_freq=16000)
waveform = resampler(waveform)


# Squeeze the tensor to remove the channel dimension
waveform = waveform.squeeze()


# Convert tensor to numpy array
waveform_numpy = waveform.numpy()
```

Make the prediction

In this project, we will utilize the Hugging Face pipeline to make predictions using a pre-trained model. The pipeline feature in Hugging Face provides a user-friendly interface to work with pre-trained models. It simplifies the process, especially for tasks that involve complex steps. For more detailed information, you can refer to the pipeline documentation available at the following link: **https://huggingface.co/docs/transformers/main/en/quicktour#pipeline**.

Refer to the following code:

```
pipe = pipeline(
  "automatic-speech-recognition",
  model="openai/whisper-large-v2",
```

```
  chunk_length_s=30,
  device=device,
)
prediction = pipe(waveform_numpy, batch_size=8)["text"]
print(prediction)
```

The accompanying notebook provides the end-to-end implementation example.

Text-to-speech

Let us now go over a project.

Project 2: Implementing text-to-Speech

In this project, we introduce a personal touch to a text-to-speech system using **speaker embeddings**. These embeddings act like voice fingerprints, capturing the unique aspects of our voice. Instead of utilizing a pre-existing one, we record our own voice to create a custom voice fingerprint. This personalized voice print is subsequently incorporated into our speech generation system, influencing the manner in which it converts written words into spoken ones.

In the end, we subject our system to a test. We provide it with a piece of text and allow it to perform its conversion magic, transforming that text into speech.

Import necessary packages using the following code:

```
import os
import torch
from speechbrain.pretrained import EncoderClassifier
import torchaudio
import torchaudio.transforms as T
from transformers import SpeechT5Processor, SpeechT5ForTextToSpeech
from transformers import SpeechT5HifiGan
```

Declare function for creating speaker embedding

The **microsoft/speecht5_tts** model requires both text input and a speaker embedding. The speaker embedding captures unique characteristics of individual speakers, allowing downstream applications to recognize and differentiate between speakers in different audio contexts. If you prefer to use pre-built speaker embeddings based on various characteristics, you can obtain them from the **Matthijs/cmu-arctic-xvectors** model.

However, in the following example, we will record our own audio and create our own speaker embedding using the **speechbrain/spkrec-xvect-voxceleb** model. The subsequent section will present a function to extract the speaker embedding from the raw audio waveform.

Refer to the following code:

```
model_name = "speechbrain/spkrec-xvect-voxceleb"


speaker_classifier = EncoderClassifier.from_hparams(
    source=model_name,
    run_opts={"device": device},
    savedir=os.path.join("/tmp", model_name)
)


def compute_speaker_embedding(audio_data):
    with torch.no_grad():
        embeddings = speaker_classifier.encode_batch(torch.tensor(audio_
data))
        embeddings = torch.nn.functional.normalize(embeddings, dim=2)
        embeddings = embeddings.squeeze().cpu().numpy()
    return embeddings
```

Perform speaker embedding

The file **audio_sample2.wav** contains a recording of my voice. You have the option to record your own voice, which can be a few seconds long. The subsequent code will pre-process the raw audio data and extract the speaker embedding based on the provided audio data.

Refer to the following code:

```
waveform, sample_rate = torchaudio.load('/Users/premtimsina/Downloads/
audio_sample2.wav')


# If audio is stereo, convert to mono
if waveform.shape[0] > 1:
    waveform = waveform.mean(dim=0)


# Resample the waveform to 16kHz
resampler = T.Resample(orig_freq=sample_rate, new_freq=16000)
```

```
waveform = resampler(waveform)


# Squeeze the tensor to remove the channel dimension
waveform = waveform.squeeze()


speaker_emb=compute_speaker_embedding(waveform)
speaker_emb=torch.tensor(speaker_emb).reshape(-1,512)
print(speaker_emb.shape)
```

Declare model

Let us describe what the following modes do:

- **Processor:** The SpeechT5Processor is responsible for processing the input text for the TTS system. It handles tasks such as tokenization, encoding, and preparing the input data for the TTS model.

- Vocoder models are utilized to convert the synthesized speech into the final waveform or audio signal. The SpeechT5HifiGan model specifically employs the HiFi-GAN architecture, which is a high-fidelity generative adversarial network. This model enhances the quality of the generated speech waveform, ensuring that the output is clear, natural, and pleasant to listen to.

- The SpeechT5ForTextToSpeech model is the core component of the TTS system. It takes the processed input from the processor, speaker embedding, vcoder and performs the text-to-speech conversion.

Refer to the following code:

```
processor = SpeechT5Processor.from_pretrained("microsoft/speecht5_tts")
model = SpeechT5ForTextToSpeech.from_pretrained("microsoft/speecht5_tts")
vocoder = SpeechT5HifiGan.from_pretrained("microsoft/speecht5_hifigan")
```

Perform TTS

Lastly, we will carry out the TTS task and listen to the audio generated based on the provided text and speaker embedding. As you listen, you will observe that the speaker style closely resembles the characteristics of the raw audio you previously recorded to create the speaker embedding. This demonstrates the ability of the TTS system to replicate the desired speaker's voice and produce synthesized speech that aligns with the provided input.

Refer to the following code:

```
inputs = processor(text="This is Harry. I live in New York City", return_
tensors="pt")
```

```
speech = model.generate_speech(inputs["input_ids"], speaker_emb,
vocoder=vocoder)
from IPython.display import Audio
Audio(speech, rate=16000)
```

The accompanying notebook provides the end-to-end implementation example.

Audio to audio

Audio-to-audio processing with transformers is an innovative approach to handle various audio tasks like speech enhancement, source separation, music translation, and even voice transformation. Audio-to-audio processing can be thought of as a transformation function where the input and output both are audio signals but with different characteristics. For example, a noisy audio signal can be the input, and the output would be a denoised version of the same audio. Some applications of audio-to-audio Transformers are:

- **Speech enhancement**: In this application, the transformer model learns to filter out the noise and enhance the speech quality.

- **Source separation**: Transformers can be used to separate different audio sources in a mixed signal.

- **Music translation**: Transformers can convert music from one style to another, essentially learning the characteristics of different music styles and applying them to input audio.

- **Voice transformation**: In voice transformation, the transformer model learns the unique features of a source and target voice. It then takes an audio input in the source voice and transforms it to sound like the target voice.

Project 3: Audio quality improvement through noise reduction

In the following code snippet, we are leveraging the power of the **SpeechBrain** library to enhance audio quality. SpeechBrain, a versatile Python library built on PyTorch, provides an array of pre-trained models catering to a multitude of audio-related tasks. These tasks encompass speech recognition, speech diarization, speech enhancement, among others. Specifically, for our audio enhancement objective, we will employ the **speechbrain/metricgan-plus-voicebank** model, renowned for its pre-trained capabilities.

Download the noisy audio

The audio clip has background noise that sounds like a busy city. In the following bit of code, we will be getting this audio from GitHub and saving it onto our computer:

```
import urllib.request
```

```
# URL of the audio file
url = "https://raw.githubusercontent.com/bpbpublications/Building-
Transformer-Models-with-PyTorch/main/ chapter10_AudioTasks/audio_noisy.wav"
filename = "audio_noisy.wav"


# Download the file from `url` and save it locally under `filename`:
urllib.request.urlretrieve(url, filename)
```

Load the model and pre-process the audio signal

In the following code, we load the audio from a file, pre-process the audio to make it single channel and 16kHz, and finally normalize the audio:

```
import torch
import torchaudio
from speechbrain.pretrained import SpectralMaskEnhancement
from IPython.display import Audio
# load the model
enhance_model = SpectralMaskEnhancement.from_hparams(
    source="speechbrain/metricgan-plus-voicebank",
    savedir="pretrained_models/metricgan-plus-voicebank",
)
#load the audio
waveform, sample_rate = torchaudio.load(filename)


# If your waveform is stereo (2 channels) you can convert it to mono (1
channel) like this:
waveform = torch.mean(waveform, dim=0, keepdim=True)


# Usually, the SpeechBrain's pre-trained models expect audio at 16kHz,
# so you might need to resample your audio if it's not at 16kHz:
if sample_rate != 16000:
    resampler = torchaudio.transforms.Resample(orig_freq=sample_rate, new_
freq=16000)
    waveform = resampler(waveform)


# Now your waveform tensor is ready to be used with the enhancement model.
```

```
# But remember to normalize the audio data before using it:
noisy = waveform / torch.max(torch.abs(waveform))


# Listen to the noisy audio
print("Noisy audio:")
display(Audio(noisy.squeeze().detach().numpy(), rate=16000))
```

Perform voice enhancement removing the noise

In the next bit of code, we are going to use our pre-trained model to improve the sound of the audio. After we do that, we will save the cleaned-up audio and listen to it, to see how well our model did. Refer to the following code:

```
# Add relative length tensor
enhanced = enhance_model.enhance_batch(noisy, lengths=torch.tensor([1.]))


# Saving enhanced signal on disk
torchaudio.save('enhanced.wav', enhanced.cpu(), 16000)
# Load and listen to the enhanced audio
print("Enhanced audio:")
enhanced_audio = torchaudio.load('enhanced.wav')[0]
torchaudio.save('enhanced.wav', enhanced.cpu(), 16000)
display(Audio(enhanced_audio.detach().numpy(), rate=16000))
```

Conclusion

This chapter examined key speech processing tasks and how transformer models handle them. We dissected **TTS**, **ASR**, and Audio-to-Audio conversion, focusing particularly on speech enhancement. These topics were clarified through detailed examples.

We started by exploring the basics of speech processing and transformers. Next, we delved into TTS, detailing its functioning and applications. This was followed by a deep dive into ASR, underlining its role in converting speech into written text. Finally, we ventured into the realm of Audio-to-Audio conversion and speech enhancement, revealing how they enhance audio signal quality.

This chapter demonstrated the versatility of transformers in managing complex speech tasks, providing valuable knowledge for implementing these models effectively. It showcased the promising future of transformers in the sphere of audio and speech technology.

Quiz

1. **What does Automatic Speech Recognition (ASR) convert?**

   a. Text into speech

   b. Spoken language into text

   c. Input audio into output audio

   d. Different languages into another

2. **Which model is used for Automatic Speech Recognition (ASR) in the first project?**

   a. microsoft/speecht5_tts

   b. Whisper

   c. espnet/kan-bayashi_ljspeech_vits

   d. facebook/wav2vec2-base

3. **What is the purpose of pre-processing the audio in the first project?**

   a. To convert audio into a text file

   b. To convert audio to a video file

   c. To meet the requirements of the Whisper model

   d. To convert audio into different languages

4. **What does 'Voice Activity Detection' task do?**

   a. Detects presence or absence of voice [Correct Answer]

   b. Translates voice in one language into another

   c. Transforms input audio into output audio

   d. Classifies audio into different categories

5. **What format does the Whisper model require the audio signal to be in?**

   a. Stereo format and sampled at 44kHz

   b. Monochrome format and sampled at 16kHz

   c. Stereo format and sampled at 16kHz

   d. Monochrome format and sampled at 44kHz

6. **What audio format does 'torchaudio' support?**

   a. MP3

   b. WAV

   c. Both A and B

   d. Neither A nor B

7. **What does a speaker embedding capture in a Text-to-Speech system?**

   a. The unique aspects of an individual's voice

   b. The text that needs to be converted into speech

   c. The background noise of a speaker's environment

   d. The language of the spoken words

8. **In the function `compute_speaker_embedding`, what does the line `embeddings = speaker_classifier.encode_batch(torch.tensor(audio_data))` do?**

   a. It normalizes the audio data

   b. It converts the audio data into text

   c. It encodes the audio data into speaker embeddings

   d. It saves the audio data into a file

9. **In the 'Perform TTS' section, what is the function of the 'Audio' class from the `IPython.display` module?**

   a. It generates speaker embeddings

   b. It resamples the waveform

   c. It allows us to listen to the generated speech

   d. It processes the input text

10. **What is Audio-to-audio processing?**

    a. It's a way to convert audio signals into text

    b. It's a transformation function where the input and output both are audio signals but with different characteristics

    c. It's a method of encoding and decoding audio files

    d. None of the above

11. **What is the role of the 'speechbrain/metricgan-plus-voicebank' model in Project 3?**

    a. It is used to download audio from the web

    b. It is used for audio quality enhancement

    c. It is used to save audio files

    d. None of the above

12. **What does 'waveform = torch.mean(waveform, dim=0, keepdim=True)' do in the code?**

    a. It converts a stereo waveform to mono

    b. It resamples the waveform to 16kHz

    c. It normalizes the waveform

    d. None of the above

13. **What task is SpeechBrain library known for?**

    a. Image recognition

    b. Natural language processing

    c. A multitude of audio-related tasks

    d. All of the above

Answers

1. b.

2. b.

3. c.

4. a.

5. b.

6. c.

7. a.

8. c.

9. c.

10. b.

11. b.

12. a.

13. c.

CHAPTER 11

Transformer Architecture for Tabular Data Processing

Introduction

In the modern era of data analytics and machine learning, we are not limited to unstructured data types like text, images, or audio; structured or tabular data holds significant value as well. The potential of transformers when applied to structured data is immense and offers an intriguing area for exploration. This chapter seeks to illustrate the application of transformer-based architectures to the realm of tabular data.

We will delve into three such transformer architectures designed specifically for structured data processing: **Google's TAPAS**, **TabTransformer**, and **FT Transformer**.

Structure

The chapter is organized as follows:

- Tabular data representation using transformer
- TabTransformer architecture
- FT Transformer architecture

Objectives

By the end of this chapter, the reader will be introduced to **Google's TAblePArSing (TAPAS)** model, demonstrating its ability to interpret and respond to queries regarding tabular data. We will also explore the **TabTransformer** model, discussing its use of the self-attention mechanism of transformers in processing tabular data, and how this approach helps capture complex relationships between features. Then, the reader will also understand the FT transformer and how it is different from the TabTransformer. Lastly, the chapter will impart an understanding of the underlying architecture of each model, with a specific focus on their unique components, how they operate, and the reasons behind their design.

System requirements

For detailed instructions on setting the environment, please follow instructions at **https://github.com/bpbpublications/Building-Transformer-Models-with-PyTorch/blob/main/General/SettingVirtualEnvironment.ipynb.**

Activate virtual environment:

```
conda activate transformer_learn
```

To proceed with the coding tasks outlined in this chapter, please install the necessary packages as follows:

```
pip install transformers
```

```
pip install datasets
```

```
pip install accelerate
```

```
pip install bitsandbytes
```

```
pip install sentencePiece
```

```
pip install speechbrain
```

Tabular data representation using transformer

Following the substantial success of representing natural language through transformer models, there has been considerable interest in applying transformer architectures to tabular data representation. Current research and applications demonstrate a broad range of potential uses in this area, including[1]:

---

[1] **https://direct.mit.edu/tacl/article/doi/10.1162/tacl_a_00544/115239/Transformers-for-Tabular-Data-Representation-A**

- **Table-based fact checking**: This application validates the veracity of textual inputs based on structured data serving as a fact-checking table.

- **Question-answering**: This encompasses posing questions in free text format and retrieving specific cells from a table or aggregating information based on the query.

- **Semantic parsing**: This involves the conversion of free text into SQL queries, enabling direct interaction with databases.

- **Table retrieval:** This task involves searching for and retrieving the table that contains the answer to a specific query or requirement.

- **Table metadata prediction**: In this scenario, given the tabular data, the model predicts associated metadata.

- **Table content population**: This functionality allows for the prediction and filling in of corrupted or missing cells/rows in a table, helping maintain data integrity.

TAPAS architecture

The Google TAPAS, Table Parser[2] model is built on top of the BERT model, one of the transformer-based models, and uses the BERT tokenizer. *Figure 11.1* shows the architecture of TAPAS. The model is designed to read tables as a form of input in addition to text. Each table's cell is a token sequence. The input is a linear sequence of tokens that includes a (CLS) token, question tokens, (SEP) token, and flatten table. Additionally, there are two classification heads attached:

- Aggregation prediction
- Cell selection

Refer to the following *Figure 11.1:*

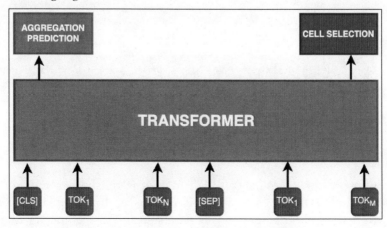

Figure 11.1: *TAPAS architecture*

---

2 **https://aclanthology.org/2020.acl-main.398.pdf**

There is additional positional encoding compared to BERT. Let us discuss each of them:

- **Token embedding**: It is the token embedding information.

- **Positional embedding**: It is the same as BERT.

- **Segment embedding**: 0 for the question and 1 for table.

- **Column embedding**: It is the index of the column.

- **Row embedding**: It is the index of the row.

- **Rank embedding:** Rank embeddings are used to encode the order of cells in a row or column.

Figure 11.2 depicts positional encoding:

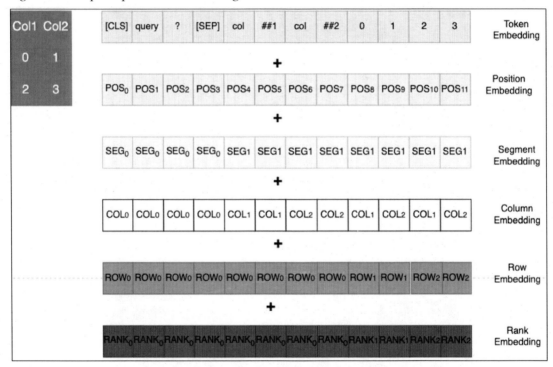

Figure 11.2: *Positional encoding on TAPAS*

Pretraining objective

The pretraining objective is similar to BERT, including masked language modeling and next sentence prediction tasks. In addition, TAPAS is pretrained using a new objective, which includes predicting whether a cell will be selected in the answer to a query about the table.

Fine-tuning

The model is fine-tuned on downstream tasks using supervised learning. For example, google/tapas-large-finetuned-wtqwas fine-tuned on the **WikiTableQuestions (WTQ)** benchmark, a complex table-based question-answering dataset. In this case, the model is trained to select the cells in the table that contain the answer.

Applications

The main application of TAPAS is a question answering from tables. Basically, there are three ways user can use the Tapas. *Table 11.1* shows those approaches:

Task	Description	
Conversational	Cell selection question	Example: Where was Nelson Mandala born?
Weak supervision for aggregation	It may involve aggregation, and model should be able to select the type of aggregation. The correct aggregator is not given to the model	Example: What is the total number of revenue on year 2020?
Strong supervision for aggregation	The correct aggregator is given to the model	

Table 11.1: *Tapas use cases*

Example

The following *Table 11.2* uses the Google TAPAS model, specifically the "google/tapas-base-finetuned-wtq" version, to answer questions about a tabular dataset. The dataset, in this case, is a simple table as shown in *Table 11.2*:

Company	CEO	Headquarters
Apple	Tim Cook	Cupertino
Microsoft	Satya Nadella	Redmond
Google	Sundar Pichai	Mountain View

Table 11.2: *Sample table*

We feed two questions to the model: *Who is the CEO of Microsoft?* and *Where is the headquarters of Google?* The model then processes the table along with these questions.

The first step in the processing is the tokenization of the table and questions. Tokenization essentially converts the table and text into a format that the model can understand and process. The tokenized table and questions are then used as input to the TAPAS model.

The TAPAS model makes predictions based on this input. Specifically, it outputs the coordinates of the cells in the table that contain the answers to the questions, and the indices of the aggregation operations. Aggregation operations refer to computations like counting, summing, averaging and so on, that might be needed to answer certain questions. However, in our case, no such operations are needed as the questions are straightforward.

We then convert these coordinates and indices into a more human-readable format, and print out the answers to the questions. The answers are the contents of the predicted cells, in case of no aggregation operation, or the name of the aggregation operation otherwise. For our example, the expected answers would be *Satya Nadella* and *Mountain View* for the two questions, respectively.

Refer to the following code:

```
from transformers import AutoTokenizer, TapasForQuestionAnswering
import pandas as pd


# Define the tokenizer and model
tokenizer = AutoTokenizer.from_pretrained("google/tapas-base-finetuned-wtq")
model = TapasForQuestionAnswering.from_pretrained("google/tapas-base-
finetuned-wtq")


# Define the data for the table
data = {
    "Company": ["Apple", "Microsoft", "Google"],
    "CEO": ["Tim Cook", "Satya Nadella", "Sundar Pichai"],
    "Headquarters": ["Cupertino", "Redmond", "Mountain View"]
}
# Convert the data into a pandas DataFrame
table = pd.DataFrame.from_dict(data)
# Define the questions (queries)
queries = ["Who is the CEO of Microsoft?", "Where is the headquarters of
Google?"]


# Tokenize the table and queries
inputs = tokenizer(table=table, queries=queries, padding="max_length",
return_tensors="pt")
# Make predictions with the model
outputs = model(**inputs)
```

```
# Extract the predicted answer coordinates and aggregation indices
predicted_answer_coordinates, predicted_aggregation_indices = tokenizer.
convert_logits_to_predictions(
    inputs,
    outputs.logits.detach(),
    outputs.logits_aggregation.detach()
)
# Iterate over the queries and print the answers
for i, query in enumerate(queries):
    if predicted_aggregation_indices[i] == 0:
        # If there is no aggregation operation (index 0), print the cells
        coords_to_answer = ' '.join([table.iat[coord] for coord in
predicted_answer_coordinates[i]])
        print(f"Question: {query}")
        print(f"Answer: {coords_to_answer}\n")
    else:
        # If there is an aggregation operation, print the operation's name
(from the list of operations)
        print(f"Question: {query}")
        print(f"Answer: {tokenizer.model.config.id2label[predicted_
aggregation_indices[i]]}\n")
```

Output:

```
Question: Who is the CEO of Microsoft?
Answer: Satya Nadella
Question: Where is the headquarters of Google?
Answer: Mountain View
```

TabTransformer architecture[3]

The fundamental concept anchoring the TabTransformer is the generation of contextual embeddings for categorical variables. Let us delve into the details of this architecture:

- **Categorical embeddings**: Each categorical feature, denoted as xi, is transformed into a parametric embedding of dimension d using a process known as column embedding.

---

[3] **https://arxiv.org/pdf/2012.06678.pdf**

- **Transformer encoder**: These embeddings of categorical features are then passed to a transformer encoder, which treats each categorical feature as a token or "word" in a sequence. This enables the model to understand and learn complex interactions between different categorical features.

- **Contextual embeddings**: Inside the transformer encoder, a self-attention mechanism is used to develop contextual embeddings for the categorical variables. The self-attention mechanism helps the model to weigh the importance and interaction of each categorical feature with every other feature within a given instance (row). It is a pivotal aspect as it allows the model to capture complex interdependencies among the categorical features.

- **Concatenation of contextual embeddings and normalized numerical variables**: Once the transformer has created contextual embeddings for the categorical variables, these are concatenated with the normalized numerical variables. This creates a comprehensive feature set, where both categorical and numerical variables are taken into account, but the former has been enriched with contextual information captured by the transformer.

- **Multilayer Perceptron (MLP)**: The concatenated data is then passed to a MLP for the final prediction. The MLP serves as the final classifier or regressor, depending on the specific task.

- **Pretraining and fine-tuning**: Like many successful transformer-based models, TabTransformer employs a two-step process of pretraining and fine-tuning. During pretraining, the model is trained on a large dataset with a reconstruction objective, learning to predict masked (hidden) columns. Once this pretraining step is complete, the model is then fine-tuned on the specific task, optimizing for the target objective (for example, classification or regression).

By leveraging the strengths of transformer architectures for handling categorical features in tabular data, TabTransformer can effectively model intricate feature relationships, leading to high-performance predictions.

Refer to the following *Figure 11.3* for a visual representation of the TabTransformer's architecture:

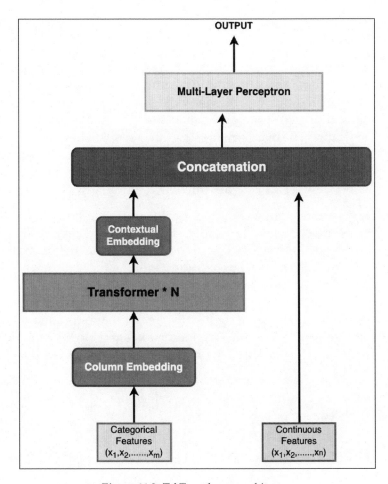

Figure 11.3: *TabTransformer architecture*

FT transformer architecture4

The main idea is to create the embedding of both numerical and categorical features and pass to transformer encoder. This approach ensures a more contextually rich representation of the input data than the TabTransformer, as it calculates self-attention across both numerical and categorical features. In contrast, the TabTransformer only applies self-attention to categorical features. Let us now go over each component in detail.

Feature tokenizer

The Feature tokenizer module is a component of the FT-Transformer model that is responsible for converting input features into embeddings.

---

[4] https://arxiv.org/pdf/2106.11959.pdf

As shown in *Figure 11.4*, the conversion process into embeddings happens differently for numerical and categorical data:

- **Numerical features**: For each numerical feature xj, the transformation involves an element-wise multiplication of the feature value xj by a learned weight vector Wj, and then an addition of a bias term bj. This is represented as: Tj = bj + xj * Wj. The multiplication by Wj allows the model to scale and adjust the influence of the numerical feature. The bias term bj allows the model to have a base representation of the feature from which adjustments can be made. For numerical features, Wj is a weight vector with dimensionality equal to the desired dimensionality d of the feature embeddings. This is represented as W(num)j $\in R^\wedge d$.

- **Categorical features**: For each categorical feature, the transformation involves a lookup in an embedding table Wj for the category in feature xj. The bias term bj is then added. A one-hot vector eTj is used to perform the lookup in the table, which retrieves the embedding for the specific category in the feature. This is represented as: Tj = bj + eTj * Wj. This method effectively gives each category in a feature its unique embedding in the d-dimensional space. For categorical features, Wj is an embedding lookup table. If Sj represents the number of unique categories for the j-th categorical feature, then the embedding lookup table Wj for this feature would have dimensions Sj by d. This is represented as W(cat)j $\in R^\wedge Sj \times d$.

Therefore, in the resulting embeddings, each feature, whether numerical or categorical, is represented in the same d-dimensional space, which makes it possible to process them uniformly in the subsequent Transformer stages of the model.

Concatenation of numerical and categorical feature

The numerical and categorical Feature embedding are concatenated. The concatenated sequence is represented by T. Then, [CLS] token is added at the beginning of the sequence. The input to the Transformer will be:

T= stack (T, [CLS])

Transformer

The input sequence is processed through the transformer encoder, which mirrors the original transformer design as proposed by *Vaswani* and colleagues. A classification or regression head, dependent on the task at hand, is affixed to the first token emanating from the final layer of the transformer encoder.

Figure 11.4 depicts the architecture of the FT Transformer:

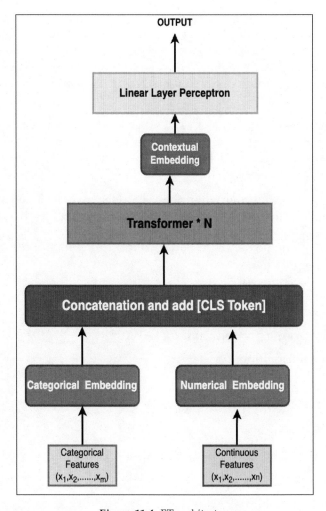

Figure 11.4: *FT architecture*

Conclusion

In conclusion, this chapter provides a comprehensive examination of the use of Transformer models for tabular data representation. Different architectures such as TAPAS, TabTransformer, and FT Transformer are explored, each employing unique strategies for handling categorical and numerical data in tables.

The Google TAPAS model demonstrates its robustness by effectively performing various tasks such as table-based fact-checking, question-answering, semantic parsing, table retrieval, table metadata prediction, and table content population.

The TabTransformer and FT Transformer models have shown to adeptly manage categorical data through their unique methodologies. The TabTransformer's utilization of contextual embeddings for categorical variables and its approach to combine these with normalized numerical variables highlights the model's capability to understand complex interactions between different categorical features. On the other hand, the FT Transformer's feature tokenizer is instrumental in effectively converting both numerical and categorical input features into embeddings, allowing for the unified processing of these features in the subsequent transformer stages.

Each of these transformer architectures brings a distinct perspective on managing tabular data, underscoring the versatility and adaptability of the transformer model. They offer promising solutions for handling tabular data, showing potential for further innovation and improvements in future research.

It is important to understand that while these models have achieved significant success, there are still many areas for exploration and improvement in handling tabular data withstransformers. The future of transformer architectures will likely see further advancements and refinements, as research continues in this exciting area of machine learning and artificial intelligence.

Quiz

1. **What is the primary application of TAPAS?**

    a. Image recognition

    b. Speech synthesis

    c. Question-answering from tables

    d. Video processing

2. **What additional encoding does TAPAS use compared to BERT?**

    a. Rank Embedding

    b. Row Embedding

    c. Column Embedding

    d. All of the above

3. **What is the first step in processing the table and questions in the TAPAS model?**

    a. The data is passed directly into the model

    b. The table and questions are tokenized

    c. The data is converted into images

    d. The data is transformed into numerical values

4. **What is the input to TAPAS?**

    a. Concat (CLS] token, question tokens, [SEP] token, and flatten table)

    b. Concat (question tokens, 2D Table)

5. **In the TabTransformer architecture, how are the categorical features initially processed?**

   a. They are normalized like numerical variables

   b. They are passed directly into the Transformer Encoder

   c. They are transformed into a parametric embedding using Column Embedding

   d. They are removed from the dataset

6. **What is the role of the Transformer Encoder in the TabTransformer architecture?**

   a. To convert numerical variables into categorical variables

   b. To treat each categorical feature as a token and learn complex interactions between different categorical features

   c. To combine the contextual embeddings with the normalized numerical variables

   d. To serve as the final classifier or regressor

7. **What mechanism does the Transformer Encoder use to develop contextual embeddings for the categorical variables?**

   a. One-hot encoding mechanism

   b. Self-attention mechanism

   c. Normalization mechanism

   d. Column embedding mechanism

8. **After the Transformer Encoder has created contextual embeddings for the categorical variables, what is the next step in the TabTransformer architecture?**

   a. These embeddings are passed to another Transformer Encoder

   b. These embeddings are concatenated with the normalized numerical variables

   c. These embeddings are normalized like numerical variables

   d. These embeddings are transformed into a parametric embedding using Column Embedding

9. **What is the role of the Feature Tokenizer in the FT Transformer model?**

   a. To convert input features into numerical data

   b. To convert input features into categorical data

   c. To convert input features into embeddings

   d. To pass input features directly into the Transformer Encoder

10. **How are numerical features processed in the FT Transformer model?**

    a. They are converted into one-hot encoded vectors

    b. They undergo an element-wise multiplication by a learned weight vector and addition of a bias term

    c. They are looked up in an embedding table

    d. They are ignored

11. **How are categorical features processed in the FT Transformer model?**

    a. They are converted into one-hot encoded vectors

    b. They undergo an element-wise multiplication by a learned weight vector and addition of a bias term

    c. They are looked up in an embedding table and a bias term is added

    d. They are ignored

12. **What is done after the numerical and categorical feature embeddings are created?**

    a. They are passed separately into the Transformer Encoder

    b. They are combined into one feature and then passed into the Transformer Encoder

    c. They are concatenated, and a [CLS] token is added at the beginning of the sequence

    d. They are normalized

Answers

1. c.
2. d.
3. b.
4. a.
5. c.
6. b.
7. b.
8. b.
9. c.
10. b.
11. c.
12. c.

## CHAPTER 12

Transformers for Tabular Data Regression and Classification

Introduction

In this chapter, we will explore the application of transformers in tabular data processing. We will also delve into the implementation of transformers such as TabTransformer, FT Transformer, and TabNet for solving classification and regression problems. By working with real-world datasets, we demonstrate the effectiveness and versatility of these models, highlighting their strengths and areas for further enhancement. Let us uncover the potential of transformers in advancing machine learning techniques.

Structure

The chapter contains the following topics:

- System requirements
- Transformer for classification
- Transformer for regression

Objectives

By the end of this chapter, the reader will have explored and implemented transformer models such as TabTransformer and FT Transformer, as well as TabNet, a popular PyTorch model for tabular data that combines decision trees and attention mechanisms. This chapter will also demonstrate the application of transformers in classification and regression tasks, and evaluate the performance of transformer models using real-world datasets.

System requirements

For detailed instructions on setting the environment, please follow instructions at **https://github.com/bpbpublications/Building-Transformer-Models-with-PyTorch/blob/main/General/SettingVirtualEnvironment.ipynb**.

Activate virtual environment:

```
conda activate transformer_learn
```

To proceed with the coding tasks outlined in this chapter, please install the necessary packages as follows:

```
pip install pytorch_tabular
```

```
pip install scikit_learn
```

Transformer for classification

In the upcoming section, we will delve into how to employ transformers for tackling classification problems. These powerful models, which have revolutionized the way we approach natural language processing tasks, are now finding their way into a variety of other domains, including tabular data. Our focus will be on three specific models, namely, TabTransformer, FT Transformer, and TabNet:

- The **TabTransformer**, developed by **Amazon Web Services (AWS)**, adapts transformer architectures for tabular data by treating the rows as sequences, much like sentences in a text. This provides a unique way to capture interactions between features in a row and between different rows.

- The **FT Transformer**, on the other hand, is a modification of the original transformer model and is specifically tailored for handling tabular data. It employs multi-headed self-attention mechanisms, allowing it to learn a much richer set of feature interactions.

- **TabNet**, another variant, integrates the best of scalable decision trees and deep learning. Its unique design allows it to learn meaningful and interpretable features that have direct implications for the decision-making process.

To demonstrate the application of these models, we will be utilizing the UCI **Adult** dataset, often referred to as the census income dataset. This dataset is a popular choice for binary classification tasks, with the objective of predicting whether an individual's income exceeds $50K per year based on various census data attributes.

Throughout this section, we will walk you through how to load the data, pre-process it appropriately for each model, train the transformer models, and evaluate their performance. We will also learn how these powerful transformer models can be effectively used for classification tasks involving tabular data.

Dataset

The **Adult** dataset, also known as the **census income** or **adult.data** dataset, is widely used in machine learning for tasks that involve classifying two different categories. It was created by *Barry Becker* from data collected by the United States Census Bureau in 1994. The main goal with this data is to predict if a person's income is over $50,000 a year based on various other pieces of information.

This dataset is made up of 15 different factors, or attributes, and one outcome variable. These attributes include a mix of categorical (like race or occupation) and continuous (like age or hours worked per week) data. These are:

- **Age:** Continuous.

- **Work class:** Private, Self-emp-not-inc, or Self-emp-inc.

- Federal-gov, Local-gov, State-gov, Without-pay, Never-worked.

- **fnlwgt:** continuous (representing the number of people the census takers believe that observation represents).

- **Education:** Bachelors, Some-college, 11th, HS-grad, Prof-school, Assoc-acdm, Assoc-voc, 9th, 7th-8th, 12th, Masters, 1st-4th, 10th, Doctorate, 5th-6th, Preschool.

- **Education-num:** continuous.

- **Marital-status:** Married-civ-spouse, Divorced, Never-married, Separated, Widowed, Married-spouse-absent, Married-AF-spouse.

- **Occupation:** categorical

- **Relationship:** Wife, Own-child, Husband, Not-in-family, Other-relative, Unmarried.

- **Race:** White, Asian-Pac-Islander, Amer-Indian-Eskimo, Other, Black.

- **Sex:** Female, Male.

- **Capital-gain:** continuous.

- **Capital-loss:** continuous.

- **Hours-per-week:** continuous.

- **Native-country:** categorical

Target

The target variable is income, which is a binary variable with two categories:

- "<=50K"

- ">50K"

Pre-process the data

We are performing data pre-processing on the UCI Adult dataset. This includes importing the dataset, assigning appropriate column names, saving the data into a CSV file, splitting the dataset into training and testing sets, and specifying the categorical, numerical, and target columns.

Code:

```
import pandas as pd

url = "http://archive.ics.uci.edu/ml/machine-learning-databases/adult/adult.data"

column_names = ['age', 'workclass', 'fnlwgt', 'education', 'education-num', 'marital-status', 'occupation', 'relationship', 'race', 'sex', 'capital-gain', 'capital-loss', 'hours-per-week', 'native-country', 'income']

data = pd.read_csv(url, names=column_names)

# Save the dataframe into a CSV file

data.to_csv('adult.csv', index=False)


# Split the data into train and test sets

train = data.sample(frac=0.8, random_state=0)

test = data.drop(train.index)


# Specify the categorical and numerical columns

cat_col_names = ['workclass', 'education', 'marital-status', 'occupation', 'relationship', 'race', 'sex', 'native-country']

num_col_names = ['age', 'fnlwgt', 'education-num', 'capital-gain', 'capital-loss', 'hours-per-week']

target_col_name = ["income"]
```

Declare the configuration

This is a critical step in the procedure. You will need to supply four configurations (most of them come with sensible default values), which will guide the rest of the process. They are:

- **DataConfig:** This is where you specify the names of the target, categorical, and numerical columns, as well as any transformations that need to be done.

- **ModelConfig:** Each model has its own specific configuration. This config not only determines the model we will train but also allows you to set the model's hyperparameters.

- **TrainerConfig:** This config allows you to tailor the training process by setting parameters such as batch size, number of epochs, early stopping criteria, and so on. Most of these parameters are taken directly from PyTorch Lightning and are passed to the underlying Trainer object during the training process.

- **OptimizerConfig:** This configuration allows you to define and utilize various optimizers and learning rate schedulers. Standard PyTorch Optimizers and Learning Rate Schedulers are supported. If you want to use custom optimizers, you can override this by using the parameter in the fit method. Remember, the custom optimizer should be compatible with PyTorch.

Refer to the following code:

```
data_config = DataConfig(
    target=target_col_name,  # target column name
    continuous_cols=num_col_names,  # numerical column names
    categorical_cols=cat_col_names,  # categorical column names
    continuous_feature_transform="quantile_normal",
    normalize_continuous_features=True
)
trainer_config = TrainerConfig(
    auto_lr_find=True,  # Runs the LRFinder to automatically derive a
learning rate
    batch_size=256,
    max_epochs=100,
    early_stopping="valid_loss",
    early_stopping_mode = "min",
    early_stopping_patience=5,
    checkpoints="valid_loss",
    load_best=True,
)
optimizer_config = OptimizerConfig()
```

```
# Specify the model configuration
head_config = LinearHeadConfig(
    layers="",
    dropout=0.1,
    initialization="kaiming"
).__dict__
```

Train and evaluate the model with three models

We are creating and training three different types of models (TabTransformer, FT Transformer, TabNet) for a classification task using the predefined configurations. After training each model on the training set, we then evaluate its performance on the test set. Refer to the following code:

```
#TabTransformer
model_config = TabTransformerConfig(
    task="classification",
    head = "LinearHead", #Linear Head
    head_config = head_config, # Linear Head Config
    learning_rate = 1e-3
)

tabular_model = TabularModel(
    data_config=data_config,
    model_config=model_config,
    optimizer_config=optimizer_config,
    trainer_config=trainer_config,
)
tabular_model.fit(train=train)
tabular_model.evaluate(test)

# FT Transformer
model_config = FTTransformerConfig(
    task="classification",
    learning_rate = 1e-3,
    head = "LinearHead", #Linear Head
```

```
        head_config = head_config, # Linear Head Config
)

tabular_model = TabularModel(
    data_config=data_config,
    model_config=model_config,
    optimizer_config=optimizer_config,
    trainer_config=trainer_config,
)
tabular_model.fit(train=train)
tabular_model.evaluate(test)

# TabNet
model_config = TabNetModelConfig(
    task="classification",
    learning_rate = 1e-3,
    head = "LinearHead", #Linear Head
    head_config = head_config, # Linear Head Config
)

tabular_model = TabularModel(
    data_config=data_config,
    model_config=model_config,
    optimizer_config=optimizer_config,
    trainer_config=trainer_config,
)
tabular_model.fit(train=train)
tabular_model.evaluate(test)
```

Evaluation

Figure 12.1 presents the benchmark results achieved from various machine learning models. On the other hand, *Table 12.1* displays the outcomes from our own experiments:

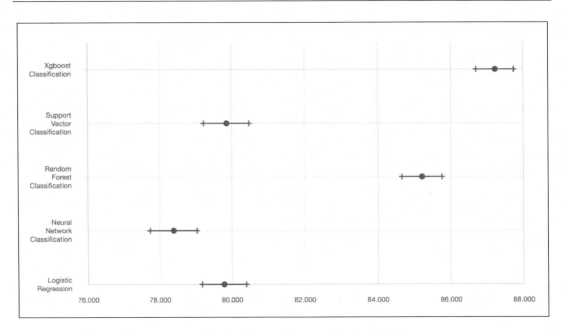

Figure 12.1: Baseline result on various algorithm1

Refer to the following *Table 12.1:*

	TabTransformer	**FT Transformer**	**TabNet**
Test_accuracy	0.843058943748474	0.85012286901474	0.845362424850463
Test_loss	0.33155241608619	0.323970586061477	0.3304014503955841

Table 12.1: Result of Our Experiments

Analysis

Figure 12.1 indicates that the best performance in several studies has been achieved using the XG-Boost model, yielding an accuracy of approximately 87%. In our case, employing the FT Transformer resulted in an accuracy of around 85%. This discrepancy suggests the potential for further investigation and experimentation.

It is essential to note that our current model's evaluation does not include cross-validation, a technique often used to assess the robustness of a model. In addition, we did not incorporate any feature transformation or feature engineering methods, which are commonly used to enhance the performance of a model.

Yet, it is impressive to see that our straightforward application of the FT Transformer still managed to achieve results that are close to the best performance recorded. This

---

[1] **https://archive.ics.uci.edu/dataset/2/adult**

reinforces the potential of transformer models and suggests that with some fine-tuning and enhancements, we may even surpass the benchmark set by XG-Boost.

Transformer for regression

In this demonstration, we will explore the application of a transformer model for regression tasks, specifically using the Ames Housing dataset.

The dataset

The Ames Housing dataset is a comprehensive record of individual residential property sales that occurred in Ames, Iowa, between 2006 and 2010. With over 80 explanatory variables, this dataset provides a plethora of information useful for predictive modeling, as it offers a rich array of factors that contribute to home values.

These factors span a wide spectrum, including:

- General attributes of the property, such as the type of dwelling, its zoning classification, proximity to amenities and roads, and the overall configuration and layout of the property and lot.

- Detailed attributes of the house itself, including the roof type, exterior materials, masonry work, and foundation type.

- Comprehensive ratings of the overall quality and condition of various parts of the house, ranging from the exterior finish to the heating system.

- Detailed information about specific areas within the house, such as the basement, garage, and porch, as well as the presence of a pool. This also includes details about the number and quality of rooms, bedrooms, kitchens, and bathrooms.

- Specifics about the sale transaction, like the type and condition of the sale, and the month and year the sale took place.

The dataset aims to predict the final sale price of each property, making this a regression problem when employing machine learning to forecast the sale price based on all the other variables.

Pre-process the data

The code presented here performs several data processing tasks for a machine learning experiment.

- Firstly, it downloads the Ames Housing dataset from a specified URL using pandas `read_csv` method, saving it to a dataframe.

- It then defines lists of the categorical and numerical columns, as well as the target column (**SalePrice**).

- The code proceeds to handle missing values in the data. For categorical columns, it fills in missing values with the most frequent value (mode) for that column. For numerical columns, including the target, it fills in missing values with the median value for that column.

- After handling missing values, the code uses **MinMaxScaler** from Scikit-learn library to scale the numerical columns. This normalization adjusts all numerical values to fall within the same range (typically 0 to 1), which is often beneficial for machine learning algorithms.

- Finally, it splits the pre-processed dataframe into a training set (80% of the data) and a test set (the remaining 20% of the data), and displays the first few rows of the resulting dataframe for verification.

Refer to the following code:

```
# Download the dataset
import pandas as pd
url = "https://raw.githubusercontent.com/wblakecannon/ames/master/data/
housing.csv"
ames_df = pd.read_csv(url)


# List of categorical and numerical columns
cat_cols = ['Garage Yr Blt', 'Mo Sold', 'Yr Sold','Open Porch
SF', 'Enclosed Porch', '3Ssn Porch', 'Screen Porch','Wood Deck
SF','Fireplaces','Year Remod/Add','Year Built','Overall Cond','Overall
Qual','MS SubClass', 'MS Zoning', 'Street', 'Alley', 'Lot Shape', 'Land
Contour', 'Utilities', 'Lot Config', 'Land Slope', 'Neighborhood',
'Condition 1', 'Condition 2', 'Bldg Type', 'House Style', 'Roof Style',
'Roof Matl', 'Exterior 1st', 'Exterior 2nd', 'Mas Vnr Type', 'Exter Qual',
'Exter Cond', 'Foundation', 'Bsmt Qual', 'Bsmt Cond', 'Bsmt Exposure',
'BsmtFin Type 1', 'BsmtFin Type 2', 'Heating', 'Heating QC', 'Central Air',
'Electrical', 'Kitchen Qual', 'Functional', 'Fireplace Qu', 'Garage Type',
'Garage Finish', 'Garage Qual', 'Garage Cond', 'Paved Drive', 'Pool QC',
'Fence', 'Misc Feature', 'Sale Type', 'Sale Condition']
num_cols = ['Lot Frontage', 'Lot Area',   'Mas Vnr Area', 'BsmtFin SF 1',
'BsmtFin SF 2', 'Bsmt Unf SF', 'Total Bsmt SF', '1st Flr SF', '2nd Flr SF',
'Low Qual Fin SF', 'Gr Liv Area', 'Bsmt Full Bath', 'Bsmt Half Bath', 'Full
Bath', 'Half Bath', 'Bedroom AbvGr', 'Kitchen AbvGr', 'TotRms AbvGrd',
'Garage Cars', 'Garage Area',   'Pool Area', 'Misc Val']
target_col = ['SalePrice']
```

```
## Perform Null Value Imputation
for col in cat_cols:
    ames_df[col].fillna(ames_df[col].mode()[0], inplace=True)

# Replace NaN in continuous columns with the median
for col in num_cols+target_col:
    ames_df[col].fillna(ames_df[col].median(), inplace=True)
ames_df = ames_df.dropna()

# Check the first few rows
print(ames_df.shape)

# Min-max scalar
from sklearn.preprocessing import MinMaxScaler

# Assuming df is your DataFrame and the columns you want to scale are in
the list 'cols_to_scale'
scaler = MinMaxScaler()
cols_to_scale=num_cols+target_col
# Fit the scaler to the columns in 'cols_to_scale'
scaler.fit(ames_df[cols_to_scale])

# Transform the columns
ames_df[cols_to_scale] = scaler.transform(ames_df[cols_to_scale])

# train, test split
train = ames_df.sample(frac=0.8, random_state=0)
test = ames_df.drop(train.index)
print(ames_df.head())
```

Define model configuration

The code for setting up a machine learning experiment with the FTTransformer model is as follows:

```
data_config = DataConfig(
    target=target_col,  # target column name
    continuous_cols=num_cols,  # numerical column names
```

```python
    categorical_cols=cat_cols,  # categorical column names
    continuous_feature_transform="quantile_normal",
    normalize_continuous_features=True
)
trainer_config = TrainerConfig(
    auto_lr_find=True,
    batch_size=256,
    max_epochs=100,
    early_stopping="valid_loss",
    early_stopping_mode = "min",
    early_stopping_patience=5,
    checkpoints="valid_loss",
    load_best=True,
)
optimizer_config = OptimizerConfig()


# Specify the model configuration
head_config = LinearHeadConfig(
    layers="", # No additional layer in head, just a mapping layer to
output_dim
    dropout=0.1,
    initialization="kaiming"
).__dict__  # Convert to dict to pass to the model config (OmegaConf doesn't
accept objects)


model_config = FTTransformerConfig(
    task="regression",
    learning_rate = 1e-3,
    head = "LinearHead", #Linear Head
    head_config = head_config, # Linear Head Config
)


tabular_model = TabularModel(
    data_config=data_config,
```

```
        model_config=model_config,
        optimizer_config=optimizer_config,
        trainer_config=trainer_config,
)
```

Train and evaluate

Here, we are running our experiment and calculating the r-squared on the test-dataset:

```
tabular_model.fit(train=train)

tabular_model.evaluate(test)

prediction=tabular_model.predict(test)

from sklearn.metrics import r2_score

r2 = r2_score(prediction['SalePrice'], prediction['SalePrice_prediction'])
print(f"R2 Score: {r2}")
```

Output:
R2 Score: 0.735613747041542

Analysis

The R-squared value achieved is decent, but there is still room for improvement through further optimization. You might consider various feature engineering strategies to boost the model's performance. Some of these strategies could include:

- Using more sophisticated methods to impute null values, such as nearest neighbors.

- Conducting feature selection to reduce the dimensionality of your data and focus on the most informative features.

- Applying feature transformations or creating new features to better capture the underlying patterns in your data.

Conclusion

In conclusion, this chapter offers an in-depth exploration of the use of transformers for tackling both classification and regression problems, specifically utilizing the TabTransformer, FT Transformer, and TabNet models. We illustrated these techniques using two real-world datasets, the adult dataset for classification and the Ames Housing dataset for regression. The results showed that these transformers can offer competitive performance with traditional machine learning models, even without extensive feature engineering. However, we also noted areas for further improvement and optimization, such as advanced null value imputation, feature selection, and feature transformation. These techniques signify the exciting potential of transformers in machine learning and suggest many avenues for future research and application.

Quiz

1. **Which three transformer models are discussed in the chapter?**

    a. TabTransformer, XG-Boost, TabNet

    b. FT Transformer, BERT, TabNet

    c. TabTransformer, FT Transformer, TabNet

    d. GPT, FT Transformer, TabNet

2. **The TabTransformer model treats rows in tabular data as sequences, similar to sentences in text data.**

    a. True

    b. False

3. **Which configuration specifies the names of the target, categorical, and numerical columns in the data?**

    a. DataConfig

    b. ModelConfig

    c. TrainerConfig

    d. OptimizerConfig

4. **Which configuration allows setting parameters such as batch size, number of epochs, and early stopping criteria during training?**

    a. DataConfig

    b. ModelConfig

    c. TrainerConfig

    d. OptimizerConfig

5. **Which configuration is responsible for defining and utilizing optimizers and learning rate schedulers?**

    a. DataConfig

    b. ModelConfig

    c. TrainerConfig

    d. OptimizerConfig

6. **Which head configuration is used in the TabTransformer model for predictions?**

   a. LinearHead

   b. MultiHead

   c. AttentionHead

   d. EmbeddingHead

7. **Which model achieved the highest accuracy in the classification task?**

   a. TabTransformer

   b. FT Transformer

   c. TabNet

   d. XG-Boost

8. **The FT Transformer achieved comparable results to the best-performing XG-Boost model.**

   a. True

   b. False

9. **What is the objective of the regression problem in the Ames Housing dataset?**

   a. Predicting the type of dwelling

   b. Predicting the condition of the house

   c. Predicting the final sale price of each property

   d. Predicting the presence of a pool

10. **What does the MinMaxScaler from Scikit-learn library do?**

    a. Removes outliers from numerical columns

    b. Scales numerical values to a specific range

    c. Performs feature selection on categorical columns

    d. Converts categorical values to numerical values

11. **What is the purpose of the head configuration in the model configuration?**

    a. To specify the learning rate for the model

    b. To define the structure of the output layer

    c. To determine the optimizer used in training

    d. To set the number of hidden layers in the model

Answers

1. c.

2. a.

3. a.

4. c.

5. d.

6. a.

7. b.

8. a.

9. c.

10. b.

11. b.

Join our book's Discord space

Join the book's Discord Workspace for Latest updates, Offers, Tech happenings around the world, New Release and Sessions with the Authors:

https://discord.bpbonline.com

## CHAPTER 13

Multimodal Transformers, Architectures and Applications

Introduction

In this chapter, we dive into multimodal transformers, AI systems that handle multiple types of data like text, images, and audio simultaneously. We will first explore how transformers consolidate various modalities into a common dimension, effectively enabling the AI to understand different languages of data. Then, we will discuss major multimodal architectures, such as ImageBind, and OpenAI's CLIP, revealing how they are pushing the boundaries of what AI can comprehend and produce. Finally, we will examine tasks related to multimodal data, spanning domains from natural language processing, and audio processing to computer vision.

Structure

The chapter is organized as follows:

- System requirements

- Multimodal architecture

- Multimodal tasks

Objectives

The objectives of this chapter on Multimodal transformers, architectures, and applications are to understand representation and thus explain how transformers process and consolidate multiple modalities into a common dimension, creating a unified language that AI systems can interpret. It will also study architectures, and delve into major multimodal architectures, including ImageBind, and OpenAI's CLIP, elucidating their design, functionality, and distinct features. The chapter will also explore MultiModal Tasks, and provide an overview of tasks related to multimodal data, encompassing various domains from natural language processing to computer vision. Lastly, there will be practical demonstrations of multimodal transformers, aiming to showcase their real-world applications and enhance the reader's understanding of the models.

System requirements

For detailed instructions on setting the environment, please follow instructions at **https://github.com/bpbpublications/Building-Transformer-Models-with-PyTorch/blob/main/General/SettingVirtualEnvironment.ipynb**. Please prepare your environment by following the given instructions:

```
conda activate transformer_learn
```

To proceed with the coding tasks outlined in this chapter, please install the necessary packages detailed as follows:

```
pip install diffusers
```

```
pip install transformers
```

```
pip install torch
```

```
pip install torchvision
```

```
pip install tqdm
```

```
pip install tensorboard
```

```
pip install accelerate
```

Multimodal architecture

Multimodal architectures refer to models that are designed to process and understand information from multiple types of data or **modalities** such as images, text, audio, and so on. The primary challenge in building such architectures is how to represent these distinct types of data in a unified manner so that the model can understand the relationships between them.

One common approach to tackle this is to map each modality into a shared high-dimensional space, known as an embedding space. Each data modality is processed through its own specialized neural network (such as a convolutional neural network for images or a Transformer for text), which transforms the raw data into a dense vector representation, or embedding. These embeddings are designed such that they capture the essential characteristics of the original data, but are represented in the same format, regardless of the original data type.

Once all modalities are represented in the same space, the model can easily compare, relate, and combine information across modalities. For instance, in the shared embedding space, the text description *a red apple* and an image of a red apple should be close together, as they represent the same concept.

There are various techniques to learn these embeddings, such as using contrastive loss which encourages the model to make the embeddings of similar concepts closer together and those of different concepts further apart, regardless of the original modality. This way, multimodal architectures can achieve a more holistic understanding of the information, leveraging the strengths of each data type to enhance overall performance on tasks that require multimodal comprehension.

In the following section, we will discuss two multimodal architectures in details.

ImageBind

ImageBind is probably the most flexible and ingenious strategy for integrating diverse types of data modalities into a single representation space. This system hinges on the idea of utilizing images as a unifying element to link other data modalities, and thus the name ImageBind. Specifically, it uses the six different modalities: images, text, audio, depth, thermal, and IMU data. *Figure 13.1* shows the diagram of how image binds all the modalities into single feature dimension:

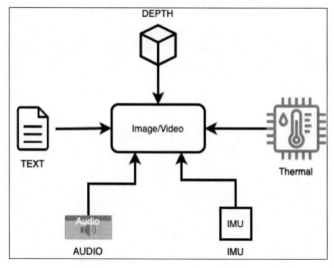

Figure 13.1: *ImageBind: Image acts as center for binding all modalities*

Let us illustrate ImageBind with a more concrete example: Suppose we have an image of a beach scene, the sound of waves crashing (audio), and a written description of the scene (text). The Transformer encoders convert the different types of data into a common form known as embedding. ImageBind use six distinct Transformer encoder, each corresponding to data modalities. In this scenario, there are two data pairs (image, sound of waves) and the pair (image, scene description). Here we can see that, the image acts as a binding agent, linking the audio and text data. The optimization process utilizes a technique called InfoNCE loss (variation of contrastive loss), a measure of the similarity between embeddings. This technique steers the learning process of the Transformer encoders, urging them to generate embeddings that are as similar as possible for an image and its corresponding modality (like the sound of waves or the scene description). This way, the model learns to align the different data modalities in the shared embedding space.

The magic of ImageBind lies in its ability to understand relationships between different data types without explicitly seeing all possible combinations. For instance, if we introduce a new modality such as the temperature at the beach (thermal data), ImageBind can infer a relationship between this new modality and the existing ones (like the sound of waves). This is possible because ImageBind has learned to associate both the temperature data and audio data with images. Leveraging the image as a common reference point, ImageBind can infer a relationship between temperature and audio data. This impressive emergent behavior opens up a wide range of possibilities, allowing ImageBind to perform complex tasks such as matching text to audio, even when it has not been trained on such data pairings. This significantly enhances ImageBind's versatility and applicability across diverse real-world scenarios.

Demonstration

You can follow the link (**https://imagebind.metademolab.com/demo**) to play with ImageBind.

You can also run the experiment following the tutorial (**https://github.com/facebookresearch/ImageBind**) to create the embedding of different modalities.

CLIP

OpenAI's **Contrastive Language–Image Pretraining (CLIP)** is a model designed to understand information from both images and text. The model has two main components:

- **Vision Transformer (ViT):** The visual part of the model is based on the transformer architecture. The input image is divided into a fixed number of patches, which are then linearly embedded and processed sequentially by the transformer. The output of the ViT is an embedding that represents the content of the image.

- **Transformer language model:** The text part of the model is a transformer-based neural network that is trained to understand and generate human language. It is similar to models like GPT, with the key difference being that it is trained to understand text in the context of images. It takes a sequence of tokens (words, or parts of words) as input and produces an embedding that represents the meaning of the text.

Pre-training objective

The objective of the pre-training phase in CLIP is to learn to correctly associate images and texts. During training, the model is presented with a batch of images and a batch of texts. It is trained to maximize the similarity between each image and its corresponding text while minimizing the similarity between each image and all other texts in the batch.

This is achieved using a contrastive loss function, specifically, the **Noise Contrastive Estimation (NCE)** loss. The model is encouraged to produce embeddings such that the dot product of the embedding of an image and its corresponding text is higher than the dot product of the embedding of the image and the text of any other image-text pair in the batch.

Applications and usage

CLIP can be used for a wide range of tasks that involve understanding and generating information about images and text. Some examples include:

- **Zero-shot classification**: Given a set of class names and an image, CLIP can predict the class of the image without needing any examples of that class during training. This is done by comparing the embedding of the image to the embeddings of the class names and predicting the class with the highest similarity.

- **Text-to-image synthesis**: Given a textual description, CLIP can generate an image that fits the description.

- **Image-to-text synthesis**: Given an image, CLIP can generate a textual description of the image.

- **Cross-modal search**: Given a query in one modality (for example, text), you can search for content in another modality (for example, images).

Multimodal tasks

Multimodal machine learning algorithms can be crafted for a myriad of tasks. Take, for instance, identifying potential health issues in patients. This involves creating a classifier that utilizes a patient's structured data (tabular data), clinical notes (natural language processing), chest X-rays (imaging), and heart sounds (audio). This aligns with how doctors usually diagnose patients, considering all modalities of information. Furthermore, multimodal input is indispensable in other tasks such as text-image association, audio transcription, and more. In the upcoming section, we will delve deeper into tasks where multimodal data plays a crucial role.

Table 13.1 illustrates the major multimodal tasks[1]:

Task	Description	Models
Feature extraction	Convert text sequence into single vector representation. Essential for text search, information retrieval, or other multiple downstream tasks.	intfloat/e5-large-v2, facebook/bart-large
Text-to-image	Generate image by giving text prompt	runwayml/stable-diffusion-v1-5, DALL-E 2
Image-to-text	Generate text description of image	openai/clip-vit-large-patch14, nlpconnect/vit-gpt2-image-captioning
Text-to-video	Generate video from text description	damo-vilab/text-to-video-ms-1.7b
Visual question answering	Q&A based on the image. For example, provide the image and ask question like, how many male are in the picture?	Salesforce/blip-vqa-base
Document question answering	For example, given invoice pdf, ask what is the invoice number	magorshunov/layoutlm-invoices

Table 13.1: Multi-modal tasks

In the following sections, we will discuss in detail some most important multi-modal tasks.

Feature extraction

Feature extraction is a crucial step in many machine-learning tasks. In the context of text data, feature extraction involves transforming a text sequence into a single vector representation that captures the essential meaning and characteristics of the text.

Let us consider an example: a movie recommendation system. Here, the feature extraction model can take movie reviews (text data) and convert them into vector representations. These vectors can then be compared to determine the similarity between different movies, based on the content of their reviews. In this way, the system can recommend movies that have received similar reviews, thereby personalizing the recommendations for each user.

---

[1] **https://huggingface.co/models**

The following code demonstrates how we can use facebook/bart-large to extract features from input text:

```
from transformers import BartTokenizer, BartModel

tokenizer = BartTokenizer.from_pretrained('facebook/bart-large')
model = BartModel.from_pretrained('facebook/bart-large')

inputs = tokenizer("Hello, my dog is cute", return_tensors="pt")
print (inputs)
outputs = model(**inputs)

last_hidden_states = outputs.last_hidden_state
# The shape is in form of (batch_size, seq_len, embedding_dim)
print(last_hidden_states.shape, '\n')
print(last_hidden_states)
```

Following is the output from the preceding code:

```
# this is tokenized input

{'input_ids': tensor([[    0, 31414,     6,   127,  2335,    16, 11962,
2]]), 'attention_mask': tensor([[1, 1, 1, 1, 1, 1, 1, 1]])}

#shape of last hidden state, this is shape of vector representation of
input data

# (batch_size=1, seq_len=8,embedding_dim=1024)

torch.Size([1, 8, 1024])

# vector representation of input text

tensor([[[ 0.5512,   0.8389,  -1.4707,   ...,   1.3124,  -0.2047,   0.2392],
        [ 0.5512,   0.8389,  -1.4707,   ...,   1.3124,  -0.2047,   0.2392],
        [ 0.9143,   0.9399,  -1.2426,   ...,   0.9184,  -0.1838,  -0.9975],

        ...,

        [ 0.2561,   0.2253,   0.4470,   ...,   0.3447,   0.0087,   1.5508],
        [ 0.2077,  -1.3086,  -1.4295,   ...,  -0.2998,   0.1828,   0.4700],
        [-0.4893,   2.5148,  -1.5513,   ...,   0.5783,   1.0961,   0.1736]]],
       grad_fn=<NativeLayerNormBackward0>)
```

Analysis

Let us dig deeper into the above code:

- The code aims to convert the input sentence *Hello, my dog is cute* into a vector representation.

- This vector representation or encoding is obtained from the attribute **outputs. last_hidden_state**.

- The **last_hidden_state** provides the output from the final layer of the BART model.

- The shape of **last_hidden_state** is printed, which happens to be (1, 8, 1024).

- The input sentence *Hello, my dog is cute* gets tokenized into a sequence of length 8.

- The dimensions of the **last_hidden_state** tensor are interpreted as follows:

  o The first dimension, **batch_size**, represents the number of input sentences processed at once. Here, it is 1.

  o The second dimension, **seq_len**, signifies the number of tokens in the input sentence. In this case, it is 8.

  o The third dimension, **hidden_state_size**, refers to the size of the model's hidden state. For the 'facebook/bart-large' model, it is 1024.

Text-to-image

In the following code, we aim to provide a prompt, and the model should generate an image based on our prompt:

```
from diffusers import StableDiffusionPipeline

import torch

from PIL import Image

import requests

from io import BytesIO

import matplotlib.pyplot as plt


model_id = "runwayml/stable-diffusion-v1-5"

pipe = StableDiffusionPipeline.from_pretrained(model_id, torch_dtype=torch.
float16)

pipe = pipe.to("cuda")
```

```
prompt = "a photo of an cowboy man riding dinosaurs in pacaso style"

# Generate images from the prompt
image = pipe(prompt,num_inference_steps=900).images[0]
plt.imshow(image)
plt.axis('off')  # No axis for clarity
plt.show()
image.save("man_riding_dinosaurs.png")
```

The output of the above code is shown in the following figure:

Figure 13.2: Image generated by the stable diffusion model

Analysis

Let us dig deeper about the above code:

- The model **runwayml/stable-diffusion-v1-5** is utilized as the base model for image generation.

- The **StableDiffusionPipeline** class is used to encapsulate the steps involved in the model. This helps to simplify the code; otherwise, the raw model application would require significantly more lines of code.

- The variable prompt contains the textual description which represents the type of image we want to generate.

- The number of inference steps is set to 900, overriding the default of 50. This is done with the expectation that a larger number of steps will generate higher quality images.

- The **pipe** function offers several parameters for the image generation process, such as the shape of the image, among other options. You can explore more about these options in the function's documentation[2].

Image to-text

In the following code, we aim to provide an image and the model should generate the description of the image:

```
from transformers import pipeline

image_url = 'https://raw.githubusercontent.com/bpbpublications/Building-
Transformer-Models-with-PyTorch/main/ chapter8_CVTask/food_image.jpg'

image_to_text = pipeline("image-to-text", model="nlpconnect/vit-gpt2-image-
captioning")

output=image_to_text(image_url)

response = requests.get(image_url)
img = Image.open(BytesIO(response.content))
if img.mode != "RGB":
    img = img.convert(mode="RGB")

# Display the image
plt.imshow(img)
plt.axis('off')  # No axis for clarity
plt.show()
print(output[0]['generated_text'])
```

Output

Figure 13.3 shows the image provided and the corresponding description generated by the image:

---

[2] **https://huggingface.co/docs/diffusers/main/en/api/pipelines/stable_diffusion/text2img#diffusers.
StableDiffusionPipeline**

a plate of food with rice, beans, and vegetables

Figure 13.3: Model captioning output

Analysis

As you can see the description, *a plate of food with rice, beans and vegetables* is a fairly accurate description of the above picture.

Visual question answering

In the following code, we aim to provide an image and a question related to that image, and the model should generate the answer to our question. *Figure 13.3* shows the picture we are passing to the model, and our question is *Is there rice on the plate?*

Code:

```
import requests

from PIL import Image

from transformers import BlipProcessor, BlipForQuestionAnswering


# Instantiate the processor and model from the pretrained "Salesforce/blip-vqa-base"

processor = BlipProcessor.from_pretrained("Salesforce/blip-vqa-base")

model = BlipForQuestionAnswering.from_pretrained("Salesforce/blip-vqa-base").to("cuda")


# URL of the image for visual question answering

image_url = 'https://raw.githubusercontent.com/bpbpublications/Building-
```

```
Transformer-Models-with-PyTorch/main/chapter8/food_image.jpg'

# Request the image from the URL and convert it to RGB
raw_image = Image.open(requests.get(image_url, stream=True).raw).
convert('RGB')

# The question to be asked
question = "Is there rice in the plate?"

# Prepare the inputs for the model
# This includes the image and the question, transformed to tensors and
moved to the GPU
inputs = processor(raw_image, question, return_tensors="pt").to("cuda")

# Generate the answer using the model
out = model.generate(**inputs)

# Decode the output into a string answer, skipping special tokens
answer = processor.decode(out[0], skip_special_tokens=True)

# Print the answer
print(f"The answer to your question is :{answer}")
```

Output:
The answer to your question is :yes

Analysis

You can review the model accurately answer our question.

Conclusion

This exploration of multimodal Transformer models demonstrated the potential these models hold for dealing with a variety of data types and complex tasks. We used various techniques such as feature extraction for text data, text-to-image, image-to-text, and visual question answering models to leverage the versatility and robustness of transformer models. Utilizing models like BART, Stable Diffusion, ViT-GPT2, and BLiP-VQA, we showed how transformer models can efficiently understand and generate both textual and visual content, indicating a significant stride towards artificial general intelligence. However, as these models continue to evolve, it is crucial to note that their implementation also presents challenges, such as managing computational costs and handling nuanced tasks. Despite these challenges, the potential for further enhancements and innovative applications remains vast, making the field of multimodal transformers an exciting frontier in AI research and development.

Quiz

1. **What is feature extraction in the context of text data?**

    a. Comparing two texts

    b. Transforming a text sequence into a vector representation

    c. Correcting the grammar of a text

    d. Compressing the text data

2. **What does the 'outputs.last_hidden_state' represent in the BART model?**

    a. The input sentence

    b. The vector representation of the input sentence

    c. The tokenized sequence of the input sentence

    d. The sentiment of the input sentence

3. **What are the dimensions of the 'last_hidden_state' tensor in the BART model?**

    a. (batch_size, seq_len, hidden_state_size)

    b. (seq_len, batch_size, hidden_state_size)

    c. (hidden_state_size, batch_size, seq_len)

    d. (seq_len, hidden_state_size, batch_size)

4. **In the 'stable-diffusion' model, what does the variable 'prompt' represent?**

    a. The type of image to generate

    b. The number of images to generate

    c. The size of the image to generate

    d. The style of the image to generate

5. **What does the parameter 'num_inference_steps' in the 'stable-diffusion' model control?**

    a. The quality of the generated image

    b. The size of the generated image

    c. The number of images to generate

    d. The style of the generated image

6. **What does the pipeline function 'image-to-text' do?**

    a. Generates a text description of an image

    b. Converts an image into text format

    c. Converts a text into image format

    d. Generates an image based on a text description

7. **What does the 'BlipForQuestionAnswering' model do?**

    a. Converts an image into text format

    b. Generates a text description of an image

    c. Answers a question related to an image

    d. Generates an image based on a text description

8. **What is the significance of 'torch_dtype=torch.float16' in the StableDiffusionPipeline?**

    a. It determines the image size

    b. It defines the data type of the model parameters

    c. It sets the image color

    d. It determines the style of the generated image

9. **In the image-to-text pipeline, why is the image converted to "RGB" mode?**

    a. To reduce the size of the image

    b. To ensure compatibility with the model

    c. To improve the quality of the image

    d. To change the color of the image

10. **In the 'StableDiffusionPipeline', what does the '.to("cuda")' method do?**

    a. It transfers the pipeline to the GPU

    b. It saves the pipeline

    c. It prints the pipeline

    d. It compiles the pipeline

11. **In the BART model, what does the 'embedding_dim' represent?**

    a. The size of the model's hidden state

    b. The number of tokens in the input sentence

    c. The number of input sentences processed at once

    d. The number of features in the input sentence

Answers

1. b.

2. b.

3. a.

4. a.

5. a.

6. a.

7. c.

8. b.

9. b.

10. a.

11. a.

Join our book's Discord space

Join the book's Discord Workspace for Latest updates, Offers, Tech happenings around the world, New Release and Sessions with the Authors:

https://discord.bpbonline.com

CHAPTER 14

Explore Reinforcement Learning for Transformer

Introduction

Reinforcement Learning (RL) is a subfield of machine learning that focuses on how an agent can learn to behave in an environment by taking actions that maximize some notion of cumulative reward. It is fundamentally about learning to make decisions based on the consequences of previous actions. Traditionally, reinforcement learning has been intertwined with various types of algorithms and neural network architectures like **Convolutional Neural Networks (CNNs)** and **Recurrent Neural Networks (RNNs)**. These approaches have had considerable success in fields like robotics, game theory, and sequential decision-making tasks.

Recently, transformer architectures have been adapted to reinforcement learning tasks. One such model is the decision transformer, which frames reinforcement learning as a problem of ranking trajectories, thus shifting the focus from traditional action-value based methods to more direct methods of estimating the optimal trajectories. Another emerging model is the trajectory transformer, which leverages the ability of transformers to understand sequence data, hence enhancing the efficiency of reinforcement learning with its power to predict the entire sequence of future states, actions, and rewards.

In this new frontier of reinforcement learning research, the interplay of RL principles with transformers could yield sophisticated, efficient, and adaptable machine learning systems, thereby sparking advancements in the field. This chapter will explore in detail the integration of these technologies, their challenges, opportunities, and future prospects.

Structure

The book is organized as follows:

- System requirements
- Reinforcement learning
- Important technique in PyTorch for reinforcement learning
- Project 1
- Transformer for reinforcement learning

Objectives

The objectives of this chapter are to explain the fundamentals of RL and the most common tools in Pytorch, and the process of building RL model. We will walk you through the process of developing a *day trading model* using tools like Gym, Stable-baselines3, and Yfinance. The reader will also be introduced to transformer architectures for RL. We will explain decision transformer and trajectory transformer, two significant transformer architectures used in RL.

System requirements

Please prepare your environment by following the given instructions. For detailed instructions on setting the environment, please follow instructions at **https://github.com/ bpbpublications/Building-Transformer-Models-with-PyTorch/blob/main/General/ SettingVirtualEnvironment.ipynb**.

Activate virtual environment:

```
conda activate transformer_learn
```

To proceed with the coding tasks outlined in this chapter, please install the necessary packages detailed as follows:

```
pip install gym
pip install pandas
pip install yfinance
pip install stable-baseline3
pip install shimmy
```

Reinforcement learning

RL is a type of machine learning where an agent learns how to behave in an environment by performing certain actions and observing the results or feedback from those actions. Let us illustrate through the example of stock portfolio management.

Imagine you are managing a stock portfolio. In this situation, you, as the portfolio manager (the agent), interact with the complex world of the stock market (the environment) by making choices (like buying, selling, or holding onto stocks). This environment is filled with different types of information: technical data, fundamental data, recent news, and overall market trends. Based on the state of the environment, if a choice (action) leads to a good result (like making money from a stock sale or earning a dividend), it is considered a good choice and should be repeated in similar situations later. However, if a choice results in a bad outcome (like a big loss in a stock's value or missing a chance to make profit), it is seen as a bad choice and should be avoided in the future. Reinforcement learning is the tool that helps learn the best strategy (policy) for making decisions, depending on the state of the environment, to earn the most rewards.

The **reinforcement** in reinforcement learning is the feedback, or the rewards and punishments, from the environment. Positive rewards reinforce the actions that led to them, encouraging the agent to repeat those actions in the future. Negative rewards (or punishments) discourage the actions that led to them. Over time, through a lot of trial and error, the agent learns the best strategy or policy to perform well in the environment.

In a more technical language, reinforcement learning involves several key components:

- **Agent**: The learner or decision maker.
- **Environment**: The context or world where the agent operates.
- **Actions**: The set of all possible moves the agent can make.
- **States**: The situation the agent finds itself in. It is a consequence of the previous actions.
- **Reward**: The feedback that the agent gets for each action. The agent's objective is to learn a policy that maximizes the cumulative reward over time.

So, in reinforcement learning, the agent learns a policy, which is a mapping from states to actions that maximize the expected sum of rewards.

Important techniques in PyTorch for RL

Some important techniques in PyTorch for Reinforcement learning are discussed in the following section.

Stable Baseline3

Stable Baselines3 (**SB3**) is an open source library that provides high-quality implementations of state-of-the-art **RL** algorithms in PyTorch. It is the successor of Stable Baselines and Stable Baselines2, which were built with TensorFlow.

The goal of Stable Baselines3 is to collect reliable implementations of RL algorithms in one place, with unified structure and standardized code. The algorithms are made accessible via a common interface, making it easier to both use and understand them.

The library includes implementations of many popular reinforcement learning algorithms, such as **Proximal Policy Optimization (PPO)**, **Soft Actor-Critic (SAC)**, **Advantage Actor-Critic (A2C)**, and **Twin Delayed DDPG (TD3)**.

Gymnasium

This library is a branch of OpenAI's original Gym library, managed by its maintainers. Gymnasium is a freely available Python library that allows for the development and comparison of reinforcement learning algorithms. It establishes a standard API for enabling communication between learning algorithms and environments, and offers a set of environments that comply with this API.

It provides a wide variety of pre-defined environments for training and testing reinforcement learning agents, including simulations of robotics, classic control tasks, computer games, and more.

Here is a breakdown of the main components:

- **Environments:** OpenAI Gym provides a large set of environments that simulate a variety of problems an RL agent needs to solve. These environments adhere to a unified API, making it easier to develop generic algorithms that can be applied across a range of scenarios. The environments range from simple tasks like balancing a pole (`CartPole`) or controlling a mountain car, to playing Atari video games, navigating 2D and 3D mazes, and even playing board games like Go and chess.

- **Spaces:** Every gym environment comes with an `action_space` and an `observation_space`. These spaces define the form of the agent's actions and observations. For example, in the CartPole environment, the observation space represents the position and velocity of the cart and pole, while the action space represents the possible forces applied to the cart.

- **Steps:** In each environment, an agent takes a step by calling the `step()` function, which advances the environment by one step. This function returns four values: the new observation, the reward, a done flag indicating whether the episode has ended, and extra information that can be used for debugging.

- **Tasks:** Each environment encapsulates a task, or a goal that an agent needs to achieve. For instance, in the `CartPole` environment, the task is to balance a pole on a cart for as long as possible.

- **Benchmarking:** OpenAI Gym also provides tools for benchmarking, which allow you to compare the performance of different algorithms on the same tasks.

Project 1: Stock Market Trading with RL

Here, we will illustrate how to use gym and stable baseline3 to conduct a reinforcement learning.

Reinforcement learning in stock market trading

- **Objective**: Development of a day trading model utilizing reinforcement learning

- **Tools**: Gym, Stable-baselines3, and Yfinance

- **Methodology**: The environment incorporates Apple's stock price over the past 6 days. Our task is to develop a policy to:

  o Decide when to buy, hold, or sell the stock.

  o Determine the quantity to buy or sell.

- **Reward**: The reward is the subsequent value of the portfolio after the action has been taken.

- **Solution**: The attached notebook provides a complete solution, covering model development and inference[1].

- **Exercise**: Enhance the model to factor in multiple stocks. Establish a policy to:

  o Determine which stocks to buy, sell, or hold.

  o Decide on the exact amount of each stock to buy or sell.

Transformer for reinforcement learning

There are two major transformer architectures for reinforcement learning: The decision transformer and the trajectory transformer. In the following section, we will discuss both in detail.

Decision transformer

At its heart, the decision transformer[1] uses a different approach compared to usual **RL** methods. Instead of teaching a system how to choose the best action to get the most reward (something called a value function), the decision transformer reformulates the problem as a sequence modeling problem. Given a certain goal (the desired return), and information about past actions and states, it tries to predict what actions should come next to reach that goal. We will start with an examination of the decision transformer, as illustrated in *Figure 14.1*. Here are its primary elements:

---

[1] **https://github.com/bpbpublications/Building-Transformer-Models-with-PyTorch/tree/main**

- **Input**: The decision transformer's input consists of **Return (R_t)**, **State (S_t)**, and **Action (a_t)** tuples. The most recent K-step **RSA (Return, State, Action)** tuples are presented as a sequence and embedded to transform into a continuous vector representation.

- **Positional encoding**: A process called positional encoding is utilized, thus capturing the relative positions of the RSA elements within the input sequence.

- **Transformer layers**: The GPT-2 model processes the input in autoregressive manner.

- **Linear layer for output**: The culmination of the decision Transformer structure is a linear layer. This layer maps the final decoder layer of the transformer into the action space, subsequently producing a sequence of actions to achieve the intended outcome.

Refer to the following figure:

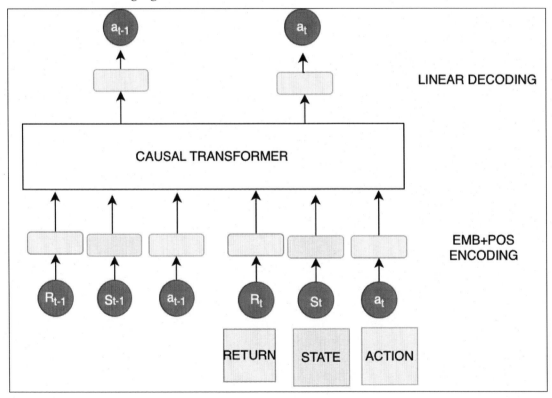

Figure 14.1: *Causal transformer*

You can follow this tutorial[2] for training your own decision transformer.

---

[2] **https://huggingface.co/blog/train-decision-transformers**

Trajectory transformer[3]

The trajectory transformer shares a similarity with the decision transformer in that they both approach the reinforcement learning task as a sequence learning problem. However, there are important distinctions, particularly in how the sequence represents the action, reward, and state. Let us delve into the details of the trajectory transformer. The architecture of the trajectory transformer is illustrated in *Figure 14.2*.

Input

A trajectory, represented by τ is a sequence comprising T states, actions, and individual rewards. This sequence can be expressed as:

$$\tau = (s_1, a_1, r_1, s_2, a_2, r_2, ..., s_T, a_T, r_T)$$

Here, states, and actions are discretized independently. Given states of N dimensions and actions of M dimensions, the trajectory τ is transformed into a sequence of length $T(N + M + 1)$:

$$\tau = \{..., s_1^t, s_2^t, ..., s_N^t, a_1^t, a_2^t, ..., a_M^t, r^t ...\}$$

$$for\ t = 1, ..., T$$

In this context, each token's subscript represents the timestep, while the superscripts on states and actions denote their respective dimensions. For instance, at a given step, the states span N dimensions, denoted as s1, …sN, and the actions occupy an M-dimensional space.

Refer to the following figure:

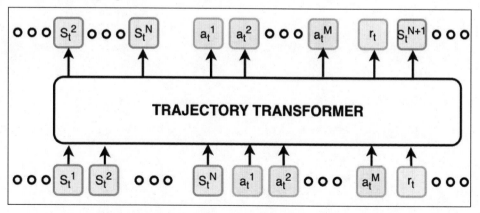

Figure 14.2: Trajectory transformer

The transformer model uses the GPT like structure with four decoders layers.

---

[3] https://arxiv.org/pdf/2106.02039.pdf

Output

The model is autoregressive and outputs the sequence of states, actions and rewards.

For a deeper understanding of trajectory transformers, kit is recommended to explore their GitHub page[4].

Conclusion

This chapter provided a comprehensive overview of RL, a powerful tool used in many areas, including game playing, robotics, finance, and healthcare. We explored the fundamental principles, key technical aspects, and practical applications of RL, using a stock portfolio management scenario as an illustrative example. We further dove into state-of-the-art RL tools and models, such as Stable Baselines3, Gymnasium, decision transformer, and trajectory Transformer.

To conclude, it is clear that reinforcement learning offers an incredibly versatile and robust approach for tackling complex decision-making tasks. transformers for RL are still in the exploratory phase; however, algorithms like the decision transformer and the trajectory transformer have shown clear indications of their potential. As technology advances and more efficient algorithms are developed, the future of RL holds immense promise, pushing the boundaries of what we can achieve in the realm of artificial intelligence.

Quiz

1. **What type of machine learning is reinforcement learning?**

    a. Supervised Learning

    b. Unsupervised Learning

    c. Semi-supervised Learning

    d. None of the above

2. **In reinforcement learning, what is the role of the agent?**

    a. To provide feedback

    b. To learn or make decisions

    c. To perform actions

    d. Both b and c

---

[4] **https://github.com/jannerm/trajectory-transformer**

3. **What are some reinforcement learning algorithms provided by Stable Baselines3?**

    a. Proximal Policy Optimization, Soft Actor-Critic, Advantage Actor-Critic, Twin Delayed DDPG

    b. Decision Trees, Random Forest, Gradient Boosting

    c. K-means, DBSCAN, Hierarchical Clustering

    d. Linear Regression, Logistic Regression, Ridge Regression

4. **What is the Gymnasium library used for?**

    a. It is used for development and comparison of reinforcement learning algorithms.

    b. It is used for text processing in natural language processing.

    c. It is used for image processing in computer vision.

    d. None of the above

5. **The transformer model in the Trajectory Transformer uses the structure similar to which model?**

    a. BERT

    b. Transformer-XL

    c. GPT

    d. None of the above

6. **In reinforcement learning, what is the goal of the agent?**

    a. To maximize the cumulative reward over time.

    b. To minimize the cumulative reward over time.

    c. To have a neutral effect on the cumulative reward.

    d. None of the above.

7. **What does the term "reinforcement" refer to in reinforcement learning?**

    a. The learning process

    b. The rewards and punishments from the environment

    c. The actions that an agent can take

    d. None of the above

8. **What are the main components of reinforcement learning?**

    a. Agent, Environment, Actions, States, Reward

    b. Dataset, Model, Training, Validation, Testing

    c. Features, Target variable, Model, Training, Validation

    d. None of the above

9. **In the context of reinforcement learning, what is a policy?**

    a. A mapping from states to actions that maximize the expected sum of rewards

    b. A specific set of actions that an agent can take

    c. The environment where the agent operates

    d. None of the above

10. **What is the primary difference between the Decision Transformer and Trajectory Transformer?**

    a. They use different algorithms.

    b. They represent the sequence of action, reward, and state differently.

    c. They use different types of reinforcement learning.

    d. None of the above.

11. **What is the purpose of the 'step' method in the StockTradingEnv class?**

    a. To initialize the environment

    b. To specify what the agent should do at each step

    c. To render the environment

    d. To reset the environment to its initial state

12. **Which Reinforcement Learning algorithm is being used in the provided project?**

    a. DQN (Deep Q-Network)

    b. A2C (Advantage Actor-Critic)

    c. PPO (Proximal Policy Optimization)

    d. SAC (Soft Actor-Critic)

13. **What kind of action space is used in the StockTradingEnv class?**

    a. Discrete action space

    b. Continuous action space

    c. MultiDiscrete action space

    d. Tuple action space

14. **What is 'gym' in the context of the provided project?**

    a. It's a reinforcement learning library that allows for the creation and manipulation of environments to train agents.

    b. It's a physical fitness related library in Python.

    c. It's a library used to download stock data.

    d. It's a machine learning algorithm used for regression analysis.

15. **Which method in the StockTradingEnv class is responsible for determining what the environment looks like at the start of each episode?**

    a. render()

    b. step()

    c. reset()

    d. close()

Answers

1. d.

2. d.

3. a.

4. a.

5. c.

6. a.

7. b.

8. a.

9. a.

10. b.

11. b.

12. c.

13. b.

14. a.

15. c.

Join our book's Discord space

Join the book's Discord Workspace for Latest updates, Offers, Tech happenings around the world, New Release and Sessions with the Authors:

https://discord.bpbonline.com

CHAPTER 15

Model Export, Serving, and Deployment

Introduction

This chapter provides a comprehensive exploration into the crucial world of machine learning lifecycle, focusing on model serialization, export, and deployment. The importance of grasping these concepts lies in the reality that machine learning models, regardless of their sophistication, yield no value unless they are effectively deployed to make predictions in real-time applications.

Structure

The chapter is structured as follows:

- System requirements
- Model export and serialization
- Exporting model On ONNX format
- Serving model with FastAPI
- Serving Pytorch model in mobile devices
- Deploying HuggingFace's transformers model on AWS

Objectives

The objective of this chapter is to provide an understanding of machine learning model deployment, specifically focusing on PyTorch models. This includes illustrating the processes involved in saving, loading, and exporting PyTorch models to interoperable formats like **Open Neural Network Exchange (ONNX)**, as well as discussing the usage of PyTorch Script and Pickle. The chapter also aims to guide the reader on how to leverage FastAPI for model serving, elucidate on serving PyTorch models on mobile devices, and offer comprehensive guidance on deploying HuggingFace's Transformers models on AWS using various services. The goal is to equip readers with the knowledge and tools needed to efficiently export, serve, and deploy machine learning models, tailored to their specific requirements and constraints.

System resources

Please follow the following instructions for setting the system environment. For detailed instructions on setting the environment, please follow instructions at **https://github.com/ bpbpublications/Building-Transformer-Models-with-PyTorch/blob/main/General/ SettingVirtualEnvironment.ipynb**.

Activate virtual environment:

```
conda activate transformer_learn
```

To proceed with the coding tasks outlined in this chapter, please install the necessary packages detailed as follows:

```
pip3 install transformers
```

```
pip3 install datasets
```

```
pip3 install torch
```

```
pip3 install torchtext
```

```
pip3 install onnx
```

```
pip3 install onnxruntime
```

```
pip3 install optimum
```

```
pip3 install fastapi[all]
```

```
pip3 install uvicorn[standard]
```

Model export and serialization

Model export refers to the process of transforming a trained machine learning model into a format that can be used independently of the original training environment. This format could be a simple binary file, a set of weights, or even a more structured format such as **ONNX** or PyTorch Script. On the other hand, model serialization is the process of converting the model into a format that can be stored or transmitted over the network and then reconstructed or deserialized back into the original model structure.

There are various formats for model export and serialization, including ONNX, PyTorch Script, and Pickle. ONNX provides a platform-independent format to represent models, which can be used across various deep learning frameworks such as PyTorch, TensorFlow, and MXNet. PyTorch Script offers a way to serialize PyTorch models by transcribing them into a subset of Python, and Pickle is a standard Python tool for serialization and deserialization. In the following section, we will discuss model export in the PyTorch Format and ONNX format.

PyTorch model export and import

For saving and loading the PyTorch models, there are three core functionalities. These three key functions are crucial when it comes to storing and retrieving models are as follows.

torch.save

This function enables the saving of serialized objects to disk, utilizing Python's pickle utility for the serialization process. It can handle models, tensors, and dictionaries comprising various objects. We can use this function to save the entire module or just the **state_dict** of the module.

Let us understand more about the **state_dict**. In PyTorch, a **state_dict** is essentially a Python dictionary object that maps each layer in the model to its corresponding parameters (tensors). It is worth noting that only layers with learnable parameters (convolutional layers, linear layers, and so on) and registered buffers (batchnorm's running mean) have entries in the model's **state_dict**. Optimizers also have a **state_dict**, which contains information about the optimizer's state, as well as the hyper-parameters used.

torch.load

Leveraging pickle's unpickling abilities, this function deserializes pickled object files back into memory.

torch.nn.Module.load_state_dict

This function is utilized to load a model's parameter dictionary using a deserialized **state_dict**.

Let us understand this through an example:

Declare the model: Here, we are declaring simple CNN model for illustration:

```
import torch
```

```python
import torch.nn as nn
import torch.nn.functional as F

class SimpleCNN(nn.Module):
    def __init__(self):
        super(SimpleCNN, self).__init__()
        self.conv1 = nn.Conv2d(3, 6, 5)    # Assuming input image channel=3
(RGB), 6 output channels, 5x5 kernel
        self.pool = nn.MaxPool2d(2, 2)
        self.conv2 = nn.Conv2d(6, 16, 5)
        self.fc1 = nn.Linear(16 * 5 * 5, 120)    # 5*5 from image dimension
        self.fc2 = nn.Linear(120, 84)
        self.fc3 = nn.Linear(84, 10)  # Assuming 10 classes for output

    def forward(self, x):
        x = self.pool(F.relu(self.conv1(x)))
        x = self.pool(F.relu(self.conv2(x)))
        x = x.view(-1, 16 * 5 * 5)  # Reshape before passing to fc layer
        x = F.relu(self.fc1(x))
        x = F.relu(self.fc2(x))
        x = self.fc3(x)
        return x


# Initialize the model
model = SimpleCNN()
```

When saving the **state_dict**, we utilize the **model.state_dict()** method to store the model's learnable parameters. It is key to note that only the model's tunable parameters are being saved in this process.

```python
# Save model state_dict
torch.save(model.state_dict(), "simple_cnn_state_dict.pt")
```

When loading and displaying the **state_dict**, it is important to recognize that the model object must be declared prior to loading the **state_dict**. The file **simple_cnn_state_dict.pt** does not contain any information linked to the model class. Another important point is, we must call **model.eval** before using the model for inference, and otherwise you will see inconsistencies in your evaluation.

Refer to the following code:

```
# Create a new model object
model2 = SimpleCNN()

# Load the state_dict into the model
model2.load_state_dict(torch.load("simple_cnn_state_dict.pt"))
model2.eval()
# Print model's state_dict
print("Model's state_dict:")
for param_tensor in model2.state_dict():
    print(param_tensor, "\t", model.state_dict()[param_tensor].size())
```

The output demonstrates that the **state_dict** is essentially a dictionary containing learnable parameters. It becomes clear that the **state_dict** encompasses the weights and biases for each layer within the neural network:

```
Model's state_dict:
conv1.weight torch.Size([6, 3, 5, 5])
conv1.bias    torch.Size([6])
conv2.weight torch.Size([16, 6, 5, 5])
conv2.bias    torch.Size([16])
fc1.weight    torch.Size([120, 400])
fc1.bias      torch.Size([120])
fc2.weight    torch.Size([84, 120])
fc2.bias      torch.Size([84])
fc3.weight    torch.Size([10, 84])
fc3.bias      torch.Size([10])
```

The key question that we must address is, Why is it standard practice to save the **state_dict** rather than the entire model? Several reasons substantiate this approach:

- **Versatility**: The **state_dict** is a Python dictionary object, hence it is easy to manage, interpret, and if required, modify. It gives the liberty to readily alter the parameters' values before injecting them into a different model.

- **Device compatibility**: The **state_dict** can be loaded onto any device regardless of its original save location. This facilitates better portability and sharing of models.

- **Efficiency in storage**: Typically, the **state_dict** takes up lesser disk space as it solely contains the model weights, unlike the entire model structure.

- **Model autonomy**: By saving the **state_dict**, we have the option to construct models that have similar structures but do not necessarily belong to the same class. This can prove advantageous in scenarios involving transfer learning.

Saving multiple models

There may be instances where your comprehensive model is composed of multiple neural networks. Take **Generative Adversarial Network (GAN)** as an example, which comprises two distinct networks: the generator and the discriminator. In such cases, it is recommended to store the entire model as a single dictionary. Here is a guide on how you can achieve this:

```
torch.save({
        'first_model_state': model1.state_dict(),
        'second_model_state': model2.state_dict(),
        'first_optimizer_state': optimizer1.state_dict(),
        'second_optimizer_state': optimizer2.state_dict(),
        # ... any other states
        }, file_path)
```

To load the model back to memory:

```
# initialize your models and optimizers first
model1 = Model1Class(*args, **kwargs)
model2 = Model2Class(*args, **kwargs)
optimizer1 = Optimizer1Class(*args, **kwargs)
optimizer2 = Optimizer2Class(*args, **kwargs)

# load the states from the file
saved_states = torch.load(file_path)
model1.load_state_dict(saved_states['first_model_state'])
model2.load_state_dict(saved_states['second_model_state'])
optimizer1.load_state_dict(saved_states['first_optimizer_state'])
optimizer2.load_state_dict(saved_states['second_optimizer_state'])

# switch to evaluation mode or training mode
model1.eval()  # or model1.train()
model2.eval()  # or model2.train()
```

Exporting model on ONNX Format

ONNX provides an open-source format for AI models, both deep learning and traditional ML. It defines an extensible computation graph model, as well as definitions of built-in operators and standard data types.

The main advantages of ONNX are:

- **Interoperability**: ONNX is supported by a variety of frameworks such as PyTorch, TensorFlow, MXNet, and tools like NVIDIA's TensorRT. You can train a model in one framework, export it to ONNX, and use it in another framework for inference.

- **Portability**: Models in ONNX format can be deployed on a variety of platforms, from cloud-based servers with powerful GPUs to edge devices like mobile phones and IoT devices.

- **Performance**: Some runtimes, like ONNX Runtime, can optimize the execution of the computation graph, leading to performance improvements.

To export a PyTorch model to ONNX format, you can use the **torch.onnx.export** function. The following code provides example of exporting and using the ONNX model for inference. When exporting a model to ONNX format, you need to provide a dummy input that matches the input your model expects. By passing through the dummy input, the exporter can infer the shape and data type of the input tensor, and these are then used in the exported ONNX graph as metadata. This allows ONNX runtime to understand what kind of input the model expects, including the shape and type.

Code:

```python
import torch
import torchvision
dummy_input = torch.randn(1, 3, 224, 224)
model = torchvision.models.alexnet(pretrained=True)
torch.onnx.export(model, dummy_input, "model.onnx")


# Inference
import onnxruntime
import numpy as np
ort_session = onnxruntime.InferenceSession('model.onnx')
# compute ONNX Runtime output prediction
ort_inputs = {ort_session.get_inputs()[0].name: np.random.
randn(1,3,224,224).astype(np.float32)}
ort_outs = ort_session.run(None, ort_inputs)
```

The accompanying notebook provides additional example of exporting and using HuggingFace models in ONNX.

Serving model with FastAPI

FastAPI is a modern, fast (high-performance), web framework for building APIs with Python 3.6+, based on standard Python type hints. It was developed as an efficient alternative to existing Python frameworks, such as Flask and Django, providing significant performance benefits and simplified syntax.

FastAPI takes advantage of Python's type checking, which makes your code more robust and simplifies debugging. It is also designed to work well with modern frontend JavaScript frameworks, which often consume RESTful APIs.

Key features of FastAPI include automatic interactive API documentation, inherent validation using Pydantic models, OAuth2 support with JWT tokens and password hashing, CORS handling, customizable exception handling, and more. It is asynchronous friendly and allows the usage of WebSockets and other web protocols.

Benefits of FastAPI

Some benefits of FastAPI are as follows:

- **Performance**: FastAPI is one of the fastest Python frameworks available, only lower than Starlette and Uvicorn, upon which it is built. It is faster than traditional frameworks and can even compete with NodeJS and Go.

- **Easy to code**: FastAPI's use of Python type hints and Pydantic models makes it easier to define API schemas, validate request data, and extract request data such as JSON fields, path parameters, and query parameters.

- **Automatic API documentation**: FastAPI generates an interactive API documentation UI automatically, making it easier for developers and users to understand and try out your API.

- **Support for modern Python features**: FastAPI supports asynchronous request handling, making it suitable for WebSockets and other scenarios requiring asynchronicity. It also supports HTTP/2 and WebSockets.

- **Robustness**: Thanks to automatic data validation and serialization using Pydantic, and Python's type hints, FastAPI applications tend to be bug-resistant and easier to debug and maintain.

Application of FastAPI for model serving

FastAPI is an excellent choice for serving machine learning models because it can quickly process incoming requests and make predictions using the model. It is also straightforward to set up routes that accept specific data types (for example, files for image processing models, JSON data for text or tabular models) and generate meaningful responses.

FastAPI's async capabilities make it possible to handle multiple requests concurrently, crucial for model serving scenarios where high throughput is necessary. Moreover, its support for Pydantic models and automatic validation ensures that the data sent to the model for prediction is correctly formatted, reducing the chance of errors.

Project: FastAPI for semantic segmentation model serving

We want to create model serving app for the food segmentation project we did in the *Chapter 8, Computer Vision Tasks with Transformers*. In the context of our food segmentation model, FastAPI provides a simple and efficient way to create an API endpoint for processing images. Users can send an image to the server, which processes the image, makes predictions using the trained segmentation model, and returns the segmented image.

Follow the given steps to do the same:

1. **Model initialization**: The Segformer model and its feature extractor are loaded when the FastAPI app is initialized. This allows the model to remain in memory, avoiding the time cost of reloading the model with each request.

   Code:

   ```
   feature_extractor = SegformerFeatureExtractor()
   model = SegformerForSemanticSegmentation.from_pretrained(
       "prem-timsina/segformer-b0-finetuned-food",
       id2label=id2label,
       label2id=label2id
   )
   ```

2. **API route definition**: FastAPI allows you to define API routes using Python decorators. In this case, the **@app.post("/segment/")** decorator is used to define a route that accepts POST requests at the "/segment/" endpoint:

   ```
   @app.post("/segment/")
   async def segment_image(file: UploadFile):
   ```

3. **Image processing**: The image sent in the request is read and converted into a format that the model can accept. This involves reading the bytes of the uploaded image and converting it into a PIL Image object.

4. **Model prediction**: The image is then passed through the feature extractor and the model to get the semantic segmentation prediction. The prediction is a 2D

array with the same dimensions as the input image, where each pixel is assigned a class label.

5. **Result conversion**: The raw prediction is then converted into an image, where each class label is assigned a specific color, creating a segmented image.

6. **Response generation**: The segmented image is returned to the client as a response. With FastAPI, it is straightforward to create various response types, including JSON, HTML, and in this case, image files.

The complete code for both server and client-side operations can be found in the corresponding GitHub repository. For deployment on the server side, the following command can be executed to launch the application:

```
uvicornmain:app --host localhost --port 8000
```

You can interact with the API endpoint through RESTful calls. Sample code for this process is available in the corresponding GitHub repository. In summary, FastAPI provides an efficient and developer-friendly way to serve machine learning models as APIs. Its performance, ease of use, and modern features make it a top choice for such use cases.

Serving Pytorch model in mobile devices

Serving a PyTorch model on mobile devices involves converting the model into a format that can be efficiently executed on mobile hardware. There are several ways to accomplish this, but here are two of the main methods:

- **TorchScript**: TorchScript is a tool offered by PyTorch that lets you turn your Python machine learning models into a form that can be run in a separate C++ program. This is helpful when you want to use your model in a different environment like a mobile or embedded device. To use TorchScript, you go through these steps:

  1. First, you adjust and improve your model in Python using either **torch.jit.trace** or **torch.jit.script**. These tools help you make your model more efficient and ready for TorchScript.

  2. Next, you turn the modified model into a script module and save it as a file using **torch.jit.save**. This process is called serialization.

  3. Finally, in your mobile application, you load this script module file using **torch::jit::load**.

  4. By following these steps, you can use the PyTorch mobile library to run your machine learning model on iOS or Android devices.

     Now, you have an exercise. There is a tutorial that shows you how to serve a specific model (DeepLabV3) on an iOS app. You can find it here **https://pytorch.org/tutorials/beginner/deeplabv3_on_ios.html**.

Your task is to go through this tutorial and apply what you learn to create an iOS app that serves a different model: the **'prem-timsina/segformer-b0-finetuned-food'** model. This exercise is an opportunity for you to apply what you have learned about TorchScript and PyTorch mobile library in a practical setting.

5   **ONNX and core ML**: Another option is to export your PyTorch model to the ONNX format, and then convert the ONNX model to Core ML format for use on iOS. This requires using the ONNX and Core ML tools, but allows your model to take advantage of the performance optimizations in Core ML. This approach might not support all types of PyTorch models, as the conversion from PyTorch to ONNX to Core ML might not support all operations used in the model. Here are the basic steps to use ONNX and Core ML:

   a. Export your PyTorch model to ONNX format using **torch.onnx.export**.

   b. Convert the ONNX model to Core ML format using the ONNX-Core ML converter.

   c. In your iOS app, load the Core ML model using the Core ML APIs.

It is important to remember that the performance of your model on mobile devices may vary, depending on the model and device. Some models might need extra tuning to run smoothly on mobile. That is why it is crucial to test your model in the environment you plan to deploy it in, to make sure that it is performing well and accurately.

Your task is to look at a tutorial about integrating a Core ML model into an app: (**https://developer.apple.com/documentation/coreml/integrating_a_core_ml_model_into_your_app**). Your goal is to understand how to serve a PyTorch model using Core ML, and apply this knowledge to create an iOS app that serves the 'prem-timsina/segformer-b0-finetuned-food' model.

Deploying HuggingFace's Transformers model on AWS

Deploying a transformers model on AWS can be done in several ways, depending on your requirements. Here we discuss two general approaches: deployment using Amazon SageMaker and using AWS Lambda and Amazon API Gateway.

Deployment using Amazon SageMaker

Amazon SageMaker is a fully managed machine learning service that provides developers and data scientists with the ability to build, train, and deploy machine learning models quickly. It provides support for deploying HuggingFace Transformer models directly. Here is one approach to deploy a pre-trained model:

1. **Create a SageMaker model**: First, you need to create a SageMaker model that specifies the S3 location of your model artifacts and the Docker image containing your inference code. HuggingFace provides pre-built Docker images for this purpose. Refer to the following code:

```
from sagemaker.huggingface import HuggingFaceModel


huggingface_model = HuggingFaceModel(
    # S3 path where the trained model is saved
    model_data='s3://my-bucket/path/model.tar.gz',
    # IAM role with the necessary permissions
    role='MySageMakerRole',
    # Transformers version used
    transformers_version='4.6',
    # PyTorch version used
    pytorch_version='2.0',
   # Python version used
    py_version='py3'
)
```

2. **Create a SageMaker endpoint**: Next, you need to create a SageMaker endpoint which will serve your model for real-time inference:

```
predictor = huggingface_model.deploy(
    initial_instance_count=1,
    instance_type='ml.m5.large'
)
```

3. **Inference**: Once your endpoint is **InService**, you can use the predict function of the predictor object to send inference requests to your endpoint:

```
result = predictor.predict("Hello, world!")
```

Deployment using AWS Lambda and Amazon API gateway

AWS Lambda is a service that lets you run code without provisioning or managing servers, while Amazon API Gateway is a fully managed service that makes it easy for developers to create, publish, maintain, monitor, and secure APIs at any scale. These two services can be used in tandem to serve a machine learning model for inference. Follow the given steps:

1. **Package your model and inference code**: First, you need to package your trained model along with the inference code (a script that loads the model and makes predictions using it) into a zip file. This zip file will be uploaded to AWS Lambda.

2. **Create a Lambda function**: Next, you create a new Lambda function, choosing **Python 3.8** as the runtime and uploading the zip file you created earlier. You need to specify the function to call within your script when the Lambda function is triggered (for example, `lambda_handler`).

3. **Create an API using API gateway**: You then create a new API using API gateway, setting the trigger of your Lambda function to be this API. This means that every time your API is hit, your Lambda function will be triggered to make a prediction.

4. **Inference**: Now you can make POST requests to your API, passing the input data for your model in the body of the request. The API Gateway triggers the Lambda function, which loads your model, makes a prediction, and returns the result.

Remember that using AWS Lambda for deploying machine learning models has limitations, especially in terms of payload size (the request/response body must not exceed 6 MB) and execution time (the maximum execution duration per request is 15 minutes). If your model is larger than the allowed limits, consider using Amazon SageMaker instead.

Note: For a more comprehensive understanding, please refer to the detailed documentation available at https://huggingface.co/docs/sagemaker/index.

Conclusion

This chapter has provided an in-depth exploration of key concepts such as model export and serialization, demonstrating methods including ONNX, PyTorch Script, and Pickle. We delved into the intricacies of saving and loading PyTorch models, highlighting the essential roles of **torch.save**, **torch.load**, and **torch.nn.Module.load_state_dict**, and the pivotal role of the **state_dict**.

Additionally, the process and benefits of exporting PyTorch models to ONNX format were discussed, emphasizing the advantages of interoperability, portability, and performance. We then examined the application of FastAPI for model serving, showcased through the creation of a model serving application for a food segmentation model. Subsequently, the potential of serving PyTorch models on mobile devices was discussed, comparing TorchScript to ONNX and Core ML, and applying these concepts through the creation of iOS apps serving the **'prem-timsina/segformer-b0-finetuned-food'** model.

Finally, deploying Hugging Face's Transformers model on AWS was explored, using methods like Amazon SageMaker, AWS Lambda, and Amazon API Gateway, providing a detailed guide on effectively leveraging these services for model deployment.

It is important to stress that the choice of model serving, export, and deployment methods should be tailored to your specific use case, model type, intended audience, and infrastructure constraints, with the hope that this chapter provides a comprehensive foundation for navigating these crucial aspects of the machine learning lifecycle.

Quiz

1. **What is model serialization in the context of machine learning?**

    a. Converting raw data into machine-readable form.

    b. Packaging a model into a format that can be stored or transferred.

    c. Automating the process of tuning model parameters.

    d. Developing machine learning models.

2. **How does ONNX enhance the usability of machine learning models?**

    a. It cleans the data for the models

    b. It serves the models

    c. It allows models to be used across different frameworks

    d. It trains the models

3. **What is FastAPI used for?**

    a. Data Visualization

    b. Model Training

    c. Building APIs

    d. Data Cleaning

4. **In the context of mobile applications, why is it beneficial to deploy machine learning models?**

    a. To provide a user interface for the model

    b. To enable on-device predictions

    c. To clean the data for the model

    d. To train the model

5. **What does the following part of the code do?**

    ```
    outputs = model(**input_tensor)
    predictions = outputs.logits.argmax(dim=1).squeeze().cpu().numpy()
    ```

    a. It performs the segmentation on the input image and converts the output to a numpy array.

    b. It computes the loss function of the model.

    c. It initializes the transformer model.

    d. It generates new input tensors for the model.

6. **What is the purpose of the following decorator in FastAPI?**

```
@app.post("/segment/")
```

    a. It defines a route for HTTP GET requests.

    b. It sets up an HTTP POST endpoint at the route "/segment/".

    c. It allows the function to handle both GET and POST requests.

    d. It provides a name for the function below it.

7. **In the context of the provided FastAPI code, why is the "async" keyword used before defining the "segment_image" function?**

```
async def segment_image(file: UploadFile)
```

    a. It turns the function into a coroutine which allows for non-blocking IO operations.

    b. It allows the function to run on multiple threads.

    c. It allows the function to be run in a separate process for parallel execution.

    d. It forces the function to complete execution before any other functions can be run.

8. **Which of the following statements about TorchScript is true?**

    a. TorchScript transforms your Python machine learning models into JavaScript code.

    b. TorchScript requires rewriting your model's architecture in C++.

    c. TorchScript uses either torch.jit.trace or torch.jit.script to prepare your model.

    d. TorchScript is a tool exclusively used for deploying models on servers.

9. **What is the correct sequence of model conversion for deploying a PyTorch model on an iOS device using ONNX and Core ML?**

    a. PyTorch -> Core ML -> ONNX

    b. PyTorch -> ONNX -> Core ML

    c. ONNX -> PyTorch -> Core ML

    d. Core ML -> ONNX -> PyTorch

Answers

1. b.

2. c.

3. c.

4. b.

5. a.

6. b.

7. a.

8. c.

9. b.

Join our book's Discord space

Join the book's Discord Workspace for Latest updates, Offers, Tech happenings around the world, New Release and Sessions with the Authors:

https://discord.bpbonline.com

## CHAPTER 16

Transformer Model Interpretability, and Experimental Visualization

Introduction

Machine learning interpretability is about understanding why a model chooses certain results. It helps us explain model outcomes. Deep learning models, like Transformers, can be very complicated. As they grow more advanced, it becomes harder to know why they decide certain things. This is especially important in areas like healthcare or self-driving cars, where model decisions can really affect people's lives. To use these models responsibly, we must understand their decisions. By understanding how a model thinks, we can make sure it is deciding things for good reasons and correct any wrong or biased choices.

Similarly, experimental logging and visualization help in fine-tuning and understanding machine learning models. Logging is recording how the model behaves during training, and visualization shows this information in charts or graphs. These tools make it easier to find and solve issues and get a clear picture of how the model operates. As models and datasets grow complex, it is crucial to log and visualize data to ensure things run correctly.

Considering the intricacy of Transformer models, in this chapter, we will explore tools and methods to interpret them. We will also see how to make these complex models more understandable. Plus, we will dive into tools that visually represent experimental data.

Structure

The book chapter is organized as:

- Explainability vs. interpretability

- Tools for explainability and interpretability

- CAPTUM for interpreting the transformer prediction.

- TensorBoard for PyTorch models

Objectives

In this chapter, we will explore the interpretation and explanation of transformer models. The chapter draws a clear line between interpretability—understanding a model's inner processes—and explainability—conveying these processes in relatable terms. Given the increasing use of transformer models in critical sectors like healthcare and autonomous vehicles, the importance of transparency is emphasized. We highlight tools like experimental logging and visualization to shed light on a model's behavior during training. The chapter introduces key tools like CAPTUM, which interprets Transformer predictions, and TensorBoard for PyTorch Models, aiding in making complex models more accessible and transparent.

Explainability vs. interpretability

Interpretability and explainability are two important concepts in the field of machine learning, often used interchangeably, but they do have distinct differences.

Interpretability is the degree to which a human can understand the inner workings of a machine learning model or how the model makes decisions based on given inputs. An interpretable model allows you to predict what is going to happen, given a change in input or algorithmic parameters. For example, linear regression models are considered highly interpretable because it is clear how changes in the input variables affect the output.

Explainability, on the other hand, is the extent to which a machine learning model's behavior can be explained in human-understandable terms. It focuses on providing understandable descriptions of how a model arrives at a decision, even if the internal workings of the model itself are not fully understood or transparent. This is often the case with complex models like neural networks and ensemble models. For instance, explaining a decision made by a deep learning model in terms of which features were most influential in driving the prediction. In the following section, we will discuss both interpretability and explainability in the context of transformer model.

Interpretability

Let us consider the self-attention mechanism in a transformer, which allows the model to focus on different words when making predictions. In the context of interpretability, we could look at the attention scores the model assigns when processing the word *intriguing*.

If the model is functioning correctly, it should *pay attention* to the word *intriguing* when trying to determine the sentiment of the sentence. We can visualize this with an attention map. The attention map might show high attention scores between *intriguing* and *not only*, and between *intriguing* and *but also*. This is because these phrases indicate that the word *intriguing* is being used in a positive context.

Explainability

In the context of **explainability**, we want to describe how the model arrived at its final prediction. For our sentiment analysis example, let us say the model correctly predicts that the sentiment of the sentence is positive.

An explainability tool like LIME could help us understand this decision. LIME creates a simplified, locally linear version of the model around the prediction we are interested in explaining. It perturbs the input sentence, gets new predictions, and weighs them based on their proximity to the original sentence.

LIME might show us that the words *intriguing* and *suspense* were highly influential in the model's decision to classify the sentiment as positive.

Tools for explainability and interpretability

When dealing with Transformer models, we have several tools and techniques that aid both in interpretability and explainability, such as:

- **Attention maps**: These are widely used for both interpretability and explainability of Transformer models. They allow us to visualize the attention weights in each layer of the model, highlighting the input tokens that each output token is attending to. For example, in a language translation task, an attention map can show which words in the source sentence are being considered while generating each word in the target sentence.

- **BERTViz**: This tool is specifically designed for the BERT model, a type of Transformer model. It visualizes attention in the model, helping with both interpretability (understanding how different parts of the model are interacting) and explainability (understanding which parts of the input sentence were most important for a particular output).

- **ExBERT**: This tool allows interactive exploration of BERT models. It provides multiple ways to analyze the model, such as neuron activations and attention distributions, thus aiding in both interpretability and explainability.

- **Local Interpretable Model-agnostic Explanations (LIME)**: While not specifically designed for Transformers, LIME can be used with any model to help explain individual predictions. It works by approximating the model locally with an interpretable one and can thus provide insights into what features the model is using to make predictions.

- **Captum**: Captum is a model interpretability library for PyTorch. It allows researchers and developers to understand how the data is being used and transformed within their models. Captum offers a wide variety of attribution algorithms that provide insights into the importance of individual features, and how they contribute to model predictions.

Several other notable tools that should be mentioned include Eli5[1], SHAP[2], and **TensorFlow Model Analysis (TFMA)**[3]. In the next section, we will demonstrate how we can use Captum for interpretability and explainability.

CAPTUM for interpreting Transformer prediction

In the following section, we will use Captum with the model **distilbert-base-uncased-finetuned-sst-2-english** to interpret the sentiment analysis of a given text. Let us explain the key components and how they work.

Model loading

We are using the pre-trained DistilBERT model fine-tuned for **sentiment analysis (SST-2).** This model classifies given text into positive or negative sentiment:

```
# Pre-trained model and tokenizer

model_path = 'distilbert-base-uncased-finetuned-sst-2-english'

model = DistilBertForSequenceClassification.from_pretrained(model_path)

tokenizer = DistilBertTokenizer.from_pretrained(model_path)

model.eval()
```

---

[1] https://eli5.readthedocs.io/en/latest/overview.html

[2] https://shap.readthedocs.io/en/latest/

[3] https://www.tensorflow.org/tfx/tutorials/model_analysis/tfma_basic

Input preparation

The function **construct_input_and_baseline** is designed to take a textual input and transform it into tensors that can be fed into a model, such as DistilBERT. In addition to the model's input tensor, the function also constructs a baseline tensor. Let us break down what is happening here, specifically focusing on the concept of the baseline tensor.

Input Tensor

Refer to the following:

- **Text tokenization**: The input text is tokenized into a sequence of integers using the model's tokenizer. This sequence represents the words and sub words in the original text.

- **Add special tokens**: Special tokens **[CLS]** and **[SEP]** are added at the beginning and end of the sequence, respectively.

- **Input IDs**: The resulting sequence of integers (**input_ids**) is converted into a tensor that can be fed into the model.

Baseline Tensor

The baseline tensor is a reference input that represents the absence or neutral state of the features you are trying to interpret. In the context of NLP, a common choice for the baseline is a sequence of padding tokens. Refer to the following:

- **Baseline Token ID**: The ID corresponding to the padding token is retrieved (**baseline_token_id**).

- **Create Baseline Sequence**: The baseline sequence is created by replacing the text's tokens with the padding token ID. The special tokens **[CLS]** and **[SEP]** are retained at the beginning and end of the sequence.

- **Baseline Input IDs**: The resulting sequence (**baseline_input_ids**) is converted into a tensor.

Example:

Suppose the input text is **"I love movies"**, and the corresponding token IDs after tokenization are **[10, 18, 27]**. The constructed input tensor and baseline tensor might look like this:

- Input IDs: [CLS_ID, 10, 18, 27, SEP_ID]

- Baseline Input IDs: [CLS_ID, PAD_ID, PAD_ID, PAD_ID, SEP_ID]

Why Baseline Tensor

The baseline tensor is used in certain attribution methods like Integrated Gradients to understand how much each feature contributes to the difference between the model's prediction for the actual input and the baseline. By comparing the model's behavior on the input to its behavior on this baseline, you can interpret how important each feature is for the prediction.

In summary, the following code snippet is constructing both the actual input to the model (reflecting the text you want to analyze) and a baseline input (reflecting a neutral or non-informative version of the text). The comparison between these two inputs will be used to understand how the model is interpreting the text.

The text and baseline are tokenized and converted into tensors. A baseline is often a reference input that represents the absence of the features of interest (for example, all padding tokens):

```python
def construct_input_and_baseline(input_text: str):

    """Constructs input and baseline tensors for the given text."""

    max_length = 768

    baseline_token_id = tokenizer.pad_token_id

    sep_token_id = tokenizer.sep_token_id

    cls_token_id = tokenizer.cls_token_id


    text_ids = tokenizer.encode(input_text, max_length=max_length,
truncation=True, add_special_tokens=False)

    input_ids = [cls_token_id] + text_ids + [sep_token_id]

    baseline_input_ids = [cls_token_id] + [baseline_token_id] * len(text_
ids) + [sep_token_id]

    token_list = tokenizer.convert_ids_to_tokens(input_ids)


    return torch.tensor([input_ids], device='cpu'), torch.tensor([baseline_
input_ids], device='cpu'), token_list


# Constructing input and baseline

input_ids, baseline_input_ids, all_tokens = construct_input_and_
baseline(text)
```

Layer Integrated Gradients

The code uses an attribution method to clarify how a model's predictions are influenced by different parts of its input, which are tokens in this case. Here is a breakdown of its key components:

- **Model output function**: The function named **model_output** is a wrapper around the model's forward pass. It extracts the prediction scores (often referred to as logits) from the model's output.

- **Setting up layer integrated gradients**: The `LayerIntegratedGradients` function is initialized with two primary components:

  o The model's forward function, represented by `model_output`.

  o The specific layer of the model we're interested in examining, which is the embeddings layer (`model.distilbert.embeddings`).

- **Attribution calculation**:

  o The code computes attributions for both sentiment classes (positive and negative). Attributions essentially give us a score, indicating how much each token influenced the prediction for each sentiment class.

- **Attribution summarization and normalization**:

  o The importance scores (attributions) for each token are aggregated by summing across the embedding dimensions.

  o These aggregated scores are then normalized to ensure that their magnitudes are comparable. The outcome is a 1D tensor, where each value signifies the relative significance of its corresponding token. For instance, if we are looking at negative sentiment, a higher score would mean that the token strongly suggests a negative sentiment.

- **Choosing attributions based on prediction**:

  o The model determines whether a given text is positive or negative in sentiment.

  o Depending on this prediction, the code selects the corresponding set of attributions, either positive or negative, to analyze further.

In essence, this approach provides an in-depth look into which words or phrases have most sway the model's sentiment prediction. Refer to the following:

```
#Model Output Function
def model_output(inputs):
    return model(inputs)[0]


#Setting Up Layer Integrated Gradients
lig = LayerIntegratedGradients(model_output, model.distilbert.embeddings)


# Attribution Calculation
target_classes = [0, 1]
attributions = {}
delta = {}
```

```
# Calculating attributions for both classes
# We will calculate the attributions for each class
for target_class in target_classes:
    attributions[target_class], delta[target_class] = lig.attribute(
        inputs=input_ids,
        baselines=baseline_input_ids,
        target=target_class,
        return_convergence_delta=True,
        internal_batch_size=1)

#Attributions summarization and normalization
neg_attributions = attributions[0].sum(dim=-1).squeeze(0) / torch.
norm(attributions[0])

pos_attributions = attributions[1].sum(dim=-1).squeeze(0) / torch.
norm(attributions[1])

# Choosing Attribution based on the Prediction
pred_prob, pred_class = torch.max(model(input_ids)[0]), int(torch.
argmax(model(input_ids)[0]))

# Selecting the attributions based on the predicted class
summarized_attr = pos_attributions if pred_class == 1 else neg_attributions
```

Visualization

Captum provides visualization tools like **viz.visualize_text** to represent the attributions visually. It shows the tokens and their corresponding importance scores, highlighting the tokens that are more influential in the model's decision. Let us understand the important aspect of the following code:

- **true_class=None**: This indicates the actual or ground-truth class for the input text. Since we are not providing any ground truth in this context, it is set to **None**.

- **raw_input_ids=all_tokens**: This provides the tokenized version of the input text (**all_tokens**) which helps in mapping attributions back to their respective words/tokens in the visualization.

- **convergence_score=delta[pred_class]**: This score measures the quality or reliability of the calculated attributions. A smaller convergence score indicates that the attributions are more reliable.

Refer to the following code:

```
score_vis = viz.VisualizationDataRecord(
                    word_attributions=summarized_attr,
                    pred_prob=pred_prob,
                    pred_class=pred_class,
                    true_class=None,
                    attr_class=text,
                    attr_score=summarized_attr.sum(),
                    raw_input_ids=all_tokens,
                    convergence_score=delta[pred_class])


# Visualizing the result
viz.visualize_text([score_vis])
```

Figure 16.1 is the captum visualization. As you can see, words *awesome* and *enjoyed* has highest attributions score for the positive sentiment predictions:

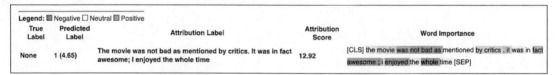

Figure 16.1: *The result of captum visualization*

TensorBoard for PyTorch models

TensorBoard, initially developed for TensorFlow, has become a vital visualization toolkit for neural network training across different frameworks. For PyTorch enthusiasts, the **torch.utils.tensorboard** integration allows them to leverage TensorBoard's robust visualization capabilities, ranging from monitoring training milestones to examining learned embeddings. To initiate TensorBoard, input **tensorboard --logdir=runs** into the terminal. By default, access to TensorBoard is available at **http://localhost:6006**.

You can visualize a variety of things related to your PyTorch models and training sessions. Here are the key visualizations you can achieve using TensorBoard with PyTorch:

- **Scalars**: Scalars refer to simple, single-number metrics that you track over time or iterations. They are typically used to log and visualize metrics that change with each epoch or iteration, such as training loss, validation accuracy, learning rate, and so on. The following code shows how you can visualize the training loss over the 100 epochs:

```
import torch
from torch.utils.tensorboard import SummaryWriter

# Create a dummy model and optimizer
model = torch.nn.Linear(10, 1)
optimizer = torch.optim.SGD(model.parameters(), lr=0.01)

# Instantiate SummaryWriter
writer = SummaryWriter()

for epoch in range(100):
    # Dummy training loop
    optimizer.zero_grad()
    output = model(torch.randn(32, 10))
    loss = ((output - torch.randn(32, 1))**2).mean()
    loss.backward()
    optimizer.step()

    # Log loss to TensorBoard
    writer.add_scalar("Training loss", loss, epoch)

# Close the writer
writer.close()
```

- **Histogram**: Visualize the distribution of tensor values, for example, layer weights. The following code demonstrates how you can visualize the model's named parameter as histogram:

```
for name, weight in model.named_parameters():
    writer.add_histogram(name, weight, epoch)
```

- **Text**: Log textual information. The following code snippet shows how you can log textual data:

```
writer.add_text('Loss_Text', 'The training loss was very low this
epoch', epoch)
```

- **Distribution**: It is just a smoother version of the histogram. You can use the same code you use for histogram.

- **Visualizing model graphs**: Beyond just scalars, you can visualize the architecture of your model. The following code shows how you can visualize the Bert Architecture:

```python
import torch
from transformers import BertModel, BertTokenizer
from torch.utils.tensorboard import SummaryWriter

# Load pre-trained BERT model and tokenizer
model_name = "bert-base-uncased"
bert_model = BertModel.from_pretrained(model_name)
tokenizer = BertTokenizer.from_pretrained(model_name)

class SimpleBERT(torch.nn.Module):
    def __init__(self, bert_model):
        super(SimpleBERT, self).__init__()
        self.bert = bert_model

    def forward(self, input_ids, attention_mask=None, token_type_
ids=None):
        outputs = self.bert(input_ids, attention_mask=attention_mask,
token_type_ids=token_type_ids)
        return outputs.last_hidden_state

model = SimpleBERT(bert_model)

# Instantiate the SummaryWriter
writer = SummaryWriter()

# Create a dummy input for the BERT model
tokens = tokenizer("Hello, TensorBoard!", return_tensors="pt")
input_ids = tokens["input_ids"]
attention_mask = tokens["attention_mask"]

# Add the BERT model graph to TensorBoard
writer.add_graph(model, [input_ids, attention_mask])

# Close the writer
writer.close()
```

- **Embedding**: Using this functionality, you can visualize the embedding of tokens in 3-D space. When you view the embeddings in TensorBoard, you will see each token (word/sub-word) positioned in the embedding space. The similar word should appear near whereas dissimilar word should appear further. Refer to the following code:

```
with torch.no_grad():
    embeddings = model(input_ids, attention_mask=attention_mask)


# Just as an example, using the tokens as metadata
# Note: We remove the [CLS] and [SEP] tokens for visualization.
metadata = [token for token in tokenizer.tokenize(text)]
embeddings = embeddings[0, 1:-1, :]  # Removing embeddings for [CLS]
and [SEP]


writer.add_embedding(embeddings, metadata=metadata)


# Close the writer
writer.close()
```

- **PR curves**: For understanding classification performance. Refer to the following code:

```
probs = model(input_data)
writer.add_pr_curve('pr_curve', true_labels, probs, epoch)
```

- **Hyperparameters**: Visualize hyperparameters. Refer to the following code:

```
hparams = {'lr': 0.1, 'batch_size': 32}
metrics = {'accuracy': 0.8}
writer.add_hparams(hparams, metrics)
```

- **Profiling**: In the case of PyTorch's torch.profiler, it is specifically designed to profile the execution of PyTorch models. When you profile a PyTorch model, here are some things you are typically interested in:

  o **Operator-level performance**: Which specific operations (for example, matrix multiplications, convolutions) are taking the most time? How long does each operation take to execute?

  o **Memory consumption**: Which operations consume the most memory? This is crucial for deep learning models which can often be memory-bound.

  o **Call stack information**: Which lines in your source code correspond to the various operations? This helps link the profiled performance data back to specific lines of your code.

o **CPU/GPU time**: How long are operations taking on the CPU versus the GPU? This can help in identifying data transfer bottlenecks, among other things.

When this information is logged to TensorBoard using **writer.add_text()**, you can visualize and analyze it, making it easier to understand the performance characteristics of your model. This is especially valuable when you are trying to optimize a model to run faster or when diagnosing performance issues. The following code snippet demonstrates how you can profile the training steps:

```
for inputs, targets in dataloader:
    with torch.profiler.profile(with_stack=True) as prof:
        train_step(inputs, targets)


    # Log the profiling results to TensorBoard
    writer.add_text("Profile", str(prof.key_averages().table()))
```

- **Visualizing image data**: For convolutional networks or any model working with image data, visualizing the input or output can be informative. Refer to the following code:

```
images = torch.randn(32, 3, 64, 64) # Simulating a batch of 32 images
grid = torchvision.utils.make_grid(images)
writer.add_image("images", grid, 0)
```

The end-to-end code for Tensorboard logging discussed above is provided in the accompanying notebook.

Conclusion

In this chapter, we dissected the subtle distinctions between interpretability and explainability within the sphere of machine learning. We delved into methods such as attention maps, LIME, and Captum to grasp the interpretability and explainability of the transformer model, highlighting a hands-on example with CAPTUM to comprehend DistilBERT's predictions. Moreover, we examined TensorBoard's adaptability for PyTorch models, emphasizing its pivotal role in tracking training phases, illustrating model structures, and gauging performance. These tools provide professionals with the requisite means to assess, hone, and enhance their models, ensuring their optimal functionality. To conclude, even if Transformers and related deep learning models seem like **black boxes**, the tools and strategies elaborated on in this chapter provide insight into these mysteries. As we amplify the influence of these models across vital societal sectors, the necessity to decipher their core mechanisms becomes ever more pressing.

Quiz

1. **Which of the following best describes the concept of "interpretability" in machine learning?**

    a. The degree to which a machine learning model's behavior can be explained in human-understandable terms.

    b. The degree to which a human can understand the inner workings of a machine learning model.

    c. A tool to visualize the attention weights in machine learning models.

    d. A method to predict the output of a model based on given inputs.

2. **What is the primary focus of "explainability" in machine learning?**

    a. Understanding the algorithms used within a model.

    b. Understanding how a model makes decisions based on given inputs.

    c. Providing understandable descriptions of how a model arrives at a decision.

    d. Predicting the output of a model based on changes in inputs.

3. **In the context of NLP, what is commonly used as a baseline tensor?**

    a. A sequence of attention scores.

    b. A sequence of padding tokens.

    c. A sequence of special tokens.

    d. A sequence of embedding layers.

4. **What is the purpose of a baseline tensor in attribution methods like Integrated Gradients?**

    a. To visualize the model's behavior on input data.

    b. To visualize the attention map of a transformer model.

    c. To understand the importance of each feature for a prediction by comparing the model's behavior on the input to its behavior on a baseline.

    d. To visualize the neuron activations in a transformer model.

5. **In the code snippet, what does the Layer Integrated Gradients (LIG) method primarily do?**

    a. Visualizes the model's forward function.

    b. Creates a simplified, locally linear version of the model.

    c. Clarifies how a model's predictions are influenced by different parts of its input.

    d. Loads pre-trained models and tokenizers.

6. **What does the viz.visualize_text function do in the code snippet provided in the chapter?**

    a. Initializes Layer Integrated Gradients.

    b. Computes attributions for both sentiment classes.

    c. Visualizes the attributions and their corresponding importance scores.

    d. Loads pre-trained models and tokenizers.

7. **What is TensorBoard primarily used for?**

    a. Profiling the execution of TensorFlow models only

    b. Visualizing training and analyzing neural network models across different frameworks

    c. Logging errors during the model training process

    d. Testing the performance of PyTorch models exclusively

8. **How do you initiate TensorBoard?**

    a. tensorboard --logdir=runs

    b. tensorboard --start=runs

    c. tensorboard --init=runs

    d. tensorboard --launch=runs

9. **Which of the following can be used to visualize the training loss over epochs in TensorBoard?**

    a. writer.add_text

    b. writer.add_histogram

    c. writer.add_scalar

    d. writer.add_image

10. **Which visualization technique enables the visualization of embeddings of tokens in 3-D space?**

    a. Scalars

    b. Histogram

    c. Embedding

    d. PR Curves

11. **What can you analyze with the profiling feature in TensorBoard with PyTorch integration?**

    a. Only memory consumption

    b. Only CPU/GPU time

    c. Only operator-level performance

    d. Operator-level performance, memory consumption, call stack information, and CPU/GPU time

12. **Where can you access TensorBoard by default?**

    a. http://localhost:8000

    b. http://localhost:6006

    c. http://localhost:5000

    d. http://localhost:3000

Answers

   1. b.

   2. c.

   3. b.

   4. c.

   5. c.

   6. c.

   7. b.

   8. a.

   9. b.

  10. c.

  11. d.

  12. b.

## CHAPTER 17

PyTorch Models: Best Practices and Debugging

Introduction

The cliché quotation, *great power comes with great responsibility* is somehow true for the transformer model. The very characteristics that make transformer models so potent, such as their deep architecture, multi-headed attention mechanisms, and large parameter count, also make them susceptible to a variety of issues during the implementation and training phases. Simple mistakes, be it in model initialization, data pre-processing, or even in the configuration of the optimizer, can lead to hours, if not days, of debugging.

This reality has ushered in the need for a structured approach to building and troubleshooting transformer models in PyTorch. As the community around the framework grows and shares its collective experiences, certain best practices and common pitfalls have come to light. Whether you are a seasoned developer looking to fine-tune your models or a newcomer eager to get your hands dirty, understanding these practices and pitfalls is crucial.

This chapter aims to be your guiding hand in this endeavor. By weaving together theoretical insights with hands-on examples, we provide a comprehensive overview of best practices when constructing transformers in PyTorch. Additionally, we delve deep into practical techniques that will empower you to swiftly identify and rectify common issues.

By the end of this chapter, you will possess the knowledge and tools needed to harness the full potential of transformer models while navigating the intricacies of PyTorch with confidence and efficiency.

Structure

The book is organized as follows:

- Best practices for building transformer models

- The Art of Debugging in PyTorch

Objectives

The primary objective of this chapter is to arm readers with a comprehensive understanding of the intricacies involved in constructing and debugging transformer models using PyTorch. Through detailed exploration of best practices, from model initialization to optimization, we aim to enhance efficiency, bolster reproducibility, and facilitate a smooth transition across diverse modeling scenarios. By demystifying the challenges, particularly in the realm of debugging, this chapter seeks to empower practitioners to confidently navigate the complex landscape of modern machine learning with transformer models.

Best practices for building transformer models

Whether you are fine-tuning a pre-trained model or training one from scratch, certain best practices can ensure your work is efficient, reproducible, and effective. In this section, we will delve deep into these practices, highlighting the nuances of both scenarios.

Working with Hugging Face

The subsequent section outlines best practices specifically for working with Hugging Face models. However, these guidelines are also relevant and applicable to other libraries.

- **Tokenization**: Choosing the right tokenizer and managing special tokens are crucial aspects. Let us dig deeper into this.

  o **Select the right tokenizer:** Always use the tokenizer that matches your chosen pre-trained model. For each model type (BERT, GPT-2, RoBERTa, and so on), you have to choose the corresponding tokenizer.

  o **Manage special tokens:** Not all models implicitly handle special tokens like `[CLS]`, `[SEP]`, `<s>`, and `<\s>`. While it is vital to ensure these tokens are incorporated where needed, it is also worth noting that not every tokenizer automatically includes them. For instance, with GPT-2, special tokens often need manual specification. Following is a code snippet demonstrating how to add special tokens for the GPT-2 model:

```
special_tokens_dict = {'bos_token': '<BOS>', 'eos_token':
'<EOS>', 'pad_token': '<PAD>'}
```

```
num_added_toks = tokenizer.add_special_tokens(special_tokens_dict)
```

- **Handling sequence length**: Be aware of the maximum length when working with models, as different models have varying token limits. For instance, BERT has a token limit of 512, while GPT-2 has a limit of 768. It is essential to ensure that your sequences do not surpass these limits. Additionally, pay attention to truncation and padding. Handling longer sequences may require truncation or other techniques, while shorter sequences might need padding. Fortunately, most Hugging Face tokenizers provide automatic padding and truncation features to streamline this process.

- **Attention masks**: Here are a few considerations related to the attention mask.

  o **Differentiate real tokens from pads**: Attention masks should be set to 1 for real tokens and 0 for padding tokens, so that the model does not pay attention to padding.

  o **Use the Tokenizer's output**: Hugging Face's tokenizer provides the attention mask automatically when you tokenize. The following code illustrates the attention mask on hugging face library:

  ```
  from transformers import BertTokenizer
  ```

  ```
  tokenizer = BertTokenizer.from_pretrained('bert-base-uncased')
  ```

  ```
  # Example sentences
  ```

  ```
  sentences = ["Hello world!", "Attention masks are important."]
  ```

  ```
  encoded_input = tokenizer(sentences, padding='max_length',
  truncation=True, max_length=10, return_attention_mask=True)
  ```

  ```
  print(encoded_input['input_ids'])
  ```

  ```
  print(encoded_input['attention_mask'])
  ```

  o The output of the above code is shown as follows. In the attention mask, 1 represents actual tokens while 0 indicates padding tokens:

  ```
  input_ids: [[101, 7592, 2088, 999, 102, 0, 0, 0, 0, 0], [101,
  3086, 10047, 2024, 2590, 1012, 102, 0, 0, 0]]
  ```

  ```
  attention_mask: [[1, 1, 1, 1, 1, 0, 0, 0, 0, 0], [1, 1, 1, 1, 1,
  1, 1, 0, 0, 0]]
  ```

- **Batching:** All sequences in a batch should have the same length. This might mean padding shorter sequences in a batch to match the length of the longest sequence. For better efficiency, consider padding to the maximum length in each batch rather than a global maximum length. Following is the example where we are doing dynamic batching. In the context of batching, it is important to grasp the variability in sequence lengths. For instance, dataset[0] and dataset[1] have different lengths of 5 and 7, respectively. The role of the **data_collator = DataCollatorWithPadding(tokenizer=tokenizer)** is crucial here. It ensures dynamic batching, where the sequence length within each batch matches the length of the longest sequence in that batch. This functionality becomes indispensable when working with real-world datasets that may contain both very short and very long sequences. Implementing this can notably accelerate the training process while optimizing computational efficiency and memory usage.

Code:

```python
from transformers import BertTokenizer, BertForSequenceClassification,
TrainingArguments, Trainer, DataCollatorWithPadding
from torch.utils.data import Dataset

# 1. Initialization
tokenizer = BertTokenizer.from_pretrained('bert-base-uncased')

# Data preparation
sentences = ["Hello world!", "I love machine learning.", "Transformers
are powerful.", "HuggingFace is great for NLP tasks."]
labels = [0, 1, 1, 0]

# Tokenize without padding and without converting to tensors
encodings = tokenizer(sentences, truncation=True, padding=False,
return_tensors=None)

# Custom dataset
class CustomDataset(Dataset):
    def __init__(self, encodings, labels):
        self.encodings = encodings
        self.labels = labels

    def __getitem__(self, idx):
        item = {key: torch.tensor(val[idx]) for key, val in self.
encodings.items()}
        item["labels"] = torch.tensor(self.labels[idx])
        return item

    def __len__(self):
        return len(self.labels)
```

```
dataset = CustomDataset(encodings, labels)

# 2. Model Initialization
model    =    BertForSequenceClassification.from_pretrained('bert-base-
uncased', num_labels=2)

# 3. Data Collator for Dynamic Padding
data_collator = DataCollatorWithPadding(tokenizer=tokenizer)

# 4. Training Arguments
training_args = TrainingArguments(
    per_device_train_batch_size=2,
    logging_dir='./logs',
    logging_steps=1,
    evaluation_strategy="steps",
    eval_steps=1,
    save_strategy="steps",
    save_steps=1,
    no_cuda=False,
    output_dir="./results",
    overwrite_output_dir=True,
    do_train=True
)

# 5. Trainer Initialization
trainer = Trainer(
    model=model,
    args=training_args,
    train_dataset=dataset,
    data_collator=data_collator
)

# 6. Training
trainer.train()
```

Let us print some samples from the dataset:

```
print('dataset[0]',dataset[0]['input_ids'])
print('dataset[1]',dataset[1]['input_ids'])
```

Output:

```
dataset[0] tensor([ 101, 7592, 2088,  999,  102])
dataset[1] tensor([ 101, 1045, 2293, 3698, 4083, 1012,  102])
```

- **Leverage pipelines from Hugging Face**: Often, leveraging Hugging Face's high-level functionalities simplifies data pre-processing, training, and inference tasks. For a comprehensive list and detailed insights, refer to the official documentation (**https://huggingface.co/docs/transformers/main_classes/pipelines**).

Table 17.1 lists a brief overview of some valuable pipelines they offer:

Higher order function	Description	Usage
Feature extraction pipeline	Extracts the model's hidden states	pipeline('feature-extraction')
Sentiment analysis pipeline	Determines if a sentence is positive or negative	pipeline('sentiment-analysis')
Text generation pipeline	Generates text based on a given prompt	pipeline('text-generation')
Text classification pipeline	Classifies texts based on given labels	pipeline('text-classification')
Token classification pipeline	Named Entity Recognition	pipeline('token-classification')
Image classification pipeline	Classifies images based on given labels.	pipeline('image-classification')
Object detection pipeline	Identifies objects within images.	pipeline('object-detection')

Table 17.1: *List of Hugging Face Pipelines*

- **Use higher level functions for training**: After diligently crafting your code and testing it, the next step is to train your model on the complete dataset in a distributed manner. Fortunately, there are advanced tools that empower you to flexibly select and fine-tune aspects like the type of device, number of available GPUs, mixed-precision training, and gradient accumulation. Three of the most prominent tools in this domain are **accelerate**, **Trainer**, and **torchrun**. It is prudent to familiarize yourself with these tools, leveraging their capabilities, rather than reinventing the wheel.

   o **Accelerate by Hugging Face**: Accelerate is a lightweight library developed by Hugging Face to simplify the sophistications of mixed precision and distributed training in PyTorch. This tool is particularly advantageous when there is a need for a direct method to harness the benefits of mixed precision training, multi-GPU, and distributed training without diving deep into modifications of existing PyTorch code. Moreover, for those seeking flexibility in training configurations without being entirely dependent on the Hugging Face ecosystem, accelerate offers an ideal solution. In the domain of distributed training, the library presents an easy approach to distribute computations over an array of devices, including CPUs and GPUs, spanning even across multiple machines. It effectively abstracts the setup intricacies of `torch.distributed`, enabling users to toggle between single and multi-GPU training with minimal alterations in the code.

o **Trainer from Hugging Face:** Hugging Face's Trainer module offers a top-notch API designed for training and checking their models. If you are using datasets and models from the Hugging Face library, this tool is perfect. It comes packed with features such as keeping track of data, saving models, and assessing them. With Trainer, you do not have to build your training process from scratch. When it comes to distributed training (using multiple GPUs or TPUs), Trainer makes things simple.

o **Torchrun:** In PyTorch, the torchrun module, formerly known as `torch.distributed.launch`, plays a crucial role in facilitating distributed training by launching multiple processes. For those leveraging PyTorch and aiming to establish distributed training without the need for additional libraries, torchrun is an ideal choice. It is particularly beneficial for those seeking granular control over the distributed setup and the training loop. Examining its distributed training capabilities, torchrun efficiently sets up the distributed environment and starts training across all available nodes or GPUs. As a foundational method for implementing distributed training in PyTorch, torchrun requires users to handle tasks like setting the distributed strategy, merging gradients, and determining device placements manually.

o **Conclusion**: If you are primarily working with Hugging Face models and datasets, `Trainer` offers a comprehensive solution. On the other hand, if you are working with pure PyTorch and have a custom training loop, or want maximum control, `torchrun` offers a direct way to set up distributed training. If you want to abstract some of the complexities, accelerate might be a good addition.

General consideration with Pytorch model

Following are the general guidelines that are applicable for general Pytorch based model:

- **Model parameters**: Use appropriate weight initialization methods (like Xavier or He initialization) depending on the activation function used.

- **Training**: Following are some guidelines related to training:

o **Autograd**: Ensure you zero out the gradients at the start of each training iteration using `optimizer.zero_grad()` to prevent accumulation.

o **Checkpoints:** Save intermediate model states during training to resume training or use the best model later. Remember to save not just the model's `state_dict` but also the optimizer's state if needed.

o **Model Modes:** Use `model.train()` before training and `model.eval()` before evaluation/testing to ensure layers like dropout and batch normalization work correctly.

o **Perform Gradient Clipping:** Gradient clipping involves limiting the value of gradients to a small range to prevent undesirable changes in model parameters during updates. Consider using gradient clipping if you notice extremely large gradients or NaN values during training. As shown in the following code, you will do gradient clipping before the `optimizer.step`:

```
# Forward pass
output = model(input_tensor)
loss = loss_fn(output, target_tensor)
# Backward pass
optimizer.zero_grad()
loss.backward()
# Gradient Clipping
torch.nn.utils.clip_grad_norm_(model.parameters(), max_norm=1.0)
# Optimizer step
optimizer.step()
```

• **Optimization**: During the training process, it is beneficial to employ learning rate scheduling techniques such as step decay or one-cycle learning rate. These methods dynamically adjust the learning rate as training progresses. Additionally, it is advisable to implement early stopping by monitoring a specific validation metric. Training should be halted once this metric ceases to show improvement.

• **Evaluation**: To ensure deterministic results, especially during evaluations, it is essential to set random seeds and turn off any non-deterministic algorithms. This ensures that results are consistent across runs. Additionally, when performing inference, it is recommended to enclose forward passes within the `torch.no_grad()` context. This action not only helps in conserving memory but also boosts the inference speed.

• **Device Management**: It is crucial to develop device-agnostic code to ensure compatibility across various hardware. One way to achieve this is by setting the device variable with the code snippet: `device = torch.device("cuda" if` `torch.cuda.is_available() else "cpu")`. This ensures that your code runs on a GPU if available, or falls back to the CPU. Additionally, when managing memory, especially on GPUs, be diligent. Utilize the `.to(device)` method to transfer tensors or models to the GPU and the `.cpu()` method to revert them back to the CPU. Proper memory management will optimize performance and prevent potential memory-related issues.

The art of debugging in PyTorch

In the realm of deep learning, even a minute error can hinder a model's ability to converge or function effectively. Debugging in PyTorch requires a keen understanding of not just the Python code, but the mathematical and computational intricacies that underlie model training. Before you can address an issue, you need to understand its nature. In a broad sense, there are three types of error: syntax, runtime, and logical error. In the following section, we will discuss in detail these errors and how we should approach debugging.

Syntax errors

These pertain directly to mistakes in the Python code structure. Often, these are the easiest to address since most **Integrated Development Environments** (**IDE**) will highlight the precise location of the error for you. Additionally, if your IDE cannot identify it, your Python interpreter will point out the error during the run. Once you identify the error, you can follow official documentation to fix the error.

Runtime errors

The Python runtime environment will raise the error during the execution of valid Python code. Let us understand a few Runtime errors and how to debug them.

Shape mismatch

One of the most common pitfalls in PyTorch involves tensor shapes. Always ensure that the tensor shapes are compatible, especially when performing operations that involve multiple tensors. *Table 17.2* lists some situations where you could encounter these issues:

	Situation	**Cause and Remedies**
Not complying with dimensional requirement	Key components such as the model, loss function, and optimizer often have specific shape requirements. For instance, PyTorch's **nn.Transformer** expects the **'src'** input to have dimensions (**sequence_length, batch_size, embed_size**). In contrast, the Transformer model from Hugging Face anticipates the input to be of shape (**batch_size, sequence_length**).	It is best practice to understand the requirements of the PyTorch component you are using and prepare the data accordingly. You might need to use operations like squeeze, unsqueeze, or transpose to prepare the data
Feedforward Networks	The shape mismatch in the feed-forward layers inside each transformer block.	Incorrect input or output feature dimensions when defining linear layers.
Input Embedding shape	The input token IDs tensor might have a shape like (**batch_size, sequence_length**), but the model expects a shape of (**batch_size, max_sequence_length**)	This could arise if some sequences in the batch are shorter than others and you have not padded them to a consistent length.
Batching Issues	If data is not batched properly, especially when using dynamic padding, the tensors in a batch might have varying sequence lengths.	Improperly handling padding can be an issue. It is often recommended to create a CustomDataSet class, which gives you more control over data preparation. For dynamic padding, you can use functions like collate_fn or other advanced methods
Positional Encoding Shape Mismatch	The positional encoding tensor's shape does not match that of the input embeddings	Using a fixed positional encoding length that does not adjust to varying sequence lengths in different batches. Another situation could be using different dimensions for Positional Encoding Vectors and embedding.
Multi-head Attention	During multi-head self-attention, if the reshaped Q, K, and V tensors' dimensions aren't properly handled.	Not reshaping or splitting the tensor correctly into multiple heads.

Table 17.2: Runtime errors related to the shape mismatch

CUDA errors

Attempting to process tensors on a CUDA device (GPU) can lead to errors if all model components, including its parameters and input data, are not consistently placed on that device. For instance, if your model resides on the GPU while your input tensors remain on the CPU, you will encounter a **`RuntimeError: expected device cuda:0`** but got device CPU. A recommended approach is to initialize a device variable at the start, or dynamically determine the appropriate device. Subsequently, consistently reference this device variable throughout your code. It is crucial to ensure that the Model, Input, Output, and Optimizer all share the same device. If the error persists despite these precautions, employ the assert statement as a safety mechanism to validate that both the model and input tensors are indeed on the same device:

```
assert tensor.device == next(model.parameters()).device, "Discrepancy
between model and tensor device placements!"
```

Loss computation issues

Using inappropriate loss functions or failing to properly align tensor shapes in the loss computation may trigger runtime error. Consider a scenario where you are building a multi-class text classification model using a transformer. If you mistakenly employ the MSELoss (a regression-based loss function) instead of **`CrossEntropyLoss`** (ideal for multi-class classification), not only will your model fail to converge effectively, but it could also throw runtime errors.

Mismatched configuration

Using a configuration that does not match the transformer's requirements can lead to issues. For instance, setting the number of heads in multi-head attention to a value that is not divisible by the embedding dimension is problematic. The best way to address these configuration mismatches is by diligently following the provided documentation.

Memory error

Memory management is crucial when working with large models like transformers in PyTorch. Frequently, developers encounter **`CUDA out-of-memory (OOM)`** errors due to overconsumption, often resulting from oversized batches or simply an enormous model architecture. To diagnose this, you can utilize PyTorch's memory profiler functions (**`torch.cuda.memory_allocated()`** and **`torch.cuda.memory_cached()`**) or employ tools like **`nvidia-smi`** for real-time monitoring.

However, identifying the problem is only half the battle. Here are several actionable strategies to mitigate memory errors:

- **Reduce batch size**: This is a straightforward adjustment, although be wary of the potential compromise on model generalization.

- **Gradient accumulation**: If a smaller batch size is not feasible due to convergence issues, consider accumulating gradients over multiple passes before performing a model update.

- **Model checkpointing**: Use PyTorch's utilities to save and reload intermediate activations, trading off memory for computation time.

- **Mixed precision training**: Implement 16-bit precision (FP16) to cut down memory requirements and potentially boost computation speeds.

- **Optimize the model**: Adopt smaller transformer variants or techniques like knowledge distillation to compress model size without sacrificing performance.

- **Clear unused variables**: Periodically purge unneeded tensors and clear the CUDA cache with `torch.cuda.empty_cache()`.

- **Gradient clipping**: By constraining gradient values to a narrow range, you can deter sudden spikes in memory usage.

- **Model parallelism**: For multi-GPU setups, distribute different model components across GPUs.

- **Efficient data handling**: Streamline data loading and augmentation processes, using PyTorch's `DataLoader` with suitable batch sizes.

- **Adjust training configurations**: Modify settings that might be inflating memory consumption, such as gradient accumulation or longer sequence lengths in transformers.

Library/Dependency errors

Deep learning libraries, given their rapid evolution and intricate interdependencies, often lead developers into a maze of compatibility issues and library interdependencies conflict. When building models or pipelines, these issues can halt progress or cause obscure errors that are challenging to debug. Here is a structured approach to mitigate these issues:

- **Using Python's virtual environment:** Creating an isolated environment for each project ensures that the libraries and their respective versions do not interfere with each other, minimizing the risk of unexpected behavior.

- **Reviewing documentation for dependencies:** Documentation provides insights into the tested and supported versions of libraries and their dependencies. Relying on this can save hours of debugging. When using HuggingFace's transformers, the documentation might specify that it is compatible with PyTorch version 2.0 or above. Installing an older version of PyTorch might result in obscure errors or even failed installations. Thus, before installing, always skim through the 'Requirements' or 'Installation' section of the library's official documentation.

- **Staying updated in a fast-moving space**: Deep learning tools change fast. Sometimes, problems in one version can be fixed in the next update, which might come out in just a few weeks or months. A good example is how older versions of the Hugging Face's transformer and PyTorch did not fully support Apple's M1/M2 chips. But in newer versions, many more models can work with these chips. So, it's good to keep an eye on the latest updates.

Logical errors

The code runs without any errors, but the output is not what is expected. Often, these are the errors which are most difficult to debug. Here are some of the most common logical errors.

- **Mismatched dataset shape**: A frequent logical error arises from incorrect data shapes, which can occur during pre-processing, training, or evaluation. For instance, while `torch.nn.Transformer` expects data in the format [`seq_length`, `batch_size`, `emb_dim`], mistakenly inputting it as [`batch_size`, `seq_len`, `emb_dim`] (a format suitable for Hugging face models) will shuffle the sequence data. This mistake will result in feeding garbage to the model. If your model is not improving, ensure your data preparation and shape align with model expectations.

- **Mismatched tokenizer and model**: Using a tokenizer from one pre-trained model but the weights from another causes misalignment in embeddings.

- **Improper padding**: Not properly handling padding tokens, leading to incorrect attention scores and inefficient training. For instance, forgetting to set `attention_mask` during training or evaluation.

- **Incorrect learning rate scheduling**: Using an inappropriate learning rate or scheduler that makes the model converge too quickly or not at all. For instance, using a large learning rate in transfer learning can lead to overfitting, especially if you are working with a limited amount of data.

- **Wrong loss function**: Using a loss function that does not raise errors but is not suited for your task can hinder model convergence. For instance, using **Mean Squared Error** (**MSE**) for binary classification is technically correct but unsuitable, likely leading to poor model performance. Always match the loss function to the problem type.

- **Not freezing pre-trained weights**: When fine-tuning, forgetting to freeze certain layers can sometimes lead to overfitting or destroying the valuable pre-trained representations.

- **Ignoring batch sizes:** Especially in transfer learning, using batch sizes that are too large or too small might not reproduce the conditions under which the model was originally trained.

- **Not shuffling training data:** Overlooking the need to shuffle training data can lead to patterns that the model might pick up on, which are not genuine features of the data.

- **Gradient imploding:** Gradient issues, especially gradient imploding, can be a critical roadblock during the training of deep learning models, including transformers in PyTorch. If you observe that your model output suddenly becomes NaN or Inf during training, it is a clear indication that you might be dealing with this problem. You can mitigate this issue by:

  o Weight initialization strategy

  o Clipping gradients

  o Choosing different activation functions

General guidelines for debugging PyTorch ML models

When an error surfaces in your PyTorch machine-learning model, it can sometimes be daunting to pinpoint its origin. Here are streamlined steps to effectively debug and rectify issues:

1. **Categorize the error**: Start by determining the nature of the error. Does it resemble any of the common pitfalls previously discussed? If so, the resolution may already be at your fingertips.

2. **Inspect data pre-processing**: Often, the root of the problem lies in data preparation. Thoroughly scrutinize this step. The optimal way to ensure accurate preprocessing is to grasp the exact input format that your model necessitates. Once you have understood this, work backward from there, designing a systematic procedure to transform your raw data to meet the model's input specifications.

3. **Print and validate**: Embrace the humble print statement. By peppering your code with print statements, you can actively monitor and verify the transformations at each step. Employ assertions in your code to validate assumptions and ensure that data retains the expected structure and values.

4. **Benchmark with established datasets**: Before fully diving into custom models tailored for specific problems, first, validate your approach using benchmark datasets with well-established performance metrics. If your tailored model falters on these datasets, it is a clear indicator that the issue likely lies in your approach rather than inherent complexities or nuances of your unique problem.

5. **Visualization and logging**: Making the invisible visible can provide invaluable insights. Use tools to visualize intermediate outputs, tensor shapes, and values. Logging, whether through traditional methods or tools like TensorBoard, can help track the model's progress over time and pinpoint when and where things go awry.

Following these guidelines systematically will empower you to identify and rectify the majority of issues that may arise during your model development journey. Remember, debugging is as much an art as it is a science. Stay patient, methodical, and persistent.

Conclusion

As we reach the end of this chapter, it becomes unmistakably clear that the revolutionary capabilities of transformer models are accompanied by inherent complexities. Given this intricacy, attention to detail is paramount during the construction of transformer models, and equally vital when undertaking the task of debugging potential bugs.

The detailed best practices outlined in this chapter, ranging from the intricacies of model initialization to the nuances of optimization, emerge as foundational keystones for architecting resilient transformer models. These principles do more than just enhance computational efficiency; they underscore the importance of reproducibility, ensuring an unobstructed transition across diverse modeling paradigms, whether one is fine-tuning an existing structure or creating new model. Moreover, the practical examples dispersed within the chapter provide readers with tangible insights, poised for direct implementation in empirical scenarios.

Debugging is an underestimated aspect of model development. While syntactical anomalies present overt hurdles, it is the covert, logical errors and runtime errors that warrant vigilant scrutiny. These errors, though insidious, can divert outcomes substantially. Therefore, the systematic debugging methodologies articulated herein are indispensable for professionals venturing into the intricate realm of deep learning via PyTorch.

Absorbing the insights of this chapter, one can significantly reduce countless hours otherwise spent on unproductive attempts at debugging transformer models. Following the recommended best practices not only prevents many pitfalls but also minimizes the potential for error.

Quiz

1. **Why is it important to select the right tokenizer in Hugging Face?**

    a. For better memory utilization

    b. To match the chosen pre-trained model

    c. For faster training

    d. To prevent model overfitting

2. **Which model has a token limit of 512?**

   a. GPT-2

   b. RoBERTa

   c. BERT

   d. TransformerXL

3. **In the Hugging Face attention mask, what value represents padding tokens?**

   a. 1

   b. 2

   c. 0

   d. -1

4. **Why is dynamic batching important?**

   a. For tokenization

   b. To consistently use the same sequence length

   c. To handle variability in sequence lengths efficiently

   d. For model initialization

5. **What is the primary use of torchrun?**

   a. For mixed precision training

   b. To simplify distributed training in PyTorch

   c. For leveraging Hugging Face functionalities

   d. To spawn multiple distributed processes in PyTorch

6. **When is gradient clipping particularly useful?**

   a. During data preprocessing

   b. When facing overfitting

   c. When encountering large gradients or NaNvalues

   d. When using a deep architecture

7. **Which method should be used to zero out the gradients at the start of each training iteration?**

   a. optimizer.empty_grad()

   b. model.zero_grad()

   c. torch.empty_grad()

   d. optimizer.zero_grad()

8. **Which mode should be activated before model evaluation or testing?**

    a. model.start()

    b. model.train()

    c. model.test()

    d. model.eval()

9. **Why is it important to use the correct model mode during training and evaluation?**

    a. To ensure tokenization is accurate

    b. To ensure model parameters are not updated during evaluation

    c. To utilize dynamic padding

    d. To ensure correct token limit

10. **When you encounter a RuntimeError: expected device cuda:0 but got device cpu, what could be the possible issue?**

    a. Syntax error in the code

    b. Memory overflow

    c. Model and input tensors are on different devices

    d. Inappropriate loss function used

11. **Which error type does not halt the program but provides unexpected output?**

    a. Syntax Errors

    b. CUDA Errors

    c. Logical Errors

    d. Runtime Errors

12. **What could be a sign that you're dealing with gradient imploding in PyTorch?**

    a. Model converges too quickly

    b. Model output becomes NaN or Inf during training

    c. Model throws a CUDA error

    d. Syntax error in the code

13. **In PyTorch, what is the primary purpose of torch.cuda.empty_cache()?**

    a. Increase memory usage

    b. Store model weights

    c. Clear the CUDA cache

    d. Manage multi-GPU setups

14. **What is a recommended strategy when encountering CUDA errors regarding tensor placement?**

   a. Increase the batch size

   b. Use a different loss function

   c. Make sure the Model, Input, Output, and Optimizer are on the same device

   d. Implement gradient clipping

Answers

1. b.

2. c.

3. c.

4. c.

5. d.

6. c.

7. a.

8. d.

9. b.

10. b.

11. c.

12. b.

13. c.

14. c.

Join our book's Discord space

Join the book's Discord Workspace for Latest updates, Offers, Tech happenings around the world, New Release and Sessions with the Authors:

https://discord.bpbonline.com

Index

Made in United States
North Haven, CT
19 May 2024

52588838R00170